Education in Canada
An Interpretation

Edited by

E. Brian Titley
Peter J. Miller

Detselig Enterprises Limited
Calgary, Alberta

E. Brian Titley
Peter J. Miller
  Department of Educational Foundations
  The University of Alberta

Canadian Cataloguing in Publication Data

Main entry under title:

Education in Canada

   Originally published: 4th ed. Edmonton :
Dept. of Educational Foundations, Faculty of
Education, University of Alberta, 1981.
  ISBN 0-920490-25-5

   1. Education — Canada — History — Addresses,
essays, lectures. 2. Canada — History —
Addresses, essays, lectures. I. Titley, E. Brian
II. Miller, Peter J.
LA411.E38 1982   370'.971   C82-091158-5

©1982 by Detselig Enterprises Limited
P.O. Box G399
Calgary, Alberta T3A 2G3

Printed in Canada   ISBN 0-920490-25-5

Contents

Acknowledgements

The idea and conceptional framework for this book grew out of lengthy meetings and discussions of a number of members of the Department of Educational Foundations, University of Alberta. The editors wish to acknowledge the valuable contributions of Robert Carney, Nick Kach, Heather Lysons, Gerald Taylor, John Young and especially Steward Hardy.

Notes on Contributors

Don Dawson is a Ph.D. Candidate in the area of Sociology of Education, Department of Educational Foundations, University of Alberta.

W.J. Eccles is Professor of History, University of Toronto.

Manoly R. Lupul is Director of the Canadian Institute of Ukrainian Studies and Professor of History of Canadian Education, University of Alberta.

Neil McDonald is Professor of History of Education, Department of Educational Administration and Foundations, University of Manitoba.

P.J. Miller is Chairman and Professor of History of Education, Department of Educational Foundations, University of Alberta.

At the time of his death in late 1981, **W.L. Morton** was Professor Emeritus, University of Manitoba.

R.S. Patterson is Professor of History of Canadian Education, Department of Educational Foundations, University of Alberta.

Brian Titley teaches in the area of History of Education, Department of Educational Foundations, University of Alberta.

J. Donald Wilson is Professor of Social and Educational Studies, Faculty of Education, University of British Columbia.

John R. Young is Associate Professor, Sociology of Education, Department of Educational Foundations, University of Alberta.

I

Introduction

Why is it that our children are required to attend school? Whose purposes is the school intended to achieve? What functions is it expected to perform? What forces have been instrumental in determining what children are required to learn, and in what kind of classrooms? What, in short, has been the story and the history of the development of our school system?

These are but a few of the fundamental questions that students and teachers must answer if they are to come to an intelligent understanding of the nature and function of the school in today's society. This book attempts to provide at least some answers by considering educational arrangements at crucial stages of Canada's past and examining a number of contemporary issues arising from these experiences. Let us begin with some theoretical considerations.

Education, in the sense of 'schooling', refers to a formal system of instruction involving teachers, pupils, curricula, textbooks, special buildings, and so on. What takes place in schools is, of course, an integrated part of a larger learning experience known as socialization. Socialization is defined as the process through which successive younger generations learn to function as responsible adults in society. The school, then, along with the family, church, etc., operates as one of society's agencies of socialization. It is an institution that is intentionally created, organized, and structured for this purpose. It seeks to impart to the young a parcel of approved behaviours, beliefs and skills.

In this sense schools are an important integrative force in society. The school's role in the socialization process provides an important means whereby a society can produce members who are willing to conform to a social order that serves the interests of the dominant social group. This is so because effective control of school systems — i.e. the power to determine curriculum content and the power to certify teachers — are invariably vested in the hands of this group. And the greater a society's ability to induce voluntary conformity and compliance, the less often it is forced to resort to rewards and coercion to preserve the status quo. In effect, the school serves as an important mechanism of social control.

Of course, this is not the only view that can be taken of the school. It can and has been seen as an important element in the generating of economic, political, social and cultural changes in society. Indeed, for many educational writers and practitioners, it was the reformist possibilities of the school that

1

drove them to devote their talents and energies to the cause of education, and particularly to that of expanding educational opportunity. And this is still a powerful factor in attracting many individuals to the profession of teaching. For questions relating to the social function of schooling have at least two kinds of answers — one kind concerning the school and its functions as they have existed in the past, the other kind concerning the school and its function as they might be in the future. They require, in fact, both a look back and a look forward, a history and an ideology.

Whether the school is seen as an institution concerned with social integration, social control and their corollary, the maintenance of the status quo, or whether it is viewed as an agency of reform, a better understanding of the nature of schooling in a given time and place can not be accomplished without reference to its relations with other social institutions, particularly those of a political, economic, religious and cultural nature. In other words, no meaningful study of the school is possible in isolation from the essential features of the society of which it is a part. For example, for most of Canada's past the school has sought to foster attitudes of loyalty to existing political institutions. It has also promoted values and attitudes that tended to strengthen acceptance of the economic system. And it has certainly tended to reinforce the moral and ethical codes of the dominant religious ideology. The social system of the school, then, has been greatly influenced by the expectations of these other institutions.

Our understanding of the function of the school in society is further enhanced by an examination of the historical circumstances under which a particular educational system came into being and of the various forces which induced change in the system over time. The educational historian, then, does not merely attempt to chronicle changes in school legislation, but seeks an explanation of why things occurred in the manner they did by analyzing the salient contemporary influences and the underlying motivations of the principal actors. Historical inquiry probes the fundamental dynamics of societies and their institutions, in order to provide an understanding of present-day situations and relationships.

Of course, not all historians are in agreement with regard to the explanations they arrive at. Therefore, it is necessary to speak of a variety of historical explanations and a number of interpretations of history. The way a historian explains or interprets history will usually depend on his/her own ideological perspective. It is not our purpose here to debate the relative merits of competing models of historical interpretation, but rather to suggest one that will be employed throughout the book. In this way we hope to create a consistent interpretive framework, one which will enable the reader to place the material contained in the series of articles in a coherent context.

This book, then, is not designed as a history of Canadian education in the conventional sense. Rather, it attempts to analyze the emergence of formal institutions of education in several regions of the country during specific historical periods and gives some attention to their subsequent transformation. In this way, it identifies particular educational traditions that have appeared and persisted over time, and whose interaction have largely determined contemporary ideas and practices.

It should also be noted that the perspective of the book is a distinctly Western Canadian one. This may be evident in the fact that the selections are largely the work of authors associated in one way or other with the West. It is certainly evident in the fact that in this book the West is viewed as the focal point of education in Canada. Thus while developments in New France and Ontario are accorded significance in their own right, they are viewed also as essential precursors to the institutional framework created in the western provinces. And educational developments in Newfoundland, the Maritimes and British Columbia, each of which have been involved in a different set of relationships with the metropoleis of Britain, the United States and Eastern Canada and have consequently a fascinating history of their own, receive no mention at all.

In examining Canadian society, one characteristic of the country readily becomes evident: its astonishing variety. And this is variety not just in the geographic sense, but also in terms of language, culture, religion and economic activities. In fact, as the mosaic metaphor implies, it could be argued that variety rather than uniformity is the distinguishing mark of Canadian society and of its education. Diversity in Canadian educational practice is not merely the consequence of making that service a provincial prerogative; it is also due to the peculiar historical experiences of each region.

Historical inquiry, then, will be the instrument with which we shall attempt to come to some understanding of the nature of Canadian education. One theme that will appear throughout the book is Canada's relations with those countries which have most influenced its development — France, Great Britain and the United States. In other words, its colonial past and its concomitant dependency on other countries for leadership in most spheres of life will be considered in order to explain the institutional framework that Canada and particularly Western Canada adopted. This pattern of domination has been termed the metropolis-hinterland relationship. The metropolis is the centre of power and influence, while the hinterland — in this case, Canada and its regions — is the area subject to its domination. The hinterland is — to employ a fashionable cliché — the victim of economic and cultural imperialism. In other words, its institutions, and in fact all aspects of life, tend to be imitative of metropolitan precedents. We would, therefore, expect to find that Canadian educational practices have owed much to those of the metropolitan centres mentioned. It should also be pointed out that this dependency relationship has existed within the country itself and is particularly evident in the domination of the West by central Canada.

But the metropolis-hinterland thesis alone does not account for the complexity and diversity of Canadian society and its institutions. Some writers have argued that the frontier was also a significant formative force. At all stages in our past, and even today to some extent, areas of white settlement were bordered by an untamed wilderness — the frontier. The frontier, it is argued, offered the tantalizing prospect of free land and its by-product, economic independence. It fostered individualism and innovation, and enabled men to escape the hide-bound traditions which they believed had shackled the minds of their ancestors. It tended to lead, therefore, to a more dynamic and future-oriented society where experimentation and change were readily accepted. As a force it tended to resent metropolitan influences, and, where it was not possible to reject them totally, at the very least to accommodate them to local circumstances. It is suggested that this frontier influence was constantly at work modifying the traditions emanating from the metropoleis — in education, as in other walks of life.

The introductory article, "The Origins of Schooling in Selected Regions of Canada: An Interpretation", explores the interaction of these metropolitan and frontier influences in determining the character of Canadian education and provides the interpretive framework for the remainder of the material in the book.

The Origins of Schooling in Selected Regions of Canada: An Interpretation

Don Dawson and Brian Titley

How has the interplay of disparate local, national and international influences worked to shape the development of education in Canada? This paper will attempt in part to answer this question by examining the concepts of frontier, hinterland and metropolis and their relationship to the origins of schooling in New France, Ontario and Western Canada.

Concepts of Frontier, Hinterland and Metropolis

The Frontier

The American historian F.J. Turner first read his now famous paper "The Significance of the Frontier in American History" to the American Historical Association in 1893.[1] At that time Turner was reacting to a statement in the 1890 census report to the effect that the frontier era in American history had come to an end. Turner suggested that historians might find an examination of the frontier very useful in explaining the development of America.

Specifically Turner saw the westward advancement of American settlements as a continuous process wherein "the frontier is the outer edge of the wave — the meeting point between savagery and civilization" which "lies at the hither edge of free land". As the American pioneer settlers learnt to adapt to the environment of the frontier the established American institutions were profoundly affected by the westward expansion. In Turner's own words,

> The peculiarity of American institutions is the fact that they have been compelled to adapt themselves to the changes of an expanding people — to the changes involved in crossing a continent, in winning a wilderness, and in developing at each area of this progress out of the primitive economic and political conditions of the frontier into the complexity of city life. . . . Thus American development has exhibited not merely advance along a single line, but a return to primitive conditions on a continually advancing frontier line, and a new development for that area.[2]

For Turner, the force behind American social development was the perennial rebirth, the continually starting anew as the line of the advancing frontier moved across the 'Great West'. The unique American western society which wiped out 'old European' characteristics, in turn reacted upon the colonies of the east. Indeed, the needs, wants and demands emanating in the west "called for important schemes of internal improvement"[3] which shaped government policy.

The conditions of the frontier in large part determined the characters of those who experienced its unforgiving wilderness. Individualism, democracy, inventiveness, idealism, *and* coarseness were the traits instilled in the frontier individuals and institutions. While many historians viewed the American west through rose-coloured glasses others recognized the rawness of the frontiersmen. A.R.M. Lower saw that "the preoccupation of a pioneer people is to better their condition. Inevitably everything tends to be sacrificed to material ends". "Life on the pioneer farm was laborious. . . . It gave the head of a new family independence and authority . . . — a sudden right to crude self-assertion".[5]

The crucial assertion of Turner's frontier thesis is not that a peculiarly 'American' personality emerged out of the isolated wilderness, but that the frontier acted as a driving force for the rest of society. That the development of the American nation was not merely a result of an orchestrated plan under the dominance of established eastern interests was a fresh insight. The reverse was seen to be true — it was predominantly the expanding west which motivated and affected the east. The west in fact was the leading force within American development in social, political, economic, and other institutional spheres.

The Hinterland and Metropolis

The concepts of 'hinterland' and 'metropolis' are used in two approaches to the understanding of social, economic and political development. The 'hinterland' refers to the relatively undeveloped country side which surrounds the 'metropolis', a large city which is the centre for trade and commerce, industry, and social development. The first, which we shall call the 'metropolis-hinterland' thesis, assumes a marked degree of mutual benefit (i.e., to hinterland as well as metropolis) from the emergence of a metropolis. The other will be referred to as 'metropolitanism'. In this approach the emphasis is upon the exploitation of the hinterland for the benefit and development of the metropolitan centre. Let us examine each of these approaches in turn. First the 'metropolis-hinterland' theory.

The metropolis-hinterland relationship was the main theme of N.S.B. Gras' book, *An Introduction to Economic History.*[6] As the title suggests his was an *economic* interpretation. According to this interpretation a large outstanding town would grow into an economic metropolis, the hinterland of which was the outlying area. He lists four stages in the emergence of an economic metropolis:

1. Organizing the Market — this includes handling goods brought in from the hinterland for consumption through distribution in a wholesale exchange market.

2. Industrial Development — the manufacture of commodities in demand, *for* the metropolis and *in* the metropolis.

3. Development of Transportation — roads, canals, railways, steamships, post, etc. throughout the hinterland and centering on the metropolis.

4. Development of Financial Organization — banking, commercial institutions, and stock exchanges in the metropolis.

A town which grows into a city, and subsequently develops through these four stages is then a metropolis — the powerful economic centre and stimulus for growth in the hinterland. But, "Interdependence of the parts is really the key to the whole situation, . . . the centre is also dependent upon the outlying area with its towns, villages and scattered homesteads".[7] Without the workers raw materials, and agricultural products supplied by the hinterland the metropolitan centre could not grow and could not continue to expand. Therefore, as the metropolis develops many benefits 'spillover' to the surrounding hinterland areas. These benefits include jobs, increased availability of manufactured goods, and overall economic stimulation.

Those who use the metropolis-hinterland concept within the framework of 'metropolitan dominance' or 'metropolitanism' assert the metropolis-hinterland relations are neither reciprocal nor equal. The metropolis is seen to be the hard pressing, dynamic, organizing force behind a pattern of societal development which exploits and controls the hinterland exclusively for its own benefits. As a result the hinterland becomes dependent upon the metropolis and consequently lacks the power to resolve its own problems of development. Hence, *"hinterland* means, in the first instance, relatively underdeveloped or colonial areas which export . . . to the city",[8] and *"metropolis* signifies the centres of economic and political control located in the larger cities".[9] While metropolitan dominance is especially evident in economic matters it also has profound social consequences. Indeed, it is difficult to understand hinterland society without reference to the metropolis. As Usher points out,

> Most traditional discussions of metropolis-hinterland relations begin with the metropolis and examines the hinterland only to explain the growth and predominance of the metropolis. . . . My own bias (is to) . . . examining the metropolis as a means of explaining current conditions in the hinterland.[10]

But we must also recognize that there exists a tendency for hinterland self-assertion and resistance to metropolitan control. Davis, for example, states that "the symbiotic metropolis-hinterland model assumes: first, a conflict of interest between metropolis and hinterland; and, second, a tendency on the part of the hinterland groups and interests to fight back eventually against their metropolitan exploiters".[11]

We have, then, three distinct though not unrelated conceptual approaches to societal development:

(a) "Frontierism" wherein the frontier is the dynamic driving force which affects all of society, including the metropolitan areas,

(b) "Hinterland-metropolis" relations wherein the emergence of an outstanding metropolitan centre is of mutual benefit to both itself and surrounding hinterland regions,

(c) "Metropolitanism" wherein the dominant metropolitan area is the driving force which exploits the hinterland.

There are difficulties in employing any one of those three approaches by itself. The basic criticism of the interpretive power of the first approach, frontierism, is that it oversimplifies complex social phenomena. The "very simplicity which renders the Turner thesis so attractive should also render it an object of suspicion".[12] Moreover, it undervalues "the non-material environment: that of ideas, traditions and institutions".[13] Though G.F.G. Stanley rejects the frontier thesis saying that the pioneer is usually "imitative" rather than "creative", he is compelled to add, "I do not mean to suggest that the frontier develops no new habits or customs. Adaptation to environment is nature's first law".[14] Despite the weaknesses of the frontier approach one cannot easily disregard the effects of the frontier on social development. However, while the frontier may well be isolated it does not exist in a vacuum and its patterns of social development are not completely independent of the hinterland and the metropolis.

The second approach, stressing mutual benefit for hinterland and metropolis, implies a distinction between the metropolis and the hinterland.The implication is that those areas immediately surrounding the metropolis will be the greatest benefactors of the metropolitan economy. However, the hinterland is not uniform throughout its different areas. Within it different regions and subordinate metropoleis may exist "having, to a greater or lesser degree, territorial and cultural integrity, (as well as) distinctive ways of life".[15] Hence, all areas of the hinterland will not benefit equally from the growth of the metropolis. Those closest to the frontier will probably not experience any great benefits or development.

The third approach, metropolitanism, ignores the fact that the people very near the open frontier had their own special interests, sheer survival being the most obvious. This obvious interest in sheer survival is most clearly visible then in those areas at the periphery of metropolitan dominance or, as Turner would say, at the 'frontier line'. Consequently we shall consider the hinterland as that area between the metropolitan center and the line of frontier. Seen in this light metropolis, hinterland, and frontier exercise a reciprocal influence upon each other. The driving force behind societal development is not only 'frontierism', nor is it merely 'metropolitanism'. Neither is it wholly exploitative nor is it always beneficial to all. It is a process involving the frontier, the metropolis, and the hinterland area, sometimes in harmony and sometimes in conflict.

Frontier, Hinterland, and Metropolis in Canada

It has been mentioned that one must be cautious not to over-simplify Turner's frontier thesis and that any mythical romanticization of the frontier should be avoided. Turner generated his frontier thesis to emphasize the unique historical phenomena of the American West, and though he felt that some generalizations could be made he realized its limitations. Many Canadian historians, however, have not been as careful using 'frontierism' as might be hoped. As J.M.S. Careless points out,

> In pursuing this promising theme, however, these writers took over the general approach and mood of Turner and company — the frontier and its agrarian population as emblematic of native democratic progressive, perhaps even of 'Good' forces in the history of the continent — rather than the precise frontier thesis, which received little direct application in Canada.[16]

The 'precise' frontier thesis, as we have seen, refers to the dynamic role of the continuously expanding frontier in shaping national policy and influencing social development. Some critics claim however, that Turner's ideas are not applicable to Canada at all.

In attempting to refute the validity of the frontier thesis for Canada some historians examined the original frontier experience in New France, now Quebec. Some maintained that the Canadian 'habitants' had "created on the banks of the St. Lawrence a replica of the French society which they had left".[17]

> Thus we have autocratic, feudalistic Catholic New France side by side with self-governing, individualistic, Puritan Protestant New England. The frontier, if it possessed the peculiar qualities attributed to it by American historians, should have produced in each a similar pattern in contemporary society.[18]

Nevertheless, other historians held that Turner's thesis was of considerable value in explaining Canadian social development. A.L. Burt, for example, explained that the wilderness interior and the abundance of land were the best explanatory factors for the extent to which the society of New France deviated so dramatically from that of the Mother country.[19] To Lower, it was a "a tribute to the essential truth in Turner's analysis that French life and society in America departed considerably from authoritarianism and in spirit approached English life and society in America".[20] New France was in fact more 'new' that it was 'France'.

Similarly the society of Upper Canada was influenced as much by local frontier conditions as it was by the 'mother' land, Britain. Even the United Empire Loyalists were products of the frontier environment.

> On the surface every Loyalist vehemently upheld British institutions; after all had he not left his home or been forced to do so for just this reason? Deep down, however, the society he had come from was a society based not on privilege and class, but on democratic and equalitarian principles born of the frontier and the New World.[21]

Moreover, most post-Loyalist American settlers were attracted to Canada not out of latent British patriotism but by the promise of free land. In 1812 four-fifths of the population in Upper Canada was estimated to be Americans who had come *after* the Loyalists, while a later estimate suggests that in many parts of Upper Canada in 1812 American immigrants outnumbered all other inhabitants two to one.[22] It is evident that directly and indirectly the frontier affected both Upper Canada and New France; certainly they were more than mere replicas of British or French society.

The frontier concept is even more applicable to an understanding of the development of the Canadian west. That vast area between the Rockies and the Red River — 'The Great Lone Land' — was sparsely settled during the first half of the 1800's. Testaments to the frontier conditions of Canada's west are as numerous and compelling as any of those from its southern neighbour.

> The isolation, remoteness, and great distances increased helplessness in the pathetic struggle against severe winter, grasshoppers, prairie fires, floods, and the frequent threat of civil unrest in a mixed frontier population, (and only those) hardened by generations of marginal existence could have survived.[23]

In many respects the development of the Canadian West paralleled that of the United States. While it is held that the Canadian western frontier was "never so lawless as the American frontier", in the 1870's "tales of rampant lawlessness, drunken orgies, and Indian unrest had reached the ears of the authorities at Ottawa".[24] Although it may well be true that the later bulk of prairie immigration was conducted under the watchful eye of the R.C.M.P., this is not unlike the American experience. In the U.S. "the frontier reached by the Pacific Railroad, surveyed into rectangles, guarded by the United States Army, . . . moved forward . . . in a different way than the frontier reached by the birch canoe or the pack horse".[25] Turner himself identified the expanding 'waves' of American frontier line as much the same as the pattern of frontier settlement in the 'Dominion of Canada'. In the frontier of both countries more orderly immigration followed the initial settlement. Nevertheless, whether the influence of frontier society in Canada is sufficient enough to be seen as the major driving force in Canadian national development is open to question.

Let us turn now to the metropolis-hinterland conceptual framework. W.L. Morton more than any Canadian historian embraced the classical interpretation of metropolis-hinterland relations which Gras had originally proposed.[26] He felt that the west had an identifiable and unique history of its own despite the dominance of Central Canada. The metropolis-hinterland approach "recognized the transplantation of economic, political, and social institutions from older settled areas to the frontier, and still enabled one to escape the implied interpretation of Canadian history as simply the imperialist expansion of Central Canada".[27] It was the interplay between metropolis and hinterland (or frontier) which was crucial, not an unidirectional account of the metropolitan dominance. The cities of Central Canada, according to Harold Innis, grew at a rapid 'cyclonic' rate in *response* to the furious exploitations of the frontier. The metropolitan centres were as much caught up by the swirl of exploitation as were the hinterlands.[28] From either Morton's or Innis' point of view the hinterland is seen to have its own existence quite apart from the metropolis, and to be a contributing factor in Canadian societal development.

In his article "Canadian Society and History as Hinterland Versus Metropolis", A.K. Davis sees the "retaliative reaction of the prairie hinterlands" as part of a process "wherein hinterland successfully wins successive concessions from metropolis".[29] So, despite the heavy emphasis in 'metropolitanism' upon the dominance and exploitation of the hinterland by the metropolis, the tendency of the hinterland to fight back assures it a prominent role. Hence, regardless of the difference in emphasis of the 'metropolis-hinterland' relations model or the more one-sided 'metropolitism' approach to Canadian history, the process of interaction of hinterland with metropolis (be it in conflict or cooperation) is the creative driving force.

Education in New France, Ontario, and Western Canada

Of all social institutions none are more profoundly affected by the impacts of the forces of the metropolis, hinterland, and frontier than schools. If the creative and formative power of the frontier is emphasized then the forms of education, both formal and informal, are seen as a response to local conditions. As such they are both relevant and dynamic. If the reciprocal relationship between metropolis and hinterland is stressed then schools, their curricula, teachers, and methods, are viewed as originating in the metropolis and being transformed to suit the needs of the hinterland. In the case of metropolitan dominance, education, including formal schooling, is interpreted as originating exclusively in the metropolis. Let us see how these approaches to education and schooling help illuminate educational developments in New France, Ontario and Western Canada.

New France

New France, which designates the area of French settlement along the St. Lawrence and in Acadia between the beginning of the seventeenth century and 1760, was in most respects a colonial society. This meant that it was in large measure effectively ruled from its mother country or metropolis, France. Given this reality, and the conventional wisdom that colonies are imitative in nature, it was natural that the institutional framework of the new society would be modelled closely on metropolitan precedents. Consequently, we find that New France had a ruling aristocratic oligarchy, an established church, and a system of feudal land tenure — arrangements which were characteristic, not only of France, but of most European countries at the time. It is evident that France, or the metropolis, was one of the chief forces in shaping the nature of the North American colony.

Among the major institutions transferred to the new world from the old in the process of colonization was the Roman Catholic church. In France this was the church which received the homage of the majority of the population and which also received the official sanction of the state. It was strongly influenced by the Gallican tradition — which meant in effect that it was subject more to the will of the king than to that of the pope.[30] In many respects, it was a branch of the civil service. It had long been a major force for social control and cohesion in the old country where it operated schools, colleges, hospitals, poorhouses, seminaries and churches and had made itself an indispensable institution in the lives of the people. As the seventeenth century progressed it attempted to create a similar network of operations in New France, with the same purpose in mind. It aimed to reproduce in the colony the social relations and cultural patterns that prevailed in France.[31]

As has been indicated, among the activities with which the church concerned itself in seventeenth century France, was the provision of education. In fact, it held a virtual monopoly with regard to the operation of schools. The Catholic church, of course, was still imbued with the spirit of the Counter Reformation. This movement had inspired it not only to reform itself, but also to reform society. A sound Catholic education was perceived to be an effective means to this end. In fact the Counter Reformation had given birth to a number of new religious orders and congregations whose specific purpose was the establishment and operation of schools.

This was the tradition from which education in New France sprang. The operation of schools in the colony became a strict ecclesiastical prerogative and teaching was usually done by such religious as the Ursuline nuns and the Jesuit fathers whose crusading zeal was unquestionable. The role of the state was merely to encourage and support the church in her endeavours by providing occasional subsidies and giving legal sanction to ecclesiastical activities.[32]

A most remarkable feature of the educational efforts of the church in New France was the striking similarity it bore, in scope, content, method and intent, to its efforts in France. The Ursuline nuns, for instance, though they did make some attempt to teach Amerindian girls,[33] concentrated their attention on providing an elite type of education for the daughters of the wealthy, and some primary instruction for the daughters of the poor — precisely the activities for which they were noted in the mother country.

It was much the same in the case of the Jesuit fathers. They were, of course, prominently involved in the attempted evangelization of the Amerindian population, but their educational endeavours on behalf of the colonists were centered on the provision of that type of advanced instruction which was their forte in Europe. Consequently, among their first accomplishments in New France was the establishment of a college in Québec in the 1630's. Nevertheless, they discovered a shortage of boys with the appropriate educational prerequisites and they were therefore obliged to offer primary-level instruction for some years in order to raise up a suitable clientele.[34] This was an expedient made necessary by the somewhat primitive state of the frontier community at the time.

By 1650 the Jesuit college in Québec was ready to offer the rigorous curriculum of the *Ratio Studiorum*, the classical fare which was de rigueur in their colleges in France and elsewhere. As Pére Camille de Rochemonteix noted:

> Le Collège de Québec était une reproduction en petit, mais complète des Collèges de France".[35]

It should be noted that the Jesuits who taught at the Collège de Québec were all from metropolitan France.[36] Under these circumstances, it is not surprising that they should model their schools on the familiar.

But the frontier environment also spawned religious congregations of its own. Among these were the Brothers Hospitallers of the Cross, founded by by François Charon, a Canadian, in 1694. These men devoted their time to the teaching of crafts to orphans. This was an eminently useful and much appreciated activity in the colonial setting.

The work of the sisters of the Congregation was in a similar vein. This was a Canadian community of religious women whose members went in pairs to rural parishes teaching the rudiments of literacy and religion to poor boys and girls.[37] Their work appears to have been greatly valued by the common people. Their rules, which allowed for flexibility and mobility were much more in harmony with the realities of life on the edge of the frontier than those of cloistered nuns, such as the Ursulines.

This suggests some innovation and adaptation on the part of the church and its functionaries to the needs of the new society. After all, New France was never much more than a sparsely populated strip of settlement clinging precariously to the St. Lawrence. Surrounded by a hostile wilderness, it faced a constant threat of annihilation by both the Iroquois and the English. These conditions shaped the character and lives of the Canadiens. Warfare, exploration, the clearing and cultivation of land, and the construction of buildings and fortifications were the activities that made most demands on their time. For education to be relevant under such circumstances, it had to be above all, practical. New France was, in Eccles' words, the Sparta, not the Athens of North America.[38]

It was in recognition of this reality that courses in navigation, hydrography and other practical sciences were added to the program of studies at the Jesuit Collège de Québec in the 1680's and 1690's. There was, evidently, a great demand for such 'useful' knowledge among colonial youth. In fact, Father Charlevoix, who taught at the college for a number of years in the early 18th century, noted that the Canadiens had "an excellent genius in mechanics" while they showed little interest in the more abstract academic disciplines.[39]

Education in New France, then, was the product of two sets of interacting influences. Because the society was a hinterland of France, its institutions were modelled closely on those of that country. It meant that one of the most distinguishing features of its educational institutions was that they were controlled strictly by the Roman Catholic clergy. Yet the schools in the new world were never precise reproductions of those in the old, at least in the things they emphasized. Because the society was on the edge of the wilderness, frontier influences dictated a certain practical orientation to life. The Canadiens appreciated education only to the extent that it proved useful in this practical sense, and the church schools, while never abandoning their classical/liberal foundations, responded by offering 'useful' knowledge and skills as well.

Ontario

As the nineteenth century opened, Upper Canada was a struggling frontier society of pioneer farmers — mainly United Empire Loyalists who had fled the fledgling American republic to live under British institutions and to recoup lost fortunes. The embryonic nature of the colony precluded the provision of extensive educational services and the schools that did exist were the product of private initiative and were limited in their scope and impact. Seventy years later Upper Canada had been transformed into Ontario, the most populous and economically developed province in the Dominion of Canada. By the same time a comprehensive and uniform system of education at both the primary and secondary levels had been brought into existence, ensuring that virtually all Ontarians received some modicum of schooling. This school system owed much to the metropolitan influences of Great Britain and the United States, and to other European countries also. And yet in its totality it was a unique adaptation to the conditions and requirements of Upper Canadian society in the mid-nineteenth century.

Attempts to improve the availability of schooling in Upper Canada in the early decades of the nineteenth century were only modestly successful. The principle of state aid to both grammar and common schools was established, but not on a scale that would have allowed for extensive instructional facilities. The creation of a 'system' of education was really the work of Egerton Ryerson, who held the post of Superintendent of Education between 1846 and 1876. During the years of Ryerson's incumbency a series of education acts brought into being a scheme of mass schooling at the elementary level that had the following characteristics: state control; social comprehensiveness; non-denominationalism; a standardized curriculum; trained teachers; compulsory attendance; public support from property taxation; and absence of fees.[40] At the same time the existing private grammar schools were brought steadily under state control and became the secondary component of the system of education.

But why was such a monolithic educational edifice necessary in the first place? Ryerson perceived, and his fellow members of the ruling oligarchy shared his perception, that there were present in Upper Canadian society certain difficulties which posed a threat to the status quo.

Perhaps foremost among these was the question of political loyalty. The rebellions of 1837 shocked the establishment of Upper Canada into the realization that a large number of people in the society did not unquestioningly accept the British form of government and were flirting dangerously with American-style republicanism. Ryerson believed that the right kind of schooling could combat effectively this tendency and thus ensure the continuity of the political status quo.[41]

Crime and immorality were further difficulties which the school would be able to control. The rising crime rate was blamed on the poor, especially the immigrant urban poor. Improper socialization in lower class families predisposed the young to lives of criminality and intemperance. Ryerson believed that public education would expose the lower class child to a superior environment and superior adult role models and thus reform his life.

Also of concern was the question of class conflict in Upper Canada. Ryerson had no wish to eliminate the class divisions in society, but he believed that conflict between the classes posed a danger to the established order of things. He therefore hoped to establish feelings of harmony and mutual interest among the classes. Again, the schools could be used to this end by placing children of all social strata in the same classrooms and by inculcating the ideas of duty and social responsibility.[42]

These were some of the problems in Upper Canadian society which Ryerson confidently predicted education would control. And he promised more. He persuaded the business interests who were to finance his school system that the regimen of the classroom would impart to the working classes those habits of 'discipline, punctuality and good conduct' essential to the factory method of production.[43]

Of course Ryerson's system of public education was not an instant creation nor was it totally original in conception. It was built on an educational tradition of both British and American origins which the Loyalists had brought with them to Upper Canada, and it also borrowed freely from contemporary educational developments in Britain, the United States, France and Prussia.

Perhaps the most obviously British educational legacy to Upper Canada in its formative years was the tradition of the grammar school. John Graves Simcoe, Lieutenant-Governor of the colony during the 1790's, and himself a product of the elite schools of England, believed that resources should be concentrated on providing a quality education to the few who could benefit from it. The greatest need was for classical grammar schools and a university, tied preferably to the Anglican church. Simcoe made little progress in his own day towards achieving this ideal, but a decade or so after his departure the legislature passed the District Public (Grammar) School Act of 1807 which provided for the creation of a grammar school in each district. It was a plan firmly modelled on the British tradition of providing education for the elite, as Simcoe had advocated, and it formed the basis of the secondary system for Ontario.[44]

On the other hand, the system of common schools, which also appeared in the early decades of the nineteenth century, owed much to American influences. The Loyalists, though they came to British North America to live under British law and institutions, were in many ways products of their American experience. They had come from a society that was far more democratic and egalitarian than contemporary Britain and were consequently less tolerant of rigid class structures and oligarchic government. In addition, they had come from a society with a well-established educational tradition — one of popular schooling provided in locally supported, non-sectarian institutions.[45]

It was on these foundations that Ryerson erected his educational monolith. And in doing so he looked for guidance to the United States and to the major countries in Western Europe — Great Britain, France and Prussia. These were the centres of economic and military power at the time and it was natural for backward, colonial Upper Canada to look to such metropoleis for leadership and inspiration. Immediately upon his appointment as Superintendent, Ryerson spent a year in Western Europe studying the systems of education in operation there to assist him in the formulation of his own plans.

He also visited Horace Mann, who was creating a school system in Massachusetts.[46]

Ryerson's creation, then, exhibited characteristics that were borrowed shamelessly from the countries that he visited. The supremacy of the state in education was a concept most highly developed in France and Prussia at the time and this had a particular appeal for Ryerson who was determined that he, as Superintendent, would be the final authority on educational matters in Upper Canada. The system he established was consequently highly centralized with power in the hands of the state, not churches.

A logical corollary of this was that schooling would be non-sectarian. This idea had a respectable lineage in the United States where the separation of church and state was a fundamental constitutional tenet. Ryerson, perhaps because of his Methodism, admired this American tradition and excluded the churches, though not Christian morality, from education.

But how would the school system be financed? The Americans again provided the answer: local property taxation. This practice was most firmly established in the state of New York and had even won the admiration of such Upper Canadian conservatives as Mahlon Burwell in the 1830's.[47] Ryerson's determination to educate everyone led him to persuade his establishment colleagues that this efficient American method of raising revenue was also necessary in Upper Canada.

One of the most admirable features of the school systems of Western Europe as far as Ryerson was concerned was their uniformity, especially in the area of curriculum. The Superintendent believed that the use of standardized, graded textbooks as in Ireland, Prussia and France, was far superior to the situation in Upper Canada where a wide diversity of texts, often unsuitable, was employed. He particularly admired the readers that were used in the Irish national schools as they were pro-British in sentiment and he obtained permission to use them in his system — a deliberate borrowing from the imperial metropolis.[48]

The Irish national school system also featured a uniform program of teacher education in a 'normal school'. Ryerson felt that such a program was essential in order to create a cadre of competent and loyal teachers to replace the suspect characters frequently found conducting classes in the colony. Therefore, one of his first steps was the establishment of the Toronto Normal School with a model school attached where student teachers could observe and practice. It was almost a replica of what he had seen in Dublin.

The hinterland status of Upper Canada vis-a-vis the metropolitan centres of Western Europe and the United States had obviously much to do with the way in which educational practices in these centres were copied in the establishment of her school system. But there was more to it than the simple imitative nature of colonial societies or the inferiority complex of the colonial mind. The borrowing was, after all, selective. And the criterion of selection was a perceived utility. There was a "sense of crisis" in Upper Canada brought about by rapid social change. Under such circumstances education was seen to be a vital agent of social cohesion. Gidney has argued plausibly that the "undeveloped social and institutional infrastructure" of the society precluded the provision of adequate educational facilities by bodies other than the state.[49] The colony's population was spread thinly over a large area. Its communities were of mixed religious composition. There was no philanthropic aristocracy nor were there well-established churches. In these conditions only the state had sufficient resources to set up a comprehensive network of schools, and consequently it did.

In other words, the conditions characteristic of a hinterland area, and the proximity of the frontier, dictated massive state intervention if education were to be provided. While ideas were borrowed freely from metropolitan areas, the end product was an educational innovation ideally suited to the conditions prevailing in the hinterland. It is worth noting, for instance, that the strong central educational authority that Ryerson established in the 1840's had no counterpart in contemporary England. The school system that emerged in Ontario, then, was in many respects a unique adaptation.

Western Canada

By 1870 the future character of Canada's prairie regions was as yet undetermined. What sort of society would be created there? What language would dominate? What model of education would be established? One thing was certain. The future did not lie with the native Indians, who by that time were already experiencing the hardships resulting from the buffalo slaughter. The land had been 'bought' by the federal government with the obvious intention that it would be settled by whites. But both Francophones and Anglophones already lived in the West and the real question was: which of these groups, representing as they did the two major linguistic groupings in central Canada, would dominate?

The outcome depended on one factor: migration. As it turned out, the vast majority of those who did move to the West were English-speakers, mainly from Ontario. What it meant was that as time passed, French-speakers, both in the newly created province of Manitoba, and in the North-West Territories (the area of present-day Alberta and Saskatchewan) rapidly became a powerless minority and it was left to the Anglo majority to determine the shape of the new society. Predictably enough, the institutional framework would be modelled closely on the familiar — Ontario.

Of course by the 1870's Ontario was no longer a pioneer society, but a rapidly industrializing province which had become the centre of economic and political power in Canada — in effect, a metropolitan centre in its own right. It also had a well-established school system — the creation of Egerton Ryerson. The system was non-sectarian, publicly supported and imposed with compulsory attendance laws and was an intrinsic element in the social fabric.

In the decades that followed, that system was to be transferred to the West, largely as a consequence of the migration of Ontarians, but also due to the increasing political and economic power of Ontario. Intimately connected with this transfer was the concept of Canadian national identity then emerging in English Canada — a concept characterized by loyalty to the British Empire and her political traditions.[50] The 'English-Protestant' dimensions of Canadian nationalism were most pronounced in Ontario. Ontarians viewed themselves as the real Canadians and looked on the West as their natural *Lebensraum*.[51] To ensure that their concept of identity and their cultural traditions were to determine the character of the new society, the Ryersonian system of education, with its emphasis on control and conformity, had to be transplanted.

The part of the western hinterland first effected by the influence of the Ontarian metropolis was the province of Manitoba. When that province came into being in 1870, its population was divided on a fairly even basis between English-speaking Protestant and French-speaking Catholic factions. The 'dual nationality' was given official recognition in the Act which established the province and it led to the creation of a system of separate denominational schools for each faction — an arrangement similar to that prevailing in Québec at the time.[52]

But the influx of English-speaking Protestants from Ontario quickly disrupted this neat balance and ultimately determined, as has been indicated, that the province, and the North-West as well, would be remade in the image of Ontario. The establishment of the Manitoba Normal School with prominent Ontario educator, David J. Goggin, as its principal, showed that an essential feature of the Ryersonian system was being adopted in the West.[53]

A far more significant step in this direction was the abolition, in 1890, of the official status of French and of separate denominational schools. Education then became the province of a centralized government department in the true Ryersonian spirit.[54] A subsequent experiment with bilingual schools of several varieties was brought to an end by the government of T.C. Norris in 1916. Compulsory school attendance was introduced, followed quickly by a repeal of the section of the Public School Act allowing for bilingual instruction. The English language was now to be imposed on all in spite of minority protests.

These measures were taken not just out of anti-French and anti-Catholic prejudice. They also represented a response to the fear of the 'Balkanization' of the West by immigrants. The diverse peoples coming from Europe to the province had to be assimilated into the English-Canadian cultural milieu.[55] The Ryersonian educational model, which provided a uniform learning experience for all, was the great instrument to be employed to this end.

Events followed a similar pattern in the old North-West Territories. In the 1870's and 1880's separate schools for Roman Catholics and French language rights were permitted in recognition of the substantial French-Catholic population of the area. But as the 1880's progressed the North West Council, and the Legislative Assembly that replaced it in 1888, were increasingly dominated by the English-speaking Protestant element. Most of these were recent arrivals from Ontario and Britain and had little sympathy for Catholicism or the French language. It meant that the character of the new society, as in Manitoba, was to be determined by "the numerical and political ascendancy of English-speaking Protestants".[56]

The two pivotal characters in these developments were Frederick Haultain, the chief executive of the North-West administration, and David Goggin who was Superintendent of Education between 1893 and 1902. Haultain was an Ontarian who believed that education should play a vital role in the North-West. He favoured "uniform instruction, uniform examinations, and uniform attainments of teachers" — fundamental tenets of the Ryersonian system.[57] Goggin, who was also an Ontarian, held similar views. He had the full confidence of Haultain and was given a free hand in directing education. In fact, as Superintendent of Education, he seemed to play the same role that Ryerson had played in Ontario. All aspects of the system received his attention: teacher training, qualification, the curriculum, finance, and so forth. In all respects he was the Tsar of education.[58]

That education would better serve the purposes of the administration, it had to be brought effectively under public control. As the 1880's progressed private, ecclesiastical and locally controlled schools were subjected to ever-increasing measures of government regulation. In 1892 the Territorial Assembly abolished the denominational Board of Education and brought all schools under the control of a Council of Public Instruction. In 1901 the noose of state control was tightened further with the creation of a Department of Education. Though separate Catholic schools were allowed under the system, government regulations ensured that they differed little from public schools — a situation virtually identical to that prevailing in Ontario.[59]

Not only was the school system of the North-West modelled closely in its structure on Ryersonian precedents, but it was also designed to serve similar purposes. Certainly the assimilation of immigrants to the English-Canadian cultural norm was one of its chief aims. Haultain admitted that the "function and mission" of the school was to "mould and assimilate all families making the prairies their home".[60] Goggin was also a strong advocate of Anglo-conformity. He insisted that "a common school and a common tongue are essential if we are to have a homogeneous citizenship". He spoke of the "unifying influence of the schools", especially with regard to the immigrant population.[61] To achieve this end the standardized curriculum was heavily punctuated with patriotic poems and songs that praised the glories of the British Empire.

The systems of public education established both in the province of Manitoba and in the North-West Territories bore striking similarities to that created in Ontario. That Ontarians were instrumental in the process made this natural enough. And the school promoters of the West had the same preoccupation with social control. Not only would education on the prairies serve to weld all the diverse immigrants into one pre-conceived national whole, but it would also serve as a palliative for the ills of society. As Daniel McIntyre, superintendent of public schools in Winnipeg put it in the 1890's, education was a safeguard against revolution and violence.[62] These were sentiments with which Egerton Ryerson would have heartily agreed.

The influence of metropolitan Ontario was all important in giving shape and purpose to education in the hinterland West in those early formative years. And it was an influence that continued. Despite the establishment of Normal Schools in Winnipeg and Regina, the West's dependency on Ontario-trained teachers lasted well into the twentieth century.[63] And the textbooks used in western schools were usually published in Ontario.[64] Innovations in Canadian education generally originated in Ontario and spread west from there. For example, kindergartens and technical/vocational schools were first adopted in Toronto and were later imitated throughout the province and later in the West.[65] As C.E. Phillips has put it:

> In the development of its educational system Ontario was often enabled by its size to do first and more thoroughly what newer and smaller provinces could attempt only partially and belatedly. Until the end of World War I, the western provinces frankly copied Ontario practice.[66]

As time passed, however, the West and its educational system developed characteristics of their own as Ontario domination came to be resisted. In the 1930's, for instance, the provinces of Alberta and Saskatchewan became leading innovators in adult and rural education and in 'progressive' curriculum reform. Of course these were not totally original concepts and they were inspired in many respects by the example of an increasingly influential metropolis — the United States.

Conclusion

The Canadian West experienced the archetypical frontier stage of development during most of the nineteenth century. Schools that existed during this period played but the limited role assigned to learning in such a society. It was only when the West was drawn into a symbiotic hinterland relationship with central Canada towards the end of the century that any systematic educational facilities were provided. But it is well to remember that central Canada itself had also experienced a frontier stage and a hinterland relationship with a metropolitan centre. The fact that the entire Canadian frontier experience was not prolonged did not reduce its effect on societal development. It was precisely this ongoing process of adaptation to the incessant, continuously expanding frontier line which helped shape the character of Canadian institutions. Although one can point to specific instances of metropolitan Ontario dominance in the educational systems of the West, the development of education in central Canada itself was an adaptive response to frontier conditions. The educational system of Ontario was never a carbon copy of that of Britain. Nor had the schools of New France been blind imitations of those of France. The institutions we have inherited, then, are the outcome of the dynamic resolution of the legacy of the frontier heritage, the reactive potential of the hinterland, and the force of metropolitan influence.

Notes

[1] F.J. Turner, "The Significance of the Frontier in American History" in *Annual Report of the American Historical Association for the Year 1893*, (Washington, Government Printing Office, 1894).

[2] *Ibid.*, pp. 199-200.

[3] F.J. Turner, *op. cit.*, p. 203.

[4] Lower, quoted in C. Berger, *The Writing of Canadian History*, (Toronto: Oxford University Press, 1976), p. 122.

[5] C.E. Phillips, *The Development of Education in Canada*, (Toronto: Gage, 1957), p. 100.

[6] N.S.B. Gras, *An Introduction to Economic History*, (New York: Harper, 1922).

[7] *Ibid.*, p. 187.

[8] A.K. Davis, "Canadian Society and History as Hinterland Versus Metropolis", in Horn and Sabourin, eds., *Studies in Canadian Social History*, (Toronto: McClelland and Stewart, 1974), p. 452.

[9] *Ibid.*, p. 453.

[10] P. Usher, "Hinterland Culture Shock", *Canadian Dimension*, Vol 8, No. 8, August 1972, p. 28.

[11] A.K. Davis, *op. cit.*, p. 453.

[12] G.F.G. Stanley, "Western Canada and the Frontier Thesis", *The Canadian Historical Association Report*, 1940, p. 105.

[13] J.M.S. Careless, "Frontierism, Metropolitanism, and Canadian History", in R. Cook, C. Brown, and C. Berger, eds., *Approaches to Canadian History*, (Toronto: University of Toronto Press, 1967), pp. 75-76.

[14] G.F.G. Stanley, *op. cit.*, p. 106.

[15] P. Usher, *op. cit.*, p. 28.

[16] J.M.S. Careless, *op. cit.*, p. 68.

[17] C. Berger, *The Writing of Canadian History*, (Toronto: Oxford University Press, 1976), p. 119.

[18] G.F.G. Stanley, *op. cit.*, p. 106.

¹⁹A.L. Burt, "The Frontier in the History of New France", *The Canadian Historical Association Report*, 1940.

²⁰A.R.M. Lower, *Colony to Nation*, (Toronto: Longmans, 1957), p. 48.

²¹J.D. Wilson et. al., *Canadian Education: A History*, (Scarborough, Ontario: Prentice-Hall, 1970), p. 191.

²²M. Smith, *A Geographical View of the Province of Upper Canada*, (Philadelphia: Thomas & Desilver, 1813), p. 62. See also *Proceedings of the Thirty-Ninth Convention of the Ontario Education Association*, Toronto, 1900, p. 275.

²³J.D. Wilson, et. al., *op. cit.*, p. 243.

²⁴C. Berger, *op. cit.*, p. 119. See also G.F.G. Stanley, *op. cit.*, p. 111.

²⁵F.J. Turner, *op. cit.*, p. 10.

²⁶W.L. Morton, *The Kingdom of Canada*, (Indianapolis: Bobbs-Merrill, 1963).

²⁷C. Berger, *op. cit.*, p. 243.

²⁸*Ibid.*, p. 117.

²⁹A.K. Davis, *op. cit.*, p. 450 and p. 453.

³⁰Gerald Cragg, *The Church and the Age of Reason 1648-1789*, Pelican History of the Church, Vol. IV, (Reprinted 1972), pp. 21-25.

³¹Cornelius Jaenen, *The Role of the Church in New France*, (Toronto: McGraw-Hill Ryerson, 1976), viii.

³²Louis-Philippe Audet, *Histoire de l'enseignement au Québec*, Tane I (Montreal: Holt, Rinehart et Winston, 1971), p. 122.

³³Cornelius Jaenen, *Friend and Foe: Aspects of French-Amerindian Cultural Contact in the Sixteenth and Seventeenth Centuries*, (Toronto: McClelland and Stewart, 1976), pp. 171-175.

³⁴Jaenen, *Role of the Church, op. cit.*, p. 98.

³⁵Audet, Histoire, *op. cit.*, p. 175.

³⁶Jaenen, *Role of the Church, op. cit.*, p. 101.

³⁷*Ibid.*, p. 106.

³⁸W.J. Eccles, *The Canadian Frontier, 1534-1760*, (Albuquerque: University of New Mexico Press, 1974), p. 100.

³⁹Jaenen, *Role of the Church, op. cit.*, p. 109.

⁴⁰R.D. Gidney, "Making Nineteenth Century School Systems: the Upper Canadian Experience and its Relevance to English Historiography", *History of Education*, Vol IX, No. 2 (1980), p. 111.

⁴¹Neil MacDonald, "Egerton Ryerson and the School as an Agent of Political Socialization" in N. McDonald and A. Chaiton (eds.) *Egerton Ryerson and His Times*, (Toronto: Macmillan, 1978), pp. 98-99.

⁴²Alison Prentice, *The School Promoters*, (Toronto: McClelland and Stewart, 1977), p. 124.

⁴³Steven Schecter, "Capitalism, Class and Educational Reform in Canada" in L. Panitch (ed.), *The Canadian State: Political Economy and Political Power*, (Toronto: University of Toronto Press, 1977), p. 374.

⁴⁴J. Donald Wilson, "Education in Upper Canada: Sixty Years of Change" in J.D. Wilson, R.M. Stamp and L.P. Audet (eds.), *Canadian Education: A History*, (Scarborough: Prentice-Hall, 1970), pp. 193-4.

⁴⁵*Ibid.*, p. 191.

⁴⁶J. Donald Wilson, "The Ryerson Years in Canada West", in Wilson, Stamp and Audet, *op. cit.*, p. 217.

[47]G.M. Craig, *Upper Canada: The Formative Years 1784-1841*, (Toronto: McClelland and Stewart, 1963), p. 187.

[48]J.D. Wilson, "Ryerson Years", *op. cit.*, p. 219.

[49]R.D. Gidney, *op. cit.*, pp. 113-116.

[50]Robert M. Stamp, "Canadian Education and the National Identity" in A. Chaiton and N. McDonald (eds.), *Canadian Schools and Canadian Identity*, (Toronto: Gage, 1977), pp. 29-37.

[51]Alan H. Child, "The Ryerson Tradition in Western Canada", in McDonald and Chaiton (eds.) *Egerton Ryerson and His Times, op. cit.*, p. 280.

[52]Cornelius Jaenen, "The Manitoba School Question: An Ethnic Interpretation" in Martin L. Kovacs (ed.), *Ethnic Canadians: Culture and Education*, (University of Regina: Canadian Plains Studies, 1978), p. 317.

[53]A.H. Child, *op. cit.*, p. 285.

[54]W.L. Morton, "Manitoba Schools and Canadian Nationality, 1890-1923", (Canadian Historical Association *Report*, 1951).

[55]C. Jaenen, "Manitoba School Question", *op. cit.*, p. 322.

[56]Neil MacDonald, "Canadian Nationalism and North-West Schools, 1884-1905", in A. Chaiton and N. McDonald (eds.), *Canadian Schools and Canadian Identity, op. cit.*, p. 59.

[57]A.H. Child, *op. cit.*, p. 285.

[58]Neil MacDonald, "David J. Goggin, Promoter of National Schools", in R.S. Patterson, J.W. Chalmers and J.W. Friesen (eds.), *Profiles of Canadian Educators*, (D.C. Heath, 1974), p. 174.

[59]A.H. Child, *op. cit.*, p. 293.

[60]*Ibid.*, p. 287.

[61]Neil MacDonald, "David J. Goggin", *op. cit.*, p. 178.

[62]A.H. Child, *op. cit.*, p. 289.

[63]C.E. Phillips, *op. cit.*, p. 229.

[64]A.H. Child, *op. cit.*, p. 281.

[65]R.M. Stamp, "Evolving Patterns of Education: English Canada from the 1870's to 1914", in Wilson, Stamp, Audet, *op. cit.*, p. 323

[66]C.E. Phillips, *op. cit.*, p. 224.

II

Education in New France

The initial rationale for the establishment of the colony of New France was profit. French merchants, hoping to make fortunes in the fur trade, helped plant the settlement in return for monopoly privileges. This gave the struggling community a dual economic base — the fur trade and agriculture — enterprises whose interests were often, ironically, at odds with each other.

To the desire for profits and free land was added a third impulse which aided the success of the venture — the missionary spirit of the Catholic Counter-Reformation. For habitants and fur-traders were accompanied to the new world by Catholic religious — men and women zealous to spread their beliefs among the pagan natives, and, of course, determined to provide spiritual guidance to the settlers.

After decades of precarious struggle New France was granted royal government in the 1660's as part of an overall policy of aggressive imperialism persued by Louis XIV's minister, Colbert. This gave the colony a distinct purpose — military and economic — and secured its ultimate survival. Royal government also tended to buttress the hierarchical structure of society, concentrating decision making in the hands of officials and augmenting the power of the Catholic church. There was little development of democratic ideas or institutions and the paternal absolutism of the regime seems to have been generally accepted.

New France was very much a society modelled on the conventions and prejudices of the mother country. In addition to an authoritarian system of government, the colony also employed the feudal system of land tenure known as the seigneurial system. This was a system that prevailed in France until the time of the revolution. What it meant was that New France was divided very much into distinct classes: those who owned land — seigneurs, and those who rented it from them — habitants.

Yet, In Eccles' article, "Society and the Frontier", we see that the attempts to transplant the social structure of France to the new world were somewhat frustrated by conditions on the frontier. The social distance between seigneur and habitant in New France was not as great as in the metropolis. The necessity of carving a new society out of the wilderness created a sense of cooperation between landlord and tenant that could not have existed in Europe at the time. Nor was the habitant an oppressed peasant — the abundance of land and food gave him an independence of spirit that resulted in the mitigation of the worst features of feudal obligations. As time passed French Canadian society developed many unique characteristics of its own. This was often remarked on by visitors from France, who were sometimes astonished at the difference they perceived. In other words, frontier influences were significant in determining the shape of the new society.

As has been mentioned, the Roman Catholic church, whose spiritual and moral supremacy were virtually unquestioned in seventeenth century France, was also transferred to the new world. There, it claimed for itself a position of power and influence similar to that which it held in the metropolis. Perhaps the best illustration of its dominance is its monopoly in educational matters which led logically to control over the minds of the people.

Brian Titley's article, "Tradition, Change and Education in French Canada", documents the educational activities of the church in the colony. Inspired by the crusading zeal of the Counter Reformation, the church claimed to be the sole authority in such matters. Education had a distinct moral purpose above all. As such, it was essentially an exercise in social control — ensuring that the populace accepted ecclesiastical supremacy in many spheres of life. It was also distributed proportionately to one's position on the social scale. This model of education — elitist and moral in conception — was firmly established in the settlement during the French Regime and survived the conquest with surprising resiliency. In fact, it was not uprooted until the events of the Quiet Revolution in the 1960's.

The study of schooling in New France shows us the origin of a particular Canadian tradition in education — that associated with the Catholic church and the French language. Not only did it form the basis of the school system in the province of Quebec, but was also transferred to other parts of the country by French Canadians. We meet it once more in the early days of the settlement of the prairies, where it competed with the other major educational tradition — that associated with state control, Protestantism and the English language.

Society and the Frontier*

W.J. Eccles

Of the more tangible factors that influenced Canadian society there can be no doubt that geography was very important. The St. Lawrence River and certain of its tributaries dominated life in the colony. The land suitable for agricultural settlement stretched in a narrow band along the St. Lawrence, wider on the south shore than on the North. Near Quebec the Laurentian Shield, scraped nearly bare long ago by an advancing ice age, meets the river. Below this point only small pockets of land at river mouths were suitable for agriculture. Above Quebec, on the north shore, the Shield draws away from the river to a distance of some forty miles at Montreal. On the south shore the belt of fertile land is quite wide between Quebec and Montreal but becomes a narrow ribbon along the river toward Gaspe. West of Montreal there is also good land but on both the St. Lawrence and Ottawa rivers, rapids make communications difficult. Consequently throughout the French regime land settlement was concentrated in the St. Lawrence Valley from a point a few miles west of Montreal to a little below Quebec, with pockets of settlements on both sides lower down the river.

Prior to 1663 the number of settlers and the amount of land cleared grew very slowly. in 1634 the first seigneurial grant was made to Robert Giffard by Richelieu's Company of New France. During the ensuing thirty years some seventy other seigneuries were granted. The Company sent a few settlers to the colony but in the main let this responsibility fall to the seigneurs who, for the most part, lacked the means to engage in a large-scale immigration program. The religious orders did bring out a goodly number of servants, laborers, and settlers; and the crown from time to time sent detachments of soldiers to aid in the colony's defense. By these means the population slowly grew, and stretches of forest near the three areas of settlement, Quebec, Trois-Rivières, and Montreal, were cleared back from the shores of the river. In 1640 the total French population in the colony — settlers, soldiers, clergy, fur trade company employees — numbered only about 240; by 1663, largely as a result of the efforts of the religious orders, this number had increased to some 2500. After the latter date, under the stimulus of the crown, settlement increased very rapidly; by 1669 the population had increased by two thirds, and by the end of the century it was at approximately the 15,000 mark, doubling thereafter each generation to a total of some 70,000 at the Conquest.[1]

The Canadian Frontier, 1534-1760 (Albuquerque: University of New Mexico Press, 1974), 83-102. Reproduced with the kind permission of the publisher.

The St. Lawrence dictated the pattern of settlement in another way. It was the main means of communication in the colony, in summer by canoe or sailing bargue, in winter by sleigh on the ice. The need for roads was thus obviated until the eighteenth century. Every settler desired land on the river, and the land holdings early took on the peculiar pattern that has endured to the present day, that of narrow strips running back from the river. Survey lines separating seigneuries ran at right angles to the river and as the generations succeeded each other the individual holdings became increasingly narrow. According to the law of the land, the *Coutume de Paris*, a seigneur's eldest son inherited the manor house and half the domain land; the rest was divided among the remaining children. The children of the humbler settlers, the *censitaires*, inherited equal parts of the parental land. After a few generations many of the individual holdings became too narrow to be worked efficiently, and in 1745 the intendant forbade anyone to build a house or barn on land narrower than one and a half arpents (approximately 100 yards) by thirty or forty linear arpents in depth. Those who contravened the *ordonnance* were fined 100 *livres* and their buildings were torn down at their expense.

By the eighteenth century the pattern was well established. Along both banks of the St. Lawrence from Quebec to Montreal the farms stretched back from the river, the houses and barns on the river bank spaced a few hundred yards apart. Every few miles there was a seigneurial manor house and a mill, and eventually a steep-roofed stone church. Later in the century concessions were taken up in the second range and another row of narrow strip farms stretched back from the rear of the first, with a roadway between the two. To anyone travelling by river up to Montreal nearly all of New France passed in review.

This pattern of land settlement was not without its disadvantages. Until the end of the seventeenth century the Iroquois were an almost constant menace, and with the homes spaced in this fashion mutual aid in times of attack was almost impossible. Individual farms and their occupants could be destroyed all too easily before aid could be mustered. While the Iroquois assaults were at their height stockaded forts had to be built in the exposed seigneuries where the people could take refuge with their livestock, abandoning their homes to the depredations of the enemy. Attempts by some of the royal officials to have the settlers live in villages with their concessions radiating our like spokes of a wheel, were not very successful. The Canadians insisted on having river frontage and living apart, lords of their own little domains, with access to the wider world beyond by way of the river.

By the mid-eighteenth century the farm houses in the first range and the churches, were nearly all of stone, thick-walled, substantial; steep Norman roofs were modified by a graceful curving wide eave, to afford shade in the hot Canadian summers. Peter Kalm, a Swedish professor of natural history who visited Canada in 1749, going by boat from Montreal to Quebec remarked:

The country on both sides was very delightful to-day, and the fine state of its cultivation added to the beauty of the scene. It could really be called a village, beginning at Montreal and ending at Quebec, which is a distance of more than one hundred and eighty miles, for the farmhouses are never above five arpents and sometimes but three apart, a few places excepted. The prospect is exceedingly beautiful when the river flows on for several miles in a straight line, because it then shortens the distance between the houses, and makes them form one continued village. . . . We sometimes saw windmills near the farms.. They were generally built of stone, with a roof of boards, which together with its wings could be turned to the wind.[2]

The principal crop grown was wheat but the climate of the St. Lawrence Valley was not particularly suitable for this cereal. Heavy rains sometimes caused serious loss from smut; early frosts were a constant menace; and plagues of caterpillars occasionally destroyed everything growing. Yet crop failures appear to have been no more frequent than in France, where they were anticipated, on an average, once every five years.[3] In the early years the yield was high, the natural result of rich virgin soil. By the mid-eighteenth century it had declined considerably, despite the increase in the number of cattle and the consequent increased use of manure.

Peter Kalm was very critical of the inefficient agricultural methods he had observed in the English colonies. He was not less critical of those in New France; they both compared unfavorably with farming methods that he had studied in England, which he stated were the most advanced in Europe. One factor that militated against efficient agricultural production, in New France as in the English colonies, was the chronic shortage of labor. When able-bodied men could obtain land very cheaply, they were not inclined to work for others, except at excessively high wages. The wages paid skilled tradesmen were also high, resulting in a drift from the country to the three towns, which contained 25 percent of the colonial population. A much more important factor, however, was the large number of men, of necessity the young and physically fit, who were continually out of the colony on voyages to the west.

All the evidence indicates that the Canadian *habitants* and the laboring class in the towns enjoyed a higher standard of living and much more personal freedom than did their counterparts in Europe. This undoubtedly accounts, to some degree, for the difference in their attitudes and character that visitors from Europe all remarked on. But what seems to have had an even greater influence was their frequent contact, on terms of equality, with the Indian nations. Nor did they have to voyage far for this contact. Within the confines of the colony, or close by, were several resident Indian bands. Near Quebec, at Lorette, resided a band of Huron, survivors of the 1649 diaspora. A few miles south of Quebec was the Abenaki village of St. Francois, removed from Acadia to protect the colony's southern approaches from Anglo-American incursions up the Connecticut River. Near Montreal were two Indian settlements: the Mission Iroquois at Sault St. Louis and the Sulpician mission that had first been established on the lower slopes of Mount Royal, then, as the town grew, had been moved first to the north side of the island, later to the western tip, and finally across the Lake of Two Mountains to Oka. The Mission Iroquois at Sault St. Louis (Caugnawaga to the Iroquois) were originally Mohawks who had been converted to Christianity by the Jesuits and had then removed to New France the better to preserve their new faith.[4] Members of other of the Iroquois nations, after conversion, subsequently moved to Caugnawaga to spare themselves the constant taunts of their fellow tribesmen who had remained pagan.

Another reason for this Iroquois defection to Canada was the desire to avoid the Albany rum traders. Not all the Indians were incapable of resisting the temporary delights that intoxication brought; the authorities of both New France and New York were frequently asked by the chiefs of the Iroquois and Algonkin nations to keep liquor away from their villages. The governors of New France, for the most part, did their best to comply and managed to curb the abuse to a considerable degree. The same could not be said of the authorities at Albany. There, rum and whisky of such appalling quality that it was little better than poison was the main item of trade, used to get the Indians drunk before they traded their furs and then defraud them. This practice was so common that the Dutch traders at Albany were little more than Canada's secret weapon, for although many of the western Indians would bypass the French posts to go to Albany where they were given all the liquor they could drink,[5] they were not so besotted that they did not later realize the consequences. This is not to say that there were no Canadian traders willing to use liquor in the same way in their commercial dealings with the Indians. The Jesuit missionaries at Sault St. Louis waged a constant struggle to keep such traders away from their charges, and the Oka mission had removed to this site largely to keep the converts away from the taverns and unscrupulous purveyors.

The members of this latter mission were a mixture of Iroquois and northern Algonkin; the common factor was their conversion to Christianity. During the colonial wars these warriors, particularly those of Sault St. Louis, performed valiant service; indeed, the authorities at Albany were greatly concerned lest most of the Five Nations should remove to Canada. Had this occurred, Albany and all the northern settlements would have had to be abandoned. Although in expeditions against the villages of the Five Nations the Mission Iroquois could not be depended on — they frequently gave their kinsmen warning — the devastating raids on the settlements of New England were carried out by war parties composed largely of these domiciled tribesmen, combined with Canadian militia, and led by officers in the colonial regulars, the Troupes de la Marine. Thus the Canadians were closely associated with the Indians, waging war after their fashion, using their techniques and becoming as adept in the harsh, cruel methods as any Iroquois or Abenaki. There was, therefore, a demonstrable degree of truth in the opinion of the

Canadians expressed by one French officer: "They make war only by swift attacks and almost always with success against the English who are not as vigorous nor as adroit in the use of fire arms as they, nor as practiced in forest warfare".[6]

In peacetime too, the Canadians were in constant association with the Indians. The Indians were frequent visitors to Montreal, and to prevent constant blood baths, the intendant had to set aside certain taverns for the Indian trade, allocated by nation, and strictly regulated. It is, therefore, hardly surprising that the Canadians early adopted much of the Indian way of life and became imbued with some of their character traits. Native foods such as corn, squash, and pumpkins found ready acceptance. Indian means of travel — the snowshoe, toboggan, and canoe — were quickly mastered. Many of the Canadians, who were inveterate pipe smokers, preferred to mix their locally grown tobacco with the inner bark of the cherry or dogwood tree, a custom borrowed from the Indians. In their mode of dress the *habitants* copied the Indians, with an effect rather startling to European eyes. The women, except when dressed up fine for Sunday mass, wore a short jacket or blouse and a short skirt which, Peter Kalm several times observed "does not reach to the middle of their legs".

It was during their frequent trips to the west that the Canadians were most exposed to the Indian way of life. Immediately following the establishment of royal government in 1663 the population of the colony expanded rapidly, from approximately 2500 to an estimated 15,000 by the end of the century. Of the latter number as many as five hundred of the active males were always off in the west on trading expeditions. It was during these years that senior officials, newly arrived from France, began to comment on the striking difference between the Canadians and their peers in France. Inevitably, these officials were first struck by what seemed to them the deleterious social and economic effects of the metamorphosis.

The Marquis de Denonville, governor general from 1685 to 1689, was appalled by certain attitudes and habits of the Canadians. Instead of laboring on the land, they preferred to spend their lives in the bush, trading with the Indians, where their parents, the *cures*, and the officials could not govern them, and where they lived like savages. Even when they returned to the colony these youths showed a shocking proclivity for going about half naked in the hot weather, as did the Indians. "I cannot emphasize enough, my lord, the attraction that this Indian way of life has for all these youths," Denonville wrote to the minister. But he then went on to say, "The Canadians are all big, well built, and firmly planted on their legs, accustomed when necessary to live on little, robust and vigorous, very self willed and inclined to dissoluteness; but they are witty and vivacious."[7] The intendant Jean Bochart de Champigny in 1691 wrote in much the same vein, stating, "It is most unfortunate that Canadian youths, who are vigorous and tough, have no inclination for anything but these voyages where they live in the forest like Indians for two or three years at a time, without benefit of any of the sacraments."[8]

Peter Kalm in 1749 was also much impressed by the martial qualities of the Canadians, acquired through their frequent sojourns in the west. He noted that they were exceptional marksmen: "I have seldom seen any people shoot with such dexterity as these. . . . There was scarcely one of them who was not a clever marksman and who did not own a rifle." He then went on:

> It is inconceivable what hardships the people of Canada must undergo on their hunting journeys. Sometimes they must carry their goods a great way by land. Frequently they are abused by the Indians, and sometimes they are killed by them. They often suffer hunger, thirst, heat, and cold, and are bitten by gnats, and exposed to the bites of snakes and other dangerous animals and insects. These (hunting expeditions) [sic] destroy a great part of the youth in Canada, and prevent the people from growing old. By this means, however, they become such brave soldiers, and so inured to fatigue that none of them fears danger or hardships. Many of them settle among the Indians far from Canada, marry Indian women, and never come back again.[9]

Some of the Jesuit missionaries in the west took a much more jaundiced view of the effects of the close relations between the Canadians and the Indians. Fathers St. Cosme and Carheil at Michilimackinac made that post appear, from their description, a veritable Sodom or Gomorrah, where the only occupations of the Canadians, apart from trading furs, were drinking, gambling and lechery. Things had come to such a pass that the *coureurs de bois* took Indian women with them rather than men on their trading expeditions. The men claimed that these women worked for lower wages than men demanded, and were willing to perform such chores as cutting firewood and cooking. The missionaries refused to be persuaded that other fringe benefits were not involved.[10] The governor general Vaudreuil, although he did not support the Jesuit proposal to keep the Canadians and Indians as far apart as possible, was strongly opposed to mixed marriages. He claimed that the children of mixed blood incorporated the worst character traits of both races and were a constant source of trouble. He, therefore, issued orders forbidding such marriages at Detroit, the main French post in the west at that time (1709).[11]

These complaints on the part of the missionaries have to be taken with a pinch of salt. To them, chastity, or failing this monogamy with the benefit of the marriage sacrament, was the ideal. They expected these *voyageurs* who, if married, had left their wives in the colony, to live like monks while in the west. The Indians had different moral values and chastity was not among them. Father Charlevoix, who was not a missionary, took a more tolerant view of Canadian society in the 1740's. He commented:

> Our Creoles are accused of great avidity in amassing, and indeed they do things with this in view, which could hardly be believed if they were not seen. The journeys they undertake; the fatigues they undergo; the dangers to which they expose themselves, and the efforts they make surpass all

imagination. There are, however, few less interested, who dissipate with greater facility what has cost them so much pains to acquire, or who testify less regret at having lost it. Thus there is some room to imagine that they commonly undertake such painful and dangerous journeys out of a taste they have contracted for them. They love to breathe a free air, they are early accustomed to a wandering life; it has charms for them, which make them forget past dangers and fatigues, and they place their glory in encountering them often. . . . I know not whether I ought to reckon amongst the defects of our Canadians the good opinion they entertain of themselves. It is at least certain that it inspires them with a confidence, which leads them to undertake and execute what would appear impossible to many others. . . . It is alleged they make bad servants, which is owing to their great haughtiness of spirit, and to their loving liberty too much to subject themselves willingly to servitude.[12]

These observations on the cupidity of the Canadians, coupled with their spendthrift attitude, are significant for these same traits were quite pronounced among the Indians. Like the Indian, the Canadian did not see any merit in storing up worldly goods; both looked down on those who did, and up to those who spent their money ostentatiously on good living. The Canadians too, became proud, independent, and improvident, glorying in their physical strength, their hardihood, and their contempt for danger, caring little for the morrow. One French officer commented, in 1757:

They are not thrifty and take no care for the future, being too fond of their freedom and their independence. They want to be well thought of and they know how to make the most of themselves. They endure hunger and thirst patiently, many of them having been trained from infancy to imitate the Indians, whom, with reason, they hold in high regard. They strive to gain their esteem and to please them. Many of them speak their language, having passed part of their life amongst them at the trading posts.[13]

It would seem an obvious conclusion that the Canadians had acquired this attitude from the Indians, and were able to do so because the necessities of life were relatively easily come by in Canada. In other words, this character trait was a product of relative affluence and the frontier environment. It was to no small degree the fact that the Canadians did come to share this attitude with the Indians that their individual relations with them were usually better than were those of the Anglo-Americans. Ruette D'Auteuil, the attorney general at Quebec, spoke the truth for his day when he claimed that, the price of trade goods being equal, the Indians preferred to have dealings with the French rather than with the English.[14] This view was later corroborated by a British commentator who stated that, "the French have found some secret of conciliating the affections of the savages, which our traders seem stranger to, or at least take no care to put it in practice."[15]

Not only did the Canadians travel to the far west, they also voyaged northeastward, serving as crews on fishing boats in the Gulf and in the seal- and whale-hunting expeditions along the coast of Labrador. There, too, they came in frequent contact with Indians, and also with the Eskimo. In wartime they served as privateers, preying on shipping along the New England coast. French privateer captains frequently called at Quebec to take on crews, Canadians being very highly regarded for their toughness and bellicosity.

Canadians in all sections of the colony were accustomed to make trips to distant parts of the continent and to live among peoples of an entirely different culture. The whole continent from Labrador and Hudson Bay to the Rocky Mountains and the Gulf of Mexico was their world. Unlike their counterparts in Europe who rarely moved beyond the confines of their native parish, there was nothing parochial about them; they were men of broad horizons and a continental outlook able to accommodate themselves to almost any conditions anywhere. Were life to become too restrictive in the settlements along the St. lawrence or were a wife to nag too constantly, some of them at least could hire out as *voyageurs* for the west or as crew on a voyage to Labrador, France, or the West Indies. Even those who never made such a trip could feel that the opportunity was there, and this must have given them a sense of freedom. They could not help but hear the tales of those who had voyaged far afield, of the strange peoples with stranger customs in these distant lands. They, too, shared the experience, vicariously.

Royal officials in the eighteenth century, upon first arriving in the colony, were quick to remark that the Canadians had become a distinct people with values and manners markedly at variance with those of the same class in the mother country. Usually they were quite taken aback by the attitudes and way of life of the Canadians. Only after they had been in the colony for a few years did they come to appreciate the positive side of what had at first seemed a society and people sadly in need of discipline and reform. It was the free and easy, seemingly dissolute, ways of the Canadians, their independent attitude, their insistence on being led not driven, that irked the officials, both civil and military. Other observers were struck by their profligacy, their feast or famine attitude, their recklessness. A Sulpician priest upon arrival in the colony in 1737 remarked that the bulk of the people — military officers, merchants, artisans, and *habitants* alike — were "as poor as artists and as vain as peacocks" and spend every sou they had on ostentatious living. He was shaken to see country girls who tended cows during the week, on Sundays bedecked in lace and hoop skirts, wearing their hair in the very elaborate, high-piled style known then as *a la Fontange*.[16]

Despite these shortcomings, all observers agreed that the Canadians were tough and hardy, gloried in feats of endurance that made Europeans blanch, could travel from one end of the continent to another while living off the land, and had no equal in forest warfare. It was also noted that these same men, when in their homes, were uncommonly courteous, with a natural air of gentility more usual among the nobility than the lower classes.[17] In this respect they compared very favorably with their counterparts, the peasants of France and the settlers in the English colonies. Peter Kalm was particularly struck by this and in his journal he noted that:

> The inhabitant of Canada, even the ordinary man, surpasses in politeness by far those people who live in these English provinces. . . . On entering one of the peasant's houses, no matter where, and on beginning to talk with the men or women, one is quite amazed at the good breeding and courteous answers which are received, no matter what the question is. . . Frenchmen who were born in Paris said themselves that one never finds in France among country people the courtesy and good breeding which one observes everywhere in this land. I heard many native Frenchmen assert this.[18]

It would, of course, be very easy to ascribe these peculiarities to the frontier environment of New France. There can be no doubt that the frontier had a good deal to do with this, but the changes that took place in Canadian society were very complex. It is therefore necessary to examine conditions in the colony closely to discover the various elements that differed from those of France and then decide which ones were occasioned by the frontier.

Perhaps the basic factor was the abundance of free, fertile land, and the peculiar terms of land tenure under the seigneurial regime. This meant that the Canadian *habitants* were assured of as much land as they could cultivate, and they paid for it only very modest seigneurial dues, if they paid any at all, amounting to less than 10 percent of their annual income from the land.[19] Apart from this obligation, and the tithe for the church, fixed by royal decree at one twenty-sixth of the wheat grown, the *habitants* paid no other taxes. Labor service for the seigneurs, in the form of *corvées*, was very rarely imposed and was, in fact, a violation of the *Coutume de Paris.* In the few seigneuries where it was imposed it consisted of one day's labor in March or an exemption payment of two *livres.* Parish and royal *corvées* for work on the seigneurial common land, roads, bridges, or fortifications were a form of taxation but they usually amounted to not more than three or four days of labor a year, and the seigneur was supposed to do his share, under the supervision of the militia captain.

Unlike the peasant in France who spent his life sweating, scrimping, cheating, and saving to put aside enough money to buy a small piece of land or to purchase exemption from manorial obligations, and who had to keep his little hoard well hidden, wearing rags, living in a hovel, giving every appearance of near starvation to prevent the tax collectors from seizing his savings, the Canadian could spend what he had earned without a care. He could buy land for his sons so as to have them near him and spare them the necessity of clearing virgin forest on a new seigneury, or he could spend his earnings on consumer goods and entertainment. Whereas the economics of the situation would tend to make the French peasant mean and grasping, the Canadian could afford to be openhanded, with little care for the morrow.

In 1699 the intendant Jean Bochart de Champigny commented that for the most part the *habitants* lived well, enjoying the right to hunt and fish, privileges that were stringently denied their European counterparts. In that age wood and leather were vital commodities; the Canadians had ample supplies of both. Canadians who moved to France complained bitterly of the shortage and high cost of firewood, and declared that they suffered far more from damp winter cold there than they ever had in Canada. In the eighteenth century the intendant Gilles Hocquart remarked that no one starved in Canada. Of few lands in Europe could this have been said. The normal consumption of meat was half a pound per person a day, and of white wheat bread, two French pounds a day. Moreover, the climate allowed the Canadians to keep plentiful supplies of meat, fish, and game frozen hard for use throughout the winter; but a mid-winter thaw that lasted too long could be calamitous. At the town markets fish were sold frozen and cut with a saw. Eels, taken at Quebec by the thousand, were a staple food; smoked or salted, they were described by Frontenac as the *"habitants' manna."* They were also a major export item to France, being considered far better than the European variety. Ice houses were common, making possible iced drinks and desserts all summer, not just for the wealthy as in France, but for the majority of the population. The colored ices served by the French in hot weather were a source of wonderment to visiting Indians when entertained by the governor, and their effect on the decayed teeth of certain elderly chiefs was electric.

The vitamin content of the Canadian diet, being much richer in protein, was considerably higher than that of the peasants and urban working class in France, who had to exist on coarse bread and vegetable stews with meat only on very rare occasions.[20] In Europe the bulk of the population went to bed hungry on most nights. Such was rarely the case in Canada. Mme. Marie-Isabelle Begon, widow of the governor of Trois-Rivieres, who in 1749 moved from Montreal to the family estate near Rochefort querulously asked, "Where are those good partridges we left for the servants? I would gladly eat them now".[21] It is not surprising that the fine physical stature of the Canadians occasioned frequent comment from persons recently come from France. In fact, the Canadians were better fed then than a sizeable percentage of North Americans are today.

If the Canadians had been willing to work hard, they could all have been very prosperous. Some of the royal officials, charged with improving the colonial economy, declared that the men showed a marked distaste for hard work and that the unbridled vanity of their womenfolk kept them poor. In 1699 Champigny noted: "The men are all strong and vigorous but have no liking for work of any duration; the women love display and are excessively lazy."[22] Denonville, thirteen years earlier, had also remarked that the indolence of the men and the desire of the women to live like gentle ladies kept the people poor and the colony's economy backward. Such comments have to be considered in context.

The Canadian *habitant* could provide for his basic needs without too much effort, and he preferred to devote his extra time, not to produce an agricultural surplus to please the intendant or to add to his own store of wordly goods, but to the relaxed environment of his leisure hours. He would grow enough flax or hemp to supply his own needs, but frequently declined to raise a surplus for export. Rather than raise more cattle, he raised horses; by the early eighteenth century all but the poorer families had a carriage and sleigh for social occasions, and every youth had his own horse, used not for the plow but for racing, or to pay calls on the neighborhood girls. During the War of the Spanish Succession the governor and intendant became concerned over this, claiming that in winter the men no longer used snowshoes because they always traveled by horse and sleigh. It was difficult, they stated, to find enough men who could use snowshoes when they were needed for war parties against New England. The question might well be asked; how many peasants in Europe owned horses and carriages let alone used them for mere social purposes. The average horse cost forty *livres* (roughly $80.00 in today's money) and a good one a hundred *livres* or more,[23] thus the Canadian *habitants* were relatively affluent, and this could not help but have influenced their social attitudes.

Given these conditions it is hardly surprising that the Canadians were by no means as submissive or even respectful, on occasion, toward their social superiors as was thought fitting. As early as 1675 the members of the Sovereign Council were incensed by derogatory graffiti on walls in Quebec, and several years later the intendant had to threaten stern action against those who composed, distributed, or sang songs that he regarded as libelous and defamatory of certain prominent persons in the colony. This last, however, might be regarded as merely the continuance of an old French tradition that had flourished in the days of the *Mazarinades*. Thus, rather than the frontier environment, economic affluence and the French temperament were the more significant factors here.

Much is made of the prevalence of lawlessness on the Anglo-American frontier. To a limited degree this was also true of New France, and it is significant that it was at Montreal, the fur trade and military base, the main point of contact between European and Indian cultures, more than at Quebec, that respect for law and order was sometimes lacking. In 1711 the governor and intendant had to establish a police force in Montreal, consisting of one lieutenant and three archers, to make the citizens keep the peace and to control drunken Indians. An educated soldier in the colonial troops, newly arrived in Canada, remarked that the citizens of Montreal called those of Quebec "sheep", and that the character of the latter was gentler and less proud. The Quebecers reciprocated by calling the men of Montreal "wolves", a label that the soldier thought apt since the Montrealers spent much of their time in the forest among the Indians. In 1754 an officer recommended that Quebec men be employed to transport supplies to the Ohio forts because they were much "gentler" and almost as vigorous as those from the Montreal area.

Despite the frequent tavern brawls and duels, the incidence of crimes of violence was not great. But what is much more significant is that, given the nature of the populace, accustomed to the relatively unrestrained, wild, free life that the fur trade afforded, very rarely was there any overt resistance to authority. On the few occasions when the people protested openly and vigorously something done, or not done, the authorities were able to subdue them quickly without recourse to punitive measures. Most of these manifestations — some five in all — were occasioned by high prices charged for certain commodities, leading the people to believe that the merchants were profiteering and that the authorities were delinquent in not taking steps to stop them. The heaviest penalty inflicted on the leaders of these "seditious gatherings" appears to have been less than two months in jail.[24] The conclusion to be drawn from all this is that the Canadian people had little to complain about, but when they did complain too vigorously order was maintained without the overt use of force.

The attitude of the Canadians toward the religious authorities makes it plain that their opinions had to be taken into account. When it was decided, immediately after the inauguration of royal government in 1663, to impose tithes on the people for the support of a secular clergy, the bishop stipulated that it be at the rate of one thirteenth of the produce of the land, payable in wheat. The people protested vigorously, claiming this to be more than they could afford. The Bishop reduced his demand to one twentieth, but the *habitants* and seigneurs would agree to pay only one twenty-sixth of their wheat, not of all their produce, with a five year exemption for newly settled concessions. With this the clergy had to be satisfied. That it was not enough is made plain by the fact that the crown had to provide the clergy with an annual subsidy to make up the difference between what the tithe produced and what the *cures* needed. By the 1730's however, as more land came into production, many of the parish priests were relatively well off.

Further evidence that the Canadians were anything but subservient to clerical authority is provided by the frequent *ordonnances* of the intendant ordering the *habitants* of this or that parish to behave with more respect toward the cloth; to cease their practice of walking out of church as soon as the *cure* began his sermon; of standing in the lobby arguing, even brawling, during the service; of slipping out to a nearby tavern; of bringing their dogs into church and expostulating with the beadle who tried to chase them out. Frequently the bishop thundered from the pulpit against the women who attended mass wearing elaborate coiffures and low-cut gowns. But all to no avail; décolletage remained that of the Paris salons. When Bishop St. Vallier somehow learned that female members of his flock wore nothing but petticoats under their gowns he was horrified. In a curiously phrased pastoral letter he demanded that they immediately cease to imperil their immortal souls in this manner.[25]

What the response was is not known. And a practice that might be advanced in support of the thesis that the frontier bred initiative was the Canadian custom of *mariage a la gaumine*, a form of "do it yourself" marriage ceremony which both the clergy and the civil authorities frowned on severely.[26]

At the upper end of the social scale, the most significant feature of this Canadian society was the aristocratic and military ethos that dominated it. This was not unique to Canada; it was part of the French old regime heritage. In the seventeenth century the aim of the rising, powerful bourgeois class was to gain entry into the ranks of the nobility, or at least to emulate the way of life of the aristocracy. Molière made this plain in *Le Bourgeois Gentilhomme*. Despite the fact that the Canadian economy was basically commercial and dependent largely on the fur trade, bourgeois commercial values did not dominate society; indeed, they were scorned. The ambitious Canadian merchant wished to be something more than prosperous. That was merely one rung on the ladder. The ultimate goal was entry into the ranks of the *noblesse* and receipt of the coveted Order of St. Louis for distinguished service. More than wealth, men wished to bequeath to their sons a higher social status and a name distinguished for military valor, some great achievement, or the holding of high office. The proverb, *"Bon renom vaut mieux que ceinture dorée"*, summed up the Canadian philosophy at all levels of society.[27]

Wealth was, of course, desired, and ethics frequently went by the board in its pursuit. Men who might well have been ennobled for valiant service were denied if they lacked the means to live in a fitting manner. Wealth was sought, not for itself, but to enable men to live in the style of the class they sought to enter. Father Charlevoix, the Jesuit historian, writing in the 1740's commented on one aspect of this proclivity: "There is a great fondness for keeping up one's position, and nearly no one amuses himself by thrift. Good cheer is supplied, if its provision leaves means enough to be well clothed; if not, one cuts down on the table in order to be well dressed". He then went on to compare the Canadians with the English colonists to the south: "The English colonist amasses means and makes no superfluous expense; the French enjoys what he has and often parades what he has not. The former works for his heirs; the latter leaves his in the need in which he is himself to get along as best as he can."[28]

In Canada it was in some ways much easier than in France for ambitious men to adopt the values and attitudes of the nobility and even to become ennobled. Despite the fact that society was very much status ordered, it was relatively easy for a talented, ambitious man or woman to move up the social scale. Four factors help account for this: the availability of free land, the economic opportunities presented by the fur trade, the Royal edict of 1685 which permitted members of the nobility resident in Canada to engage directly in commerce and industry, something that, with a few notable exceptions such as the manufacture of glass and paper, was not permitted in France, and the presence of a large corps of regular troops in the colony in which Canadians could obtain commissions as officers.

It is rather ironic that when the king issued the edict of 1685 allowing nobles in Canada to engage in trade, he intended merely to stimulate the colonial economy.[29] It quickly came, however, to function in a way not anticipated by Louis XIV, for if those who were of noble status could engage in trade, there was nothing to prevent merchants and entrepreneurs who were not noble from aspiring to become so, provided they fulfilled the other requirements. Thus a Canadian of humble origin could make his fortune in the fur trade, acquire a seigneury, have his sons, if not himself, commissioned in the Troupes de la Marine, and hope one day he, or his sons, would be ennobled for valiant service. Enough Canadians accomplished this feat to encourage a much larger number to govern their lives accordingly. It was the old story, few are chosen but many hear the call.

To be a seigneur, the first rung up the social ladder, was a distinct mark of social superiority, made manifest in a variety of ways; hence there was never any lack of applicants;[30] but it necessitated accepting rather onerous responsibilities and in the seventeenth century most seigneurs had a hard time making ends meet. Yet so eager were the Canadians to attach the coveted particle *de* to their names that by 1760 there were nearly 250 seigneuries in the colony. Even more significant, it is estimated that there were some 200 *arrière fiefs* or sub-seigneuries, that is, small seigneuries granted by a seigneur within his own seigneury to a friend or relative whom he wished to see get on in the world. Another significant point is that many seigneurs, the majority of whom lived in the towns and not on their lands, did not bother to collect the stipulated dues, *the cens et rentes,* from their *censitaires.* Clearly, many seigneurs were not interested in the economic aspect of land holding. The only other motive would appear to be the social prestige attached to the title. In other words, Joseph Blondeau was undoubtedly a good name, but Joseph Blondeau de Grandarpents, of even de Petitarpents, was much better.

There were some who sought to gain entry into the *noblesse* through the back door, by simply assuming a title and claiming its privileges. In 1684 a royal edict was enacted levying a fine of 500 *livres* on any Canadian who falsely claimed noble status. A few years later the intendant Champigny stated that there were many such in the colony, but in time of war he thought it unwise to initiate an enquiry lest it cool their ardor for military campaigns. He also declared that several officers had requested to be ennobled and although some of them merited it, he could not support their requests because they lacked the means to live as members of the *noblesse* should.[31] Although gaining entry into the ranks of the nobility was by no means easy, it was remarked in the mid-eighteenth century that there was a greater number of nobles in New France than in all the other French colonies combined. It was not the actual number of nobles that was important; rather it was the scale of values that they imparted to the whole of society, the tone that was set, and the influence it had on the way of life of the Canadian people.

Inextricably mingled with, and greatly strengthening, this aristocratic ethos was the military tradition of New France. In Europe wars were fought by professional armies, and civilians were not directly involved unless they happened to get in the way while a battle was being fought. This was more true of France and Britain than of other countries, since they both had sense enough to wage their wars on other nations' territory. In Canada when war came, all the settled areas were a battlefield and everyone was obliged to be a combatant. The administration of the colony was organized along military lines. The entire male population was formed into militia companies, given military training, and employed in campaigns. In 1665 the Carignan Salieres regiment arrived in the colony to quell the Iroquois; it comprised over a thousand officers and men, and many of them stayed on as settlers. This greatly enhanced the influence of the military, for at that time the total population was less than 3000. Twenty years later the Troupes de la Marine were permanently stationed in the colony, some 1300 men and 400 officers by the end of the century among a total population of 15,000.

In the campaigns against the Iroquois and the English colonies it was quickly discovered that Canadians made better officers in forest warfare than did regulars from France. Consequently this career was opened to the seigneurs and their sons. They seized on it eagerly. Youths in their teens were enrolled as cadets and served on campaigns with their fathers or elder brothers to gain experience, then were sent out in command of scouting and small raiding parties to capture prisoners for intelligence purposes. The minister, however, thought they were being enrolled at far too early an age, while still mere children, and suspected the practice was merely a means for their families to draw military pay and allowances. Mme. de Vaudreuil, wife of the governor general, declared, "It would be advantageous for the well-being of the colony to accept youths of good families as cadets in the troops at fifteen or sixteen; that would form their characters early, render them capable of serving well and becoming good officers". The minister and Louis XIV were not convinced, they ordered that cadets had to be seventeen before they could be enrolled.[32] The dominant values of Canadian society were clearly those of the soldier and the noble, the military virtues those held in highest regard.

The social circles of Montreal and Quebec, comprising the senior officials, the army officers, and seigneurs, were undoubtedly very urbane, reflecting the polish and social graces of the French *noblesse*. Certainly Peter Kalm found this society much more civilized than that which he encountered in the English colonies where few people thought of anything but making money and not spending it.[33] Some of the senior officials who came from France in the eighteenth century, men like the intendant Claude Thomas Dupuy and the Comte de la Galissoniere, took a keen interest in natural science, as had earlier the doctor and surgeon Michel Sarrazin who was a corresponding member of the

Academie Royale des Sciences, but few Canadians showed much interest in intellectual pursuits.

The parish schools provided a basic education for those who wished it, and the Jesuit college at Quebec offered facilities as good as those in the larger French provincial cities. The letters and dispatches of Canadian-born officers and merchant traders in the mid-eighteenth century demonstrate that, with the rare exception of an officer such as Claude-Pierre Pecaudy de Contre-coeur who although a competent commandant had obviously had little schooling, they were all well-educated men. They expressed themselves succinctly and quite often felicitously; their syntax was good, the subjunctive employed where required; the literary style as well as the contents of their letters make them a pleasure to read. In fact, these men appear to have been as well educated as their counterparts in the French and British armies.

Yet the colony did not develop a literary tradition; the published journals depicting life in the colony were written by men from France and were intended for a metropolitan audience. But then, Canadians would see little merit in describing what was familiar to all their compatriots. Several Canadians had large private libraries, but there was no public library. Nor was there a printing press in the colony, hence no newspaper, not because of any sinister repression of thought by the clergy, but because there was no great need there was therefore no demand for one. In these realms of activity Canada lagged far behind the English colonies. In short, New France was the Sparta, not the Athens of North America.

Notes

[1]*Chronological List of Canadian Censuses*, Bureau of Statistics, Demography Branch, Ottawa.

[2]Adolph B. Benson (ed.), *Peter Kalm's Travels in North America*, 2 vols. (New York, 1966), vol. II, pp. 416-417.

[3]Le Roi a Vaudreuil et Raudot, Versailles, 6 juillet 1709, *Rapport de la Province de Quebec*, 1942-1943 (hereafter cited as *RAPQ*), p. 408.

[4]E.B. O'Callaghan and J.R. Brodhead, *Documents Relating to the Colonial History of New York*, 15 vols. (Albany, 1856-1883), vol. IV, p. 693.

[5]Benson (ed.), *Kalm's Travels in North America*, Vol. II, p. 600.

[6]Papiers La Pause. *RAPQ*, 1931-1932, pp. 66-67.

[7]Denonville au Ministre, Que., 13 nov. 1685, Archives Nationales, Colonies, Series C11A, vol 7, pp. 89-95.

[8]Memoire instructif sur le Canada, 10 may 1691, *ibid.*, Vol. 11, pp. 262-268.

[9]Benson (ed.), *Peter Kalm's Travels in North America*, vol. 11, pp. 522, 563.

[10]Etienne de Carheil, S.J. a Champigny, Michilimackinac, 30 d'août 1702, Public Archives of Canada, Series M. vol. 204, Part 1, pp. 177-179.

[11]Vaudreuil et Raudot au Ministre, Que., 14 nov. 1709, *RAPQ*, 1942-1943, p. 420.

[12]Charlevoix, *Histoire de la Nouvelle France*, vol. II: *Journal d'un voyage fait par ordre du Roi dans l'Amerique septentrionale addresse a Madame la Duchesse de Lesdiguieres* (Paris, 1744), pp. 247-249.

[13]Papiers La Pause, *RAPQ*, 1931-1932, p. 67. See also Fernand Ouellet, "La mentalité et l'outillage economique de l'habitant canadien 1760. . ." *Bulletin des Recherches Historiques* (1956), pp. 131-136.

[14]Memoire sur les affaires du Canada, Avril 1689, *RAPQ*, 1922-1923, p. 7.

[15]*The American Gazetteer*, 3 vols. (London, 1762), vol. II, entry under Montreal.

[16]Relation d'un voyage de Paris a Montreal en Canada en 1737. *RAPQ*, 1947-1948, pp. 16-17.

[17]See Benson (ed.), *Peter Kalm's Travels in North America*, vol. II, pp. 446-447, 558; H.R. Casgrain (ed.), *Voyage au Canada dans le nord de l'Amerique septentrionale fait depuis l'an 1751 par J.C.B.* (Quebec, 1887), p. 169.

[18]Benson (ed.), *Peter Kalm's Travels in North America*, vol. II, pp. 558, 626.

[19]Richard Colebrook Harris, *The Seigneurial System in Early Canada* (Madison, Wis., 1966), p. 81.

[20]Robert Mandrou, *Introduction a la France moderne. Essai de psychologie historique 1500-1640* (Paris, 1961), pp. 17-39.

[21]Mme. Begon a son gendre, Rochefort, 8 dec. 1750. *RAPQ 1934-1935*, p. 129.

[22]Champigny au Ministre, Que., 20 oct. 1699. Archives Nationales Colonies, Series C11A, vol. 17, pp. 106-110.

[23]Benson (ed.), *Peter Kalm's Travels in North America*, vol. II, p. 536.

[24]For a revealing account of one such protestation, which could have become dangerous, and the cool way it was subdued without the *habitants* concerned being treated at all harshly, see Vaudreuil au Conseil de la Marine, Que., 17 oct. 1717, Archives Nationales, Colonies, Series C11A, vol. 38, pp. 123-124.

[25]Mandement de Jean eveque de Quebec, 26 avril 1719, ("Trivia," Cameron Nish), *William and Mary Quarterly*, 3rd Series, vol. XXIII (July, 1966), pp. 477-478.

[26]See Les Mariages a la Gaumine, *RAPQ, 1920-1921*, pp. 366-407.

[27]Mme. de Contrecoeur a son Mari, Montreal, 23 mai 1755. Fernand Grenier (ed.), *Papiers Contrecoeur et autres documents concernant le conflit Anglo-Francais sur l'Ohio de 1745 a 1756* (Quebec, 1952), p. 349.

[28]Pierre-Francois-Xavier de Charlevoix, S.J. *Histoire de la Nouvelle France*, vol. III; *Journal d'un voyage fait par ordre du Roi dans l'Amerique septentrionale addresse a Madame la Duchesse de Lesdiguieres* (Paris, 1744), p. 79.

[29]Roy au Sr. de Meulles, Versailles, 10 mars 1685, *ibid., Series B*, vol. 11, p. 99.

[30]Roland Mousnier, "L'evolution des institutuions monarchiques en France et ses relations avec l'état social," *XVII, Siècle*, 1963, nos. 58-59.

[31]Extrait des Registres du Conseil d'Etat, 10 avril 1684, Bibliotheque Nationale, Collection Clairambault, vol. 448, p. 369; Champigny au Ministre, Que., 10 mai 1691, Archives Nationales, Colonies, Series C11A, vol. 11, p. 255; Memoire Instructif sur le Canada, *ibid.*, pp. 265-267.

[32]Le Ministre a M. de Vaudreuil, Versailles, 30 juin 1707, *RAPQ 1939-1940*, p. 375; Résumé d'une lettre de Mme. de Vaudreuil au Ministre, Paris, 1709. *RAPQ,*

1942-1943, p. 416; Memoire du Roy a MM de Vaudreuil et Raudot, a Marly, 10 May 1710, *RAPQ, 1946-1947*, p. 376; Archives du Seminaire de Quebec, Fonds Verreau, carton 5, no. 62.

[33]Benson (ed.), *Peter Kalm's Travels in North America*, vol. I, 343-346, 375-376, 392-393; vol. II, pp. 446-447, 558,626, 628.

Tradition, Change and Education in French Canada

E. Brian Titley

The recent struggle to find an acceptable constitutional formula for Canada showed clearly that the country's unity is very much a fragile arrangement. For on this most fundamental of issues, Québec, again, stood alone. Nor was it simply a question of linguistic differences which a flexible federal structure could probably have accommodated. It was evident that Québec increasingly viewed itself as potentially a nation state with a distinct national consciousness developed during almost four centuries of existence. Nor had forcible incorporation into British North America in 1760 in any way destroyed this consciousness.

The educational practices of a people are often a key to their weltanschauung. As one writer so aptly stated it, "The way in which a society teaches children to face the pressures of the world tells us as much about that people as do all their statutes and parliamentary debates".[1] This article aims to examine the educational traditions of French Canada with the objective of arriving at some understanding as to why that society differs so fundamentally from the rest of the country.

The Legacy of the Counter Reformation

The Protestant Reformation of the sixteenth century represented both a doctrinal revolt and an attack on abuses in the Roman Catholic church. That church, whose spiritual and moral supremacy in Western Europe had been largely unchallenged for centuries, had grown decadent and corrupt with the passing of time. With good reason the reformers criticized the ignorance of the parish clergy, the laziness of the religious orders and the extravagance and politicing of the Papacy. The success of Luther and Calvin in shattering the unity of western Christendom by wrestling significant parts of the continent from Papal authority forced the church to face the question of internal reform. This resolve gave birth to a movement known as the Counter Reformation. Beginning around the mid-sixteenth century, its spirit was very much alive well into the seventeenth.

The General Council of the church which met periodically at Trent between 1545 and 1563 was one of the principal reforming agencies of the Catholic revival. The Council concerned itself primarily with drawing up disciplinary regulations and defining dogma, but also looked to education as part of its blueprint for change. it decreed that a seminary for the education of the clergy should be established in every diocese.[2] This meant that the demand expressed by Colet, Erasmus and Loyola for better clerical education was at last accepted.

There was a further and even more significant educational dimension to the Counter Reformation. The old monastic orders had existed primarily for the benefit of their members. The monastic life had generally represented an attempt to flee the temptations of the world and to seek perfection in hard work, prayer, fasting and other forms of mortification in the solitude of an institution largely cut off from society. But the religious revival of the sixteenth century brought about the establishment of a new type of order, most typified by the Ursuline nuns and the Society of Jesus. These differed from the others in that they sprang up to deal with specific problems of the age. While the perfection of the individual member remained an important aim, it existed in conjunction with an equally important one — as Ignatius of Loyola put it, "to seek zealously the salvation and perfection of our neighbours' soul".[3] Perfection was to be sought in the moral guardianship of others, a role to be exercised primarily through education.

The Ursuline nuns believed that they could best serve the church by educating the daughters of the wealthier classes in the spirit of the Counter Reformation. Though founded in Italy, the order had its greatest success in France where it was operating 255 schools by 1650. The Renaissance had prompted limited experiments in the education of women in latin and Greek, but the Ursulines had no inclinations in this direction. Even for the daughters of nobility they saw no need for anything beyond a basic knowledge of reading, writing, arithmetic, needlework and housekeeping, "since it was more pleasing to our Lord, and more useful to them to be virtuous than to be learned". Janelle has described the purpose of Ursuline education as follows:

> The aim of the Ursuline schools was to turn out that fine social type which is still found in the French bourgeoisie of today, a thrifty, pleasant-mannered housewife, able to 'run' a middle or even higher class home, to make a little go far, and to fulfill both her domestic and social obligations, while at the same time preserving her virtue unsullied and her piety sincere and fervent.[4]

The Society of Jesus was founded in the 1530's by a former Spanish soldier, Ignatius of Loyola, and was destined to become the church's most dynamic and aggressive religious order. The strict discipline and demanding regimen expected of members gave it an almost military resoluteness and ensured that only men exhibiting outstanding qualities in terms of self-denial, dedication and intelligence were admitted to the ranks.

Loyola had noticed that the Protestants were using education as a vehicle for the advancement of their cause and came to believe that the future of his church too would depend "much less on preachers than on teachers".[5] His plan, then, was to establish a network of secondary-type schools which would at once offer a thoroughly Catholic education to society's elite and create a sound training program for the clergy. The Jesuit colleges were astonishingly successful in their aims. The fathers became the schoolmasters of the Catholic world — or, more specifically — of its elite, and succeeded in stemming the rising tide of Protestantism in Europe and driving it back in places.

The success of Jesuit education was partly due to the *Ratio Studiorum*, a code of school regulations and pedagogical procedures which was made universal in their colleges in 1599. In an age when little attention was paid to such matters it at least provided a coherent and consistent plan of action. Curriculum content, however, showed little originality and was borrowed freely from the contemporary humanistic tradition which emphasized mastery of Latin and Greek above all, with some attention to mathematics, rhetoric, philosophy and theology. It was an education designed for both the priest and the aristocratic man of leisure.

The Catholic church also began to take a greater interest in instructing the masses as it struggled to reform itself. In the aftermath of the Council of Trent parish priests were obliged to establish schools near their churches for the teaching of basic literacy and catechism to the children of the common people. This was done with varying degrees of enthusiasm and success. It was prompted more by a fear of Protestant encroachment than by a sense of dedication to raising the intellectual attainments of the populace. Consequently its provisions were minimal and meagre at best.

In addition to these efforts by the parish clergy, the sixteenth and seventeenth centuries also witnessed the founding of several religious communities of men and women whose purpose was to provide some minimal instruction to the poor. The Brothers of the Christian Schools, established by Jean Baptiste de la Salle, is perhaps the best example of such an order. It should be stressed that this was an education designed to combat moral deviance believed to arise from ignorance. It was not conceived as a means of social mobility — a concept generally alien to the sixteenth and seventeenth century mind.

This, then, was the educational legacy of the Counter Reformation. Formal education was the exclusive domain of the Catholic clergy, whether regular or secular. It was a distinctly moral and intellectual enterprise and was administered in quantities proportionate to one's socio-economic standing. This was the legacy inherited by French Canada.

The French Regime

The Reformation and Counter Reformation represented a great religious revival in Europe. And this revival coincided with the period of European conquest and colonization that followed the first crossing of the Atlantic. Both Catholic and Protestant churches accompanied settlers to the new world in order to minister to their spiritual needs and, of course, to proselytize the pagan aboriginal inhabitants.

New France was no exception to this pattern. The French settlement along the St. Lawrence exhibited a similar institutional framework as the mother country. It was very much a stratified society. At the bottom of the social scale were slaves, servants, labourers and coureurs de bois; next in rank came artisans and habitants; above them in wealth and prestige were fur trade merchants and professionals — a sort of bourgeoisie; and at the top of the scale were the seigneurs — a land-owning class holding minor titles of nobility. The Catholic church formed a parallel social structure, although it identified very closely with the elite groups.

The church's influence in the colony was pervasive. New France was a predominantly rural society and in the small villages that dotted the country-side — often isolated from each other, especially in the winter — the parish priest was the leading social figure. His authority derived not only from his spiritual function, but from the fact that he was invariably the only person with any semblance of advanced education. His role was to ensure that the people participated in the life of the church — attending mass and the sacraments with regularity and, of course, contributing to the ecclesiastical coffers.[6]

The key to the church's influence was its control of education. Consonant with the spirit of the Counter Reformation, the instruction of the young was claimed as an exclusive ecclesiastical prerogative. Schools were owned and operated by bishops, parish priests and religious orders. It was possible for laymen to teach, but only with the approval of church authorities. As educational aims were defined in almost purely moral terms, moral criteria were those that were applied in such cases. When Bishop de Saint Vallier established rules for the operation of schools in 1703, he made this quite clear:

> Le grand-vicaire ou l'archidiacre qui fera la visite des paroisses à la place de l'évêque aura soin de s'informer: s'il y a un mâitre et une mâitresse d'école, s'ils font le catéchisme, s'ils sont de bonnes moeurs et propres pour enseigner. Il devra s'enquérir encore si le curé prend soin que les enfants ne lisent point de mauvais livres et que les filles n'aillent jamais avec les garçons dans la même école; si enfin les parents sont exacts a envoyer leurs enfants a l'école.[7]

The secular authorities never questioned the educational monopoly claimed for itself by the church. In fact the state generally supported these efforts with grants and subsidies. The idea of separating religion and education was inconceivable at the time.

As was the custom in contemporary France, the education of the common people was not a priority of the church in the colony. It was certainly believed that the poor lived lives of crime and immorality and that basic Christian instruction would save them from the worst excesses of such depravity.[8] But nothing elaborate was in mind. In the petites écoles of the parishes little was attempted beyond catechism and the rudiments of literacy and numeracy.

The parish clergy were aided in the work of instructing the lower classes by religious communities of men and women. Perhaps the most successful of these was the Congregation of Notre Dame, an order of teaching nuns founded by Marguerite Boureoys in New France (the order was granted canonical approval in 1698).[9] The nuns were uncloistered, which meant that they were free to move openly among the people to carry on their teaching work. This was a distinct advantage in the frontier environment and consequently the order grew and prospered.

But how widespread was this basic instruction? Peter Kalm, the Finnish botanist who visited New France in the eighteenth century, noted that every parish had its petite école. Unfortunately, he had not visited all seventy parishes, and the main centres he did see were probably better endowed than those elsewhere.[10] In fact evidence of literacy gleaned from marriage registers (the ability to sign one's name) suggests a great disparity between rates in urban and rural settings. Literacy, as measured by this crude device, was five times higher in towns (50 per cent as opposed to 10 per cent).[11] Nevertheless, Audet has suggested that school attendance and literacy rates in New France were comparable to those in the mother country at the time.[12]

If the educational services provided for the common people were haphazard and rudimentary at best, this could not be said of those made available for the elite. For those same religious orders, the Ursulines and the Jesuits, who had made their mark on European society by educating the offsprings of the rich and powerful, arrived in New France soon after its establishment to carry on the same work.

As early as 1639 the Ursuline convent at Québec was offering a "finishing" type of education to the daughters of the colony's elite. It was precisely the kind of schooling the nuns were noted for in contemporary France. Marie de l'Incarnation, who had brought the community to New France, believed that their work was vital in maintaining the faith of the young women who otherwise would have been corrupted by the immorality of colonial life.[13] It should also be noted that the Sisters of the Congregation operated a boarding school for the daughters of the wealthier families in Montréal.

The Collège de Québec, founded by the Jesuits in 1635, became the principal institution of advanced education for the sons of the colony's elite. It was modelled closely on the order's colleges in Europe, employing the system of instruction and organization of the *Ratio Studiorum* and the classical/liberal curriculum. Associated with the college was the Grand Séminaire which was founded by Bishop Laval in 1663. This was intended as a training institution for the parochial and missionary clergy and its students took most of their courses with the Jesuits.[14] In fact the early introduction of a full theology course at the Collège de Québec was a consequence of this association.[15]

This brings us to one of the principal functions of education as offered by the Catholic church in the colony. Schools were intended to recruit boys and girls to the religious life and to offer them the appropriate training prerequisite to the taking of final vows. Bishop Dosquet in particular was aware of the vital role played by the school in recruiting for the priesthood. He urged in 1735 that elementary instruction be provided adequately in more seigneuries. It was important, in his opinion, that priests instruct boys in Latin to prepare them for eventual admission to the seminaries. And this was particularly so in the case of the more intelligent ones, or those exhibiting suitability for the religious life.[16]

These efforts appear to have been quite successful under the French regime. By 1760 there were seventy-three secular priests in the colony, of whom four-fifths were Canadian-born.[17] At the same time there were about 215 nuns living in seven convents and all had been born in New France.[18]

Despite the importation of an elitist literary type of education to the colony, intellectual life never became a vibrant component of social reality. The absence of a printing press was hardly encouraging in itself and the books that did exist were confined to the private collections of a few individuals. Even so, literary pursuits and accomplishments were evidently not high in the priorities of Canadiens. This, after all, was to be expected. New France was never much more than a community struggling for its very existence on the edge of a hostile wilderness. Under such circumstances the immediate necessities of clearing land and building houses took precedence over activities of a more leisurely nature. Such pursuits gave the Canadiens a distinct character over time, a process which Frenchmen identified with barbarization.

Bourgainville, an aide to Montcalm, observed in 1756 that the colonists showed little interest in learning, while hunting and warfare were their consuming passions.[19] In a similar vein, Fr. Charlevoix, who taught at the Collège de Québec between 1705 and 1709, observed the following:

> Many are of the opinion that they (Canadians) are unfit for the sciences which require any depth of application, and a continued study. I am not able to say whether this prejudice is well-founded, for as yet we have seen no Canadian who has endeavoured to remove it, which is perhaps owing to the dissipation in which they are brought up. But nobody can deny them an excellent genius for mechanics; they have hardly any occasion for the assistance of a master in order to excel in this science; and some are every day to be met with who have succeeded in all trades, without ever having served an apprenticeship.[20]

Education in New France, then, was valued to the extent that it served the practical necessities of everyday life. Only an elite minority was willing or able to avail of the intellectual program offered at the Jesuit College. The vast majority of the populace received either no instruction at all or the bare rudiments, perhaps supplemented with practical training of some sort. The quantity and quality of formal education one received was linked inextricably with one's position in the social hierarchy. And instruction was always dispensed by functionaries of the Catholic church, or at least only with its approval. Education in this context had a distinctly spiritual and moral purpose. It was designed to inculcate loyalty to the church and her teachings among all sections of society. Curiously, this model of education survived almost intact in French Canada for two hundred years after the conquest.

Minority Status

The British conquest of New France in 1760 cut off the colony permanently from its mother country. Québec suddenly found itself isolated and surrounded in an increasingly English-speaking continent. Although the Québec Act of 1774 gave the official sanction of the new regime to French Canadian traditions and institutions, it could not guarantee that they would not be whittled away in time.

The existing educational structure certainly received a setback as a result of the events of 1760. Apart from the actual destruction of church property by bombardment, many religious returned to France and the conquerors placed restrictions on the activities of some orders. This meant that the church was less able to provide instruction as it had been previously.

And there were attempts to intrude British ideas into the educational realm. The new regime generally favoured a centrally controlled school system for both English and French speakers. This was opposed by French Canadians on the grounds that it threatened their language and did not recognize the essential role of the Catholic church in education. The tradition of private, ecclesiastically-directed education died hard and the populace was suspicious of state enterprise and the concept of public taxation for school support.

A series of school acts passed by the United Assembly of the Canadas in the 1840's and 1850's aimed at a compromise between these two conflicting traditions and succeeded in establishing the basic structure of education for modern Québec. The new laws allowed for the creation of school boards in each municipality, empowered to raise taxes for the construction and maintenance of elementary schools. There could be both Catholic and Protestant boards within a municipality, ensuring religious (and linguistic) separation of children. This division was further reinforced by the appointment of a board of overseers — the Council of Public Instruction — which was comprised of two departments, one for Catholics and one for Protestants. The Catholic church accommodated itself to these arrangements as they reinforced denominationalism and as clergymen could sit on school boards, which they invariably did.[21]

The new structure did not affect education at the secondary level. The small number of French Canadians who were able to avail themselves of advanced instruction did so in private schools — almost always owned and operated by the clergy. For boys, the elitist type of education that had been offered at the Jesuit Collège de Québec was imitated in several new foundations known as 'classical colleges'. These institutions existed primarily to recruit young men for the religious life and to educate those intending to study law and medicine.[22] For the daughters of the wealthy the 'accomplishments' tradition of education as epitomized in the work of the Ursulines continued to be offered in exclusive convent schools.

The establishment of Laval University under the auspices of the Séminaire de Québec in 1851 ensured that French Canadian higher education also would be firmly under ecclesiastical control.

Meanwhile, English-speakers in Québec went their separate educational way, developing their own system of secondary schools based on the grammar school model of the United Kingdom. The foundation of McGill College in 1821 provided them with an institution of higher learning.

What it meant was that English-speaking and French-speaking citizens of Québec had virtually no common educational experiences. Linguistic and religious differences were rigidly institutionalized in the school system. The achievement of confederation in 1867 did little to disrupt the status quo. Though the BNA Act delegated responsibility for education to the provinces, it also guaranteed existing denominational rights. There was no incentive to modify a system with which both sides were relatively satisfied. If provincial status for Québec had any effect educationally, it was to strengthen church influence in the order of things. This in turn meant even greater alienation between Catholic and Protestant, French and English.

By insisting on strict confessionalism in the school structure, Québec was moving against the general course of events elsewhere in the western world. Ever since the Enlightenment and the French Revolution the premier role of organized religion in social and political life was challenged by a new secularism. One manifestation of this trend was the reduction or abolition of ecclesiastical control of schooling and its replacement with state supremacy. But state involvement in education in Québec was viewed with alarm by the Catholic church. Such intervention, whenever proposed, was denounced as the harbinger of atheistic secularism, moral decay and the destruction of French Canadian society. "L'école sans Dieu!." became the warning slogan upon such occasions. So suspicious was the church of state encroachment on its jealously guarded domain that a law requiring attendance at elementary school was not brought in until 1943, and only then with decided lack of enthusiasm![23]

Mâitres Chez Nous

The Catholic church succeeded in maintaining its dominant position in Québec education and society until the 1960's, when a series of changes, now collectively labelled la Révolution tranquille, was ushered in. La Révolution tranquille, which began with the advent of Jean Lesage's Liberal government in 1960, represented a rejection of traditional Québec institutions and ideology. The power and influence of the church came to be questioned and the old phobias of secularism, socialism and modernization were finally cast off. State involvement in hitherto neglected spheres of life found acceptance as Québécois sought participation in the prosperity of industrialized North American society.

The educational changes wrought by the Lesage regime epitomized, perhaps above all else, the reform mood of the era. Despite ecclesiastical opposition, a Ministry of Education was created in 1964, symbolizing state, as distinct from church, responsibility for education.[24] The Protestant and Catholic committees of the Council of Public Instruction, previously the real power in education, were reconstituted as the Superior Council of Education whose responsibility was merely to supervise religious instruction.

State intervention in the 1960's also meant a greater co-ordination of the school system, both in structure and curriculum. The majority of schools still remained Catholic and Protestant in designation but the previous chasm between them was bridged considerably.

Rapid expansion of the educational system at all levels allowed for greater accessibility. The establishment of CEGEPs and l'Université du Québec — based, interestingly enough, on the American state university model — doomed the old elitism. Like elsewhere in Canada the 1960's was a decade of great faith in the school. The concept of investment in education as an essential component of economic expansion was widely accepted.

As Roman Catholicism lost its symbolic importance in Québec life, the French language assumed even greater significance as an emblem of identity. This was partly due to a perceived threat to the position of the language. by the early 1960's the French Canadian birth rate had fallen below the national average. To make matters worse, immigrants to the province overwhelmingly opted for assimilation into the English-speaking population. This raised the alarming spectre of the English minority increasing its proportionate strength vis-a-vis the French.

When the Liberal party, led by Robert Bourassa, returned to power in 1970 (after a Union Nationale interim since 1966), it did so on a frankly nationalistic platform, promising to strengthen the position of the French language. The Official Language Act of 1974, or Bill 22 as it became known, made French the sole official language of the province. It also restricted the right to attend English schools to those already with a working knowledge of English.[25] This was aimed particularly at the immigrant population of Montréal that overwhelmingly enrolled its children in English schools, but also at those Francophones who did likewise.

Though nationalistic in intent and purpose, Bill 22 did not go far enough to protect the French language in the opinion of the radical Parti Québécois which swept to power under the leadership of René Lévesque in November 1976. It quickly moved to take the steps it deemed necessary for such protection. The Charte de la langue française, also called Bill 101, placed severe restrictions on attendance at English schools in the province. It was stipulated that only those already resident in Québec and who had received their primary instruction in English in Canada could continue sending their children to English schools.[26] This effectively removed English education privileges from Francophones, immigrants and all future non-Quebeckers moving to the province. Bill 101 appears to be accomplishing its objective. Enrolment in English language schools fell by 15.6 per cent in the first two years of its operation.[27]

While educational change in Québec in the 1960's suggested accommodation to the modern world and rejection of the old ecclesiastical absolutism, it has not necessarily forged stronger links between the province and the rest of Canada. For modernization was accompanied by a new wave of nationalism — a nationalism that aimed at some form of sovereignty for Québec. Linked inextricably to this national consciousness was a new emphasis on the French language as a symbol of identity. And the language received even more attention as the realization dawned that its historic position in the province was threatened by both immigration and the gradual assimilation of Québécois into Anglo-American culture.

The educational changes of the 1970's, then, were of a different nature. During that decade the school came to be seen not so much as an instrument of modernization, but one of cultural protection. School legislation aimed to buttress the position of the French language in society by preventing the defection of Francophones to English language schools and by forcing newcomers to the province to give their children an education in French.

These actions, though undoubtedly justified in their historical context, have tended to exacerbate relations between Anglophone and Francophone in Québec on the one hand, and between Québécois and Canadians on the other. The new linguistic nationalism and Bill 101, its premier educational manifestation, have been important reasons why Québec felt compelled to reject the constitutional accord agreed to by the federal government and the nine provinces on 5 November 1981. That document's charter of rights, which guarantees minority language rights in each province, would probably render Québec's language legislation unconstitutional.

The outcome of this complex issue is beyond speculation at the time of writing. However, it does illustrate the fundamental cleavage that exists in Canadian society — a cleavage not just of language, but one interwoven in a bewildering set of distinct religious, cultural and educational tradtions.

Notes

[1]Donald H. Akenson, *A Mirror to Kathleen's Face: Education in Independent Ireland, 1922-1940* (Montreal and London: McGill-Queen's University Press, 1975), x.

[2]A.G. Dickens, *The Counter Reformation* (London: Thames and Hudson, 1968), p. 128.

[3]Michael Foss, *The Founding of the Jesuits* (New York: Webright and Talley, 1969), p. 127.

[4]Pierre Janelle, *The Catholic Reformation* (Milwaukee: Bruce Publishing Co., 1965), p. 133.

[5]Foss, *op. cit.*, p. 164.

[6]Cornelius Jaenen, *The Role of the Church in New France* (Toronto: McGraw-Hill, Ryerson, 1976), pp. 96-97.

[7]Louis-Philippe Audet, *Histoire de l'enseignment au Québec, Tome I 1608-1840* (Montréal/Toronto: Holt, Rinehart et Winston Ltée, 1971), p. 119.

[8]Jaenen, *op. cit.*, pp. 109-110.

[9]Audet, *op. cit.*, p. 144.

[10]Jaenen, *op. cit.*, p. 107.

[11]Roger Magnuson, *A Brief History of Quebec Education* (Montréal: Harvest House, 1980), p. 8.

[12]Audet, *op. cit.*, pp. 152-153.

[13]Jaenen, *op. cit.*, pp. 104-105.

[14]Magnuson, *op. cit.*, pp.3-4.

[15]Audet, op. cit., p. 206.

[16]Jaenen, *op. cit.*, p. 108.

[17]Louis-Philippe Audet, "The French Heritage" in J.D. Wilson, R.M. Stamp and L.P. Audet (eds.) *Canadian Education: A History* (Scarborough, Ontario: Prentice-Hall of Canada, 1970), p. 22.

[18]Jaenen, *op. cit.*, p. 117.

[19]Magnuson, *op. cit.*, p. 10.

[20]Jaenen, *op. cit.*, p. 109.

[21]L-P. Audet, "Education in Canada East and Quebec: 1840-1875", in Wilson, Stamp, Audet, *op. cit.*, pp. 172-175.

[22]L-P. Audet, "Attempts to Develop a School System for Lower Canada: 1760-1840", in Wilson, Stamp, Audet, *op. cit.*, pp. 160-161.

[23]Magnuson, *op. cit.*, p. 78.

[24]Norman Henchey, "Revolution and Education in Quebec", in Douglas Myers (ed.), *The Failure of Educational Reform in Canada* (Toronto: McClelland and Stewart, 1973), pp. 159-160.

[25]Roger Magnuson, "Language, Education, and Society in Quebec", in Hugh A. Stevenson and J. Donald Wilson (eds.), *Precepts, Policy and Process: Perspectives*

on *Contemporary Canadian Education* (London, Ontario: Alexander Blake Associates, 1977), pp. 62-68.

[26]William D. Coleman, "From Bill 22 to Bill 101: The Politics of Language Under the Parti Québécois", *Canadian Journal of Political Science*, XIV, 3 (September 1981), p. 469.

[27]*Ibid.*, p. 470.

III

Education in Ontario in the Nineteenth Century

The British North American colony of Upper Canada owed its origin to the United Empire Loyalists — men and women who had fought for or sympathized with the British cause during the American Revolution. In the aftermath of that event they fled the new republic often fearing bodily injury, or even death itself. They sought to build new lives for themselves and recoup their lost fortunes in those northern regions that had remained loyal to the crown.

Those Loyalists who moved west from Quebec and settled in the Niagara peninsula and on the northern shores of Lake Ontario were the founders of the colony of Upper Canada, later to become the province of Ontario. In many ways they were a dispossessed elite and their traumatic experiences during the revolutionary war predisposed them to an inflexible conservatism and a suspicion of change, especially if it hinted of republicanism. Loyalty to the British crown and its institutions was their distinguishing characteristic.

By 1791 the settlement had progressed so satisfactorily that it became the colony of Upper Canada and was administratively separated from Quebec, which became Lower Canada. The Constitutional Act which brought about this division recognized the essential differences between the two linguistic groups in British North America. Lower Canada, with its predominantly French-speaking population, retained the seigneurial system of land tenure and French common law. Upper Canada, on the other hand, was given distinctively British institutions in recognition of its English-speaking, Loyalist stock.

Upper Canada's ties with Britain and her anti-American sentiment were strengthened by the War of 1812 and ultimately helped in the formation of a concept of Canadian nationalism. And these ties were further reinforced by the large influx of immigrants from the United Kingdom which followed the Napoleonic Wars. This constant stream of newcomers did not abate in any degree until mid-century at which time the population had reached almost a million.

The rapid population increase and its attendant clearing of land, building of cities, canals, roads and railways meant that Upper Canada's pioneer stage was relatively short lived. By 1850 it was a thriving community and already benefitting from initial ventures into manufacturing.

With economic maturity came political maturity. Upper Canada quickly outgrew the structure of government created for it in 1791 in which power was concentrated in the hands of an appointed governor and a small oligarchy. Though an elected assembly existed, it had little real power and it was here that the grievances of those who sought a more democratic government began to be aired in the 1820's. The failure of this agitation led to the abortive rebellion of 1837 which, though unsuccessful as a military exercise, paved the way for political reform.

One reaction of the British government to these events was to create in 1841 the United Province of Canada incorporating both Upper Canada, now to be called Canada West, and Lower Canada, to be called Canada East. This arrangement remained until the two Canadas entered Confederation as the provinces of Ontario and Quebec in 1867.

It was during the 1840's that responsible government was finally achieved in the colony. In other words, the democratic principle that a cabinet be chosen from the party with most support in the assembly was accepted. And it was in this decade also that Ontario (or Canada West as it was officially designated) laid the foundations of its system of public education.

This is the topic of J. Donald Wilson's article, "The Ryerson Years in Canada West". The school system is depicted as very much the creation of one man, Egerton Ryerson. Ryerson viewed the school as an important instrument of social cohesion — so necessary in an era of rapid change. It would bind the diverse social elements together with one set of values and political beliefs. In this regard Ryerson was by no means alone. Wilson points out that in contemporary Britain and the United States, for example, other reformers also looked to the school as a mechanism of social salvation. And Ryerson looked for leadership to such places, borrowing freely ideas on school organization and curriculum as they suited his purpose. Nevertheless, the end product, the school system of Ontario, was a unique adaptation modified by local conditions, public opinion and the forces of organized religion.

Political socialization through the schools is the theme of Neil McDonald's article, "Canadianization and the Curriculum: Setting the Stage, 1867-1890". The new nation of Canada, a shaky amalgam of disparate entities unsure of its identity and future, looked to public education to forge a sense of unity and political loyalty. This was a particular concern in Ontario where the tactic employed was the "Canadianization" of the curriculum. Yet the new English-Canadian nationalism did not undermine one of the original purposes of the school — the inculcation of the Victorian puritan ethic. Canadian texts were equally redolent of a vigilant moralizing as those they replaced. Social stability remained a central aim of education and the concept of Canadian nationality was wedded to this.

What McDonald illustrates is that Ontario was becoming a metropolis in its own right. For while the move to employ purely Canadian textbooks suggests a shaking off of British metropolitan dominance, Ontario had already begun to view the west as an area for the extension of its own influence — its own hinterland and frontier. Ontarians were increasingly determined that the new society on the prairies would be English-Canadian, not French-Canadian, in character. Ontario institutions, including the school system, were therefore moved west to guarantee this outcome. McDonald's article, then, anticipates our next chapter, *Education and the Clash of Cultures in the West.*

The Ryerson Years in Canada West*

J. Donald Wilson

In front of the Ryerson Institute of Technology in downtown Toronto stands a statue of Egerton Ryerson, originally erected on the grounds of what was then the Toronto Normal School. Beneath the erect figure of Ryerson is chiselled the inscription, "Egerton Ryerson Founder of the School System of Ontario". Few people today would debate this assertion of 1889. Some historians go further in proclaiming Ryerson to be the founder of the public school system in English Canada, on the basis that the public education systems in Western Canada as they developed during the last decades of the nineteenth century were strongly influenced by the Ontario example created by Ryerson.

Ryerson's energy, unlike Strachan's and Simcoe's before him, was devoted to establishing a firm base for the educational pyramid. His primary objective was to overcome the general ignorance of the people by establishing a system of common schools for all, and leading from that, a system of grammar schools or high schools for those who could benefit from further study or desired preparation for university entrance. At the top of this integrated system was to be a provincial university, a project for which Ryerson found little time, but which has been a recurring theme ever since in Ontario higher education. Although principal of Victoria College at Cobourg for three years and an important witness of the investigations into the University of Toronto in 1860 and 1862, Ryerson actually spent little time thinking about university problems. In contrast, John Strachan devoted a large part of the last forty years of his life to the launching of two universities, King's College (now the University of Toronto), and Trinity College.

Egerton Ryerson has been presented by his biographers[1] and most Canadian historians as a great educational innovator and a sincere reformer. Most of this writing can be associated with the "hero" theory of history made familiar by Thomas Caryle. In actual fact, seen against the perspective of educational change in Western Europe and elsewhere in North America, Ryerson was only one of a multitude of men who were spearheading change made necessary by widespread social and technological advance and increasing urbanization. In France, Victor Cousin, in England, Sir James McKay-Shuttleworth, and in Massachusetts, Horace Mann were promoting educational change in much the same way as Ryerson was in Canada West. In the mid-

---

*From J. Donald Wilson, Robert M. Stamp, and Louis-Phillipe Audet (eds.), *Canadian Education: A History*, Prentice-Hall of Canada, Ltd., 1970. Reprinted with the permission of the publisher.

West of the United States, the area most nearly corresponding to Canada West in terms of development, Illinois, Indiana, Michigan, and Ohio each had its Ryerson in the 1840's and 50's.

These facts clearly show that Ryerson was by no means unique; rather, his efforts were in the mainstream of educational change which was occurring throughout the Western world in the mid-nineteenth century. The new direction that education was taking has been classified by William Boyd into four categories: social comprehensiveness, total commitment to education, linking of education with technological and social change, and heavy reliance upon action by the state, as opposed to "non-official" activity.[2] Ryerson's measures were part of this same world-wide pattern.

Seen in this light Ryerson can no longer be thought of as a radical. In fact, as a student of Ryerson has recently pointed out, he might better be termed a social conservative.[3] Like his American counterparts, Ryerson looked on the school as a vehicle for inculcating loyalty and patriotism, fostering social cohesion and self-reliance, and insuring domestic tranquility. "In a land where the people was king, it was essential to educate the sovereign."[4] And so the school would provide a base for a smooth evolution of society without any violent disruption of time-worn values or traditions. In the United States free schools were to assist in developing a unity in American culture; so too for Ryerson, free schools would ensure a loyal Upper Canadian society but within the embrace of the British Empire. For him Canada could become "the brightest gem in the crown of Her Britannic Majesty".[5]

Another problem is to determine to what extent Ryerson was a maker of history and to what extent he was made by events going on around him. Clearly the state of education in the province could not remain unaffected by urban development, the early stages of industrialization, and improvements in transportation and communications associated with the railway era. Before Upper and Lower Canada were united in 1841, Upper Canadians had been largely rural and self-sufficient. In the forties and fifties the growth of industries and urban centres, especially Toronto, changed the way of life for many settlers. As they became less and less self-sufficient, there grew up the need for specialized urban services including schools of a sophisticated nature. Thus the education of children became not only more widespread as the need for education became more widely recognized, but also more formalized and institutionalized. Trained teachers, state-run schools, compulsory property assessment and compulsory education up to a certain age are all ideas associated with Ryerson. But none was original with him. Many American states attained free schools before Ontario. In New York State the rate-bill (for the collection of fees from parents whose children were attending school) was abolished in urban schools in the 1850's and in all schools in 1853 and in Pennsylvania in 1868. In British North American free school acts were passed in Lower Canada in 1846, in Prince Edward Island in 1852, in Nova Scotia and Vancouver Island in 1865, and in Manitoba, New Brunswick and Ontario in 1871, although the actual achievement of free schools was delayed every-where except in Ontario.

Therefore the crowning achievement of Ryerson's educational career, the attainment of universal, free and compulsory education at the elementary level in 1871, was not solely the result of Ryerson's brilliance as an educational reformer but rather a combination of factors.

Ryerson's Early Life and Ideas on Education

Egerton Ryerson was the first prominent Ontario educator to be born in Canada. This fact should not be interpreted to mean he was a Canadian nationalist; his firm Loyalist background and a concomitant love for Britain always remained a central feature of his life. Ryerson was born on March 24, 1803; on a farm near Vittoria, a village just north of Lake Erie. He attended the district grammar school and an English language course given in Vittoria. At eighteen he was ordered to leave home by his Tory Anglican father because of his attraction to Methodism. He then taught for two years as an usher or assistant in the district grammar school. In 1824 he moved to Hamilton to attend the Gore District Grammar School. Six months later he suffered a nervous breakdown, and after his recovery he decided to enter the Methodist ministry as a travelling missionary or "circuit rider". His first charge took him to the Yonge Street circuit which included the town of York (Toronto), and nine adjacent townships. Later he was stationed at the Chippewa Indian mission on the Credit River where, besides preaching, he also taught the Indian children. Ryerson followed various circuits until in 1829 he was named first editor of the Methodist newspaper, the *Christian Guardian,* which position he held almost continuously until 1840.

Three years prior to this appointment, Ryerson had appeared in the lime-light of public controversy. In the summer of 1825 the indomitable John Stra-chan, soon to be named Archdeacon of York and the virtual "prime minister" of Upper Canada, preached a funeral oration on the death of Jacob Mountain, Anglican Bishop of Quebec. In his sermon Strachan not only reaffirmed the claim of the Church of England as the established church of Upper Canada, thus emphasizing its exclusive title to the income from the Clergy Reserves, but also singled out the Methodists for special ridicule. He accused their min-isters of being ignorant, self-important, and disloyal; since most of them were Americans they should be held suspect. Under the signature of "A Methodist Preacher", Ryerson later launched a blistering 12,000 word counter-attack which appeared, appropriately enough, in William Lyon Mackenzie's spirited anti-Tory newspaper, the *Colonial Advocate.*

This article marked Ryerson's first blow in his campaign for equal rights for all denominations and against special privilege for the Church of England.

It also marked another stage in the long fight against Anglican control of the Clergy Reserves. During the thirties, using the pages of the *Christian Guardian,* Ryerson supported the sale of the reserves for general education purposes. By 1840 he agreed to accept a sharing of the income from the reserves among all religious denominations in Upper Canada. Finally, in 1854, the reserves were secularized, with most of the money going to municipalities after safeguarding the vested interests of those who had shared in them by charging certain clergy stipends against the reserves.

In 1833 Ryerson made his first trip to England where he succeeded in negotiating a union between the Methodist episcopal church in Canada and the British Wesleyan Conference, operating in Upper Canada and Lower Canada respectively. This visit served to change Ryerson's views about Tories and Reformers in Upper Canada. From the time of his 1826 altercation with Strachan, Ryerson had been closely associated with Reform circles in the province; however, he now found first-hand that the ideas of the Philosophical Radicals, such as Hume and Roebuck, the patrons of most Upper Canadian Reformers, were too radical for him. Moreover, these men were atheists. Ryerson came back with kind words for the moderate Tories. His first visit to England marked an important watershed in his career. While a distinct conservative-liberal dichotomy remained in his political philosophy, the conservative element became increasingly more dominant.

Two years later Ryerson returned to England, this time to raise funds and to procure a Royal Charter for the Upper Canada Academy, an institution "for the education of Youth of the Methodist Connection, and other Youth of the Province". His efforts were rewarded and the Methodist academy grew into Victoria College, which held its first academic session in 1841 and granted its first degree in Arts four years later. Appropriately, Ryerson served as the College's first principal and delighted in seeing "his" college come into being a full two years before Strachan's King's College. In 1842 an additional triumph came in the form of an honorary Doctor of Divinity degree from Wesleyan University in Connecticut.

In 1844 Ryerson again hit the public spotlight in his celebrated defence of the Governor-General, Sir Charles Metcalfe. Metcalfe, Ryerson argued, had acted within his constitutional rights in refusing his Council's advice on certain appointments. Looking through different glasses, the Reformers accused Metcalfe of subverting the constitution. Ryerson's brilliant defence brought him due reward in the form of the post of Assistant Superintendent of Schools for Canada West, a post which two years later led to the full superintendency. Despite the political reasons that may have brought about his appointment, Ryerson was eminently suited to assume such an important position.

Almost immediately he set off on a year-long trip to Europe to study various national systems of education. On the way he stopped in Massachusetts for a few days to visit Horace Mann, his counterpart in that state, who had already acquired a considerable reputation as a common school reformer following publication of his Seventh Annual Report in 1843. During his fourteen months abroad, Ryerson spent eight of them on the continent, examining the school systems of more than twenty countries including Britain, Prussia, France, Sweden, the Netherlands, Switzerland, and Austria. He was most impressed by what he saw in France, Ireland and Prussia. On his return in 1846, he wrote a "Report of a System of Public Elementary Instruction for Upper Canada" which provides the most comprehensive statement of his philosophy of education, displays his favour for the educational systems of Ireland and Prussia, and sets the framework for the public school system that was evolved in the next three decades. It is significant that, while Strachan's 1815 plan for education in the province was only partially implemented over the next three decades, Ryerson's blueprint of 1846 was to a large extent realized within his thirty-year term of office.

Education for Ryerson was to be Christian, universal, free, and compulsory. "By religion and morality", Ryerson made clear, he did not mean "sectarianism in any form, but the general system of truth and morals taught us in the Holy Scriptures". For Ryerson the schools were proper vehicles for the dissemination of Christian principles; these Christian principles were, however, virtually synonymous with Protestant values. "Education is a public good, ignorance is a public evil", and therefore every child rich or poor should receive an education sufficient to overcome "the evils of want and poverty", and to "fit him to be an honest and useful member of the community". This conviction led Ryerson to assert that education should be compulsory — "if the parent or guardian *cannot* provide him with such an education, the *State is bound* to do so".[6]

Compulsory education would serve both social and individual ends. For one thing, an educated populace is "the best security for a good government and constitutional liberty",[7] for if the people are educated they will not be misled by demagogues. Moreover, "a country is great as it is educated and intelligent; and it is happy as it is moral and virtuous".[8] Like other nineteenth century humanitarians, Ryerson saw education as a vehicle to help man by the use of his reason to overcome ignorance and thereby, vice, crime, and juvenile delinquency. In his 1846 Report Ryerson contended that crime and pauperism were high where educational facilities were poor. The humanitarian position was reinforced by economic arguments, for, as one student points out, statistics for Toronto and other cities disclosed that in the wake of increasing urbanism and industrialism "delinquent juveniles were costing the community far more than would a ragged [pauper] school".[9] The patriotic needs of the country would also be served by free and compulsory education. While Ryerson always remained loyal to the British connection, he boldly stated as early as 1841 that the educational system of Canada West must be "not only *British*, but *Canadian*".[10]

A fourth feature of Ryerson's system of education, a corollary of the first three, was that education should be practical. Like Strachan, Ryerson saw the limitations of a classical education in "an agricultural and commercial country, where the knowledge generally in demand is plain and practical".[11] He advocated a curriculum including history, geography, linear drawing, bookkeeping, and music and emphasized the practical advantages of traditional subjects such as arithmetic. Nature study, stressed earlier by Rousseau and Pestalozzi, agriculture, because of its practical application,[12] physical education and hygiene, and political economy, which is only now being introduced into Ontario secondary schools, were included in the curriculum he pioneered.

Development of a Public School System
The Common School Act of 1846

In 1846 Ryerson was elevated from the post of Assistant Superintendent to Superintendent of Schools for Canada West with responsibility restricted for the time being to supervision of common schools. After making his report, he began drafting a bill which became the Common School Act of 1846. This was the first of a series of acts culminating in 1871 in the attainment of free and universal elementary education. Similar steps were taken to organize the province's secondary school system through legislation in 1853 and 1865 resulting, also in 1871, in the transformation of the grammar schools into "high schools" or "collegiate institutes".

The essence of Ryerson's Common School Act of 1846 was its provision for a strong central authority to prepare regulations and curricula, to authorize suitable textbooks, and to improve the quality of teaching through certification, inspection, and the erection of a normal school. Local control of education was not, however, completely abolished. The effective local administrative units were the county-based Board of Public Instruction composed of the local common school superintendents and the grammar school trustees in the county, and the Board of School Trustees composed of three trustees elected from each school section and directly responsible for operating the school in its section. Their responsibilities included the hiring and dismissal of teachers, the administration of the school according to law, and the maintenance of the school building. At the provincial level the Act of 1846 created a General Board of Education consisting of the Superintendents of Education and six other members appointed by the Governor-General. Ryerson managed, however, to hold effectively in his own hands the reins of power.

The creation of a centralized authority was probably necessary before serious improvements in education could be effected in Canada West. Estimates vary but one scholar suggests that only about half of all school-age children were attending some type of school before mid-century and these averaged about twelve months' attendance in all. In Toronto, the province's largest urban centre (population 30,775 in 1851), 1,221 out of 4,450 children were enrolled in common schools. Another 1,000 were attending private and church schools.[13] In 1844 there were twenty-five grammar schools and academies in the whole province.[14] According to Ryerson's 1846 Report, one in nine of over 2,000 school districts in Canada West had no common schools at all. By contrast, in 1867 there were 32,719 pupils attending 4,422 common schools throughout Canada West, an increase of more than 50 per cent since 1846.[15]

One of the first problems Ryerson sought to attack when he came to office was that of school textbooks. Prior to 1846 no central control over textbook selection was in force. The General Board of Education under the presidency of John Strachan (1823-1833), made some feeble attempts to provide authorized textbooks, but with slight result. In practice each local board or teacher made his own selection, or more commonly the pupils used whatever texts they could put their hands on. Consequently, there was a great variety of books in use.[16] Many of these, as explained in chapter ten, were American in origin and therefore were often republican, democratic, and anti-British in tone. Ryerson went so far as to assert that "the advocacy of their use in our Schools appears to be both anti-British and unpatriotic".[17] But in more practical terms the diversity of texts made it impossible to classify students into grades and thus make their instruction more uniform.

In his 1846 report, drawing upon the example of France and Prussia, Ryerson had urged the inauguration of a classified school system in which the work of all grades would be clearly delineated. Such a system was dependent on a series of graded texts. With a preponderance of poorly trained teachers who themselves needed textbooks to lean on, Ryerson found in the Irish National Series the answer to his problem. These texts were not only graded but they were also patriotic (in a British sense) and were devoid of denominational leanings. Not the least consideration in their appeal was their cheapness. Permission was obtained to republish them in Canada West at a price low enough to discourage competition.[18]

But in spite of the 1846 ruling against the use of "foreign books", American texts continued to be used in Upper Canadian schools. One scholar estimates that a year after the Irish books were introduced into the schools about one-half of the books used were from the United States.[19] Since American texts had long been in use, it was difficult for teachers and parents to adjust to the rapid change-over. In some cases it was simply a matter of time until the Irish Readers were more widely distributed; until then it was preferable to continue using American texts than none at all. Actually the textbook ban of the 1846 Act was not enforced until 1859 when a notice appeared in the *Journal of Education for Upper Canada* warning all schools that failure to comply made them subject to forfeiture of their share of the school grant. The practice begun by Ryerson of having the provincial educational authority prescribe texts for use in the province's schools was followed until 1950 when the Ontario Department of Education allowed local school boards to select their own texts from provincially approved lists.

The Act of 1846 also provided for a normal school. Ryerson felt strongly the necessity for proper and uniform training of teachers. His visits to France, Prussia, Ireland, and the United States convinced him that normal schools produced better teachers, and better teachers meant better schools. The best way to ensure teachers' acceptance of new ideas on methodology was by requiring that they be trained. This was of course a long-range goal but Ryerson stressed the importance of beginning at once and worked for the establishment of a normal school in Toronto that was opened in 1847. It was among the first of its kind on the continent, opening just eight years after the first Massachusetts normal school and ante-dating those of Michigan and Connecticut. In the rest of British North America, Montreal had a normal school from 1837 to 1842, New Brunswick opened its normal school in 1847 and within ten years all the other eastern colonies, except Newfoundland, had followed suit. Attached to the Toronto Normal School was a model school where student teachers could put theory into practice.

Another feature of the 1846 Act was its provision for a system of supervision and inspection — a system which became the touchstone of Ontario education for the next century. Just as the common schools were in need of a uniform system of textbooks so were they in need of a system of inspection to ensure some standard of instructional uniformity throughout the province. Prior to the passage of this act, the township superintendents, who were not educators, could neither guide nor inspire teachers. Ryerson desired a system of competent inspectors under government control rather than district or township boards.[20] Such officials could then ensure the enforcement of provincial laws and regulations, point out failings and suggest remedies, "animate teachers, trustees and parents by conversations and addresses, whenever practicable, imparting vigour by every available means to the whole school system". Ryerson added, "what the Government is to the system and what the teacher is to the school, the local inspector or superintendent of schools should be within the limits of his district".[21] These District Superintendents were superseded in the Act of 1850 by county and local superintendents who were replaced in 1871 by county school inspectors. By Confederation, larger cities such as Toronto were appointing city superintendents.

Ryerson was a strong believer in winning the support of the people to the cause of educational reform. His 1846 *Report* ends by stating, "No Constitutional Government [should] establish and render effective a system of Public Instruction without the cooperation of the people themselves".[22] With this in mind, Ryerson made five tours of the province in 1847, 1853, 1860, 1866 and 1869.[23] Each trip involved a one- or two-day visit to between twenty and forty communities. The ritual was always the same: a public meeting and then conferences with school trustees, inspectors, and teachers. Each time Ryerson emphasized a particular topic of interest; it might be the necessity of free schools, or compulsory attendance, or public libraries.

Another important vehicle used by Ryerson to publicize his ideas was the *Journal of Education* which he inaugurated in 1848. During the first five years, Ryerson published and edited the *Journal* at his own expense. Finally in 1853 after its value was apparent, the Assembly assumed financial responsibility for its publication. The material of the *Journal* included articles about new apparatus and methods employed in American and European schools, articles on school law and design, and articles encouraging experiment and innovation. Each month copies were mailed to school boards throughout the province and teachers, trustees, and superintendents were required by law to read it. Undoubtedly the *Journal* was a powerful force in publicizing Ryerson's views.

The Educational Depository, devised by Ryerson and begun in 1850, was an important aid to educational innovation. The purpose of the Depository was to provide upon request the schools of the province with approved books and apparatus. The reasonable prices, usually one-half cost, encouraged school boards to purchase their own books, maps, and globes. This practical scheme helped to spread the methodological ideas of Pestalozzi throughout Canada West (see chapter fourteen). Associated with the goals of the Depository was the impetus Ryerson gave to the creation of public libraries, allowing students an opportunity to continue reading after school libraries were closed for the day.[24]

In 1885 Ryerson established an Education Museum in Toronto. Although it was designed primarily for the use of Normal School students, teachers from all parts of the province came to visit the museum's displays that included school apparatus and emphasized the object aspects of Pestalozzi's method. Among the most prominent of the many foreign visitors was Edward A. Sheldon, principal of the Oswego Normal School in New York State. He was so impressed by what he saw that he returned home to make Pestalozzianism a vogue in the United States. (See chapter three).

Free School Movement

Perhaps Ryerson's greatest achievement was public acceptance of the idea of free schools. The term "free school" came to mean schools supported by the payment of taxes based on compulsory assessment on property owned by each citizen of a community regardless of whether or not he had children attending school.

The idea of local assessment for school support did not originate with Ryerson. John Strachan had advocated it on the New York State pattern in 1829; Mahlon Burwell had made it a central feature of his common school bills of 1832 and 1833. But just as the United States was not ready for common schools in Thomas Jefferson's time, so Upper Canada had to await the combination of leadership and the right social, economic, and political conditions. As has been mentioned, free and universal schooling was supported by a variety of people for various reasons. Some conservatives, for example, saw it as a means of curbing social radicalism while radicals were convinced it would contribute to social mobility. Conservatives and liberals alike saw the value of free schooling in inculcating loyalty to Britain and British institutions in the face of persistent republican threats from the south. Also essential for the emerging urban-industrial society were self-reliant citizens and better educated workmen. The workers themselves became increasingly aware of the desirability of education. A further argument heard in Toronto at the time was that "free education would prove . . . beneficial . . . in withdrawing from idleness and dissipation a large number of children who now loiter about the streets. . . ."[25]

Essential to an adequate common school system were citizens willing to pay for education. As pointed out in the previous chapter, this was not the case in Upper Canada in the 1830's, and by the following decade the idea was only forming in the minds of the people. But as the necessity of an educated populace was slowly accepted by the burgeoning middle class, free schooling was no longer rejected. The middle class reaction was crucial since they would bear the burden of taxation. As R.B. Splane has stated, "Much of Ontario's progress, at least from 1850, is attributable to the willingness of the people of the province to govern and tax themselves at the local level. . . ."[26]

In the original draft of his 1846 bill, Ryerson had included a clause authorizing local assessment on all inhabitants according to property. At the time he described this as "the *poor man's* clause, & at the very foundation of a system of public education". The main objection to the clause, he predicted, would come from the rich and quoted a Methodist magistrate as saying he did not wish "to be compelled to educate *all the brats* in the neighbourhood". Ryerson's reply was to emphasize that "to educate 'all the brats' in every neighbourhood is the very object of this clause of the bill; & in order to do so, it is proposed to *compel selfish* rich men to do what they ought to do, but what they will not do voluntarily".[27] This forthright statement shows Ryerson's willingness to utilize the power of the state to achieve what he held to be social justice. "In every good government, and in every good system," he urged, "the interests of the whole society are obligatory upon each member of it".[28]

Although it was another four years before provincial legislation made it optional for school boards to levy taxes on the basis of property assessment, a few boards got the jump by instituting free schools. The first region to do so was the Niagara District whose superintendent was an American-born Italian named Dexter Deverardo. Six free schools were established during 1847; by the end of the next year twenty-four of the 181 common schools in the Niagara District were free.[29] The town of Preston followed closely, opening its first free school in 1848.[30]

But the road leading to the attainment of free schools was not altogether smooth. When the Act of 1847 seemed to deny urban school boards the right to levy the old ratebill on parents, the Toronto board of trustees asked the city council to introduce property assessment to raise the necessary school costs. Urged on by opponents of free schools, the council refused the request, and the board, without funds, was obliged to close the Toronto schools from June 30, 1848 to July 2, 1849.

Opposition to free schools coalesced around several poles. Ideologically the concept was held to be an infringement of individual choice. The idea of taxing people with no children was considered tyrannous, socialistic, and according to the Standing Committee on Education in Toronto, "repugnant to British freedom and common sense".[31] A Toronto Congregationalist minister, Rev. John Roaf, charged that free schools were "introducing communism in education to the undermining of property and society".[32] A more strident British attitude was heard at a meeting in Barrie. When free schools were advocated, the speaker replied, "What do you need such schools for? There will always be enough well-educated Old Countrymen to transact all public business, and we can leave Canadians to clean up the bush".[33] Another argument held education to be an individual matter and of benefit only to the recipient. Why then should society be required to pay for it? Others argued that "What costs nothing, is valued at nothing". The effect on the teacher-pupil relationship was also called into question:

> It will destroy all the confidence and love felt towards the teacher as the employee and friend of the child's parents, and substitute for them a cold respect due to the public official. . . . Instead of the soft, familiar, and refined circle in which wise parents like to place their children, it will drive gentle youths and sensitive girls into the large herds of children with all the regimental strictness and coldness and coarseness by which such bodies must be marked.[34]

Legislative recognition of property assessment was finally given in the Act of 1850 although it remained up to each school board whether it would raise money by this method, or by voluntary subscription, or by the old ratebill charged against each child attending school, or by a combination of all of these. Because of the provision for property assessment, which formally ushered in the era of free schools, the Act of 1850 has been called the Great Charter of common school education in Upper Canada.

Building on the framework erected by this act, Ryerson spent the next two decades completing the structure. His goal was free and compulsory education first at the elementary and then at the secondary level. His strategy was clear. From Europe he wrote to J.G. Hodgins, his chief lieutenant and protégé, in 1851: "I am satisfied I have adopted the best course in having the battle of free Schools fought in each city, town & school section rather than in attempting to fight it in the Legislature".[35] By means of his *Journal of Education* as well as extensive tours of the province, Ryerson was able to win popular acceptance of the property tax at the grass-roots level.

Ryerson's efforts were aided considerably by certain social and economic changes occurring in Upper Canadian society. By 1850 most of the productive land in the southern part of Canada West had been granted. The number of inhabitants had reached 952,000 at the beginning of the decade with Toronto itself standing at 30,775. Of the total population of Canada West, 16.2 per cent lived in incorporated places. York County, which included Toronto, had an urban population of 61.2 per cent.[36] The era of railway building was in full swing; these were the days of the Great Western, the Northern Railway, and the Grand Trunk. Similarly communications had improved. A new means of rapid communication, the telegraph, made people ask "what next?" More newspapers were being published and read; the railways and cheap postal rates made wide distribution possible.

The role of the urban newspapers in spreading urban attitudes into a predominantly rural community merits special attention. The impact of urban Toronto on its surrounding hinterland was becoming more pronounced. This impact was felt not only in the economic sphere but also in terms of changing social attitudes. A crucial factor in this regard was the opinion-forming power of George Brown's *Globe*, which had the largest circulation in British America and was read religiously in countless rural households. The concurrence of liberal-conservative attitudes and the needs of the emerging urban-industrial society virtually assured the success of Ryerson's efforts in the realm of educational reform.

A mark of the province's acceptance of free schools was the fact that by 1870, 4,222 of 4,400 school sections had adopted the local assessment voluntarily. By contrast, in New Brunswick where similar legislation had made the property tax optional for school support in 1852, only a few districts and not a single county had adopted this form of taxation by 1871. When compulsory legislation was passed that year, several years of hard work was required to achieve public acceptance, whereas the passage of compulsory legislation in Ontario in 1871 caused little stir.

Grammar Schools

Not until 1850 were grammar schools put under the jurisdiction of Ryerson and the General Board of Education, by then called the Council of Public Instruction. The situation in these schools required immediate attention. Brought into being by the District Public School Act of 1807 and officially termed "grammar schools" from 1839, they continued to operate independent of any government supervision although receiving government grants. The curriculum was intended to be classical but by mid-century "fifty-six per cent of them received pupils who were unable to write. Not one pupil in six was studying Latin . . ."[37] They were, in fact, largely elementary schools and thus, besides impairing their own efficiency, were competing with and thereby injuring the neighbouring common schools. Originally intended for boys only on the English model, by 1850 perhaps one-half of these admitted girls as well as boys. The religious atmosphere was predominantly Church of England because of the origins of this type of school. This feature particularly disturbed Ryerson who opposed any sort of sectarian teaching in publicly supported schools.

Just as 1846 marked the start of a new era for the province's common schools, so did 1853 prove a milestone for grammar schools.. The passage of the Grammar School Act of that year coincided with the emergence of Canada West from the frontier stage of its development. As a first step of the grammar schools were brought under closer government control. As with the common schools, the Council of Public Instruction was empowered to make regulations regarding courses of study, textbooks, and the appointment of inspectors. The idea of centralized control of education that Strachan had sought twice to initiate, in 1815 and in 1823, now came close to realization. Trustees, however, were to be appointed by the county councils and not by the provincial government. Masters were required to be university graduates and to conduct admission examinations for all candidates. The act as amended in 1855 also permitted the "union" of grammar and common schools.

But the condition of grammar schools improved only slightly. An inspector's report of 1858 complained of the small number of classical scholars; many had principals who were not university graduates; too many held classes in rented or temporary quarters. The union school arrangement proved even less satisfactory. Then onto the stage strode an *eminence grise,* whose ideas were to be picked up by Ryerson and have a profound effect on the subsequent Ontario secondary school system.

This man was George Paxton Young (1819-1889), a Presbyterian clergyman and later University of Toronto philosophy professor. Following his appointment as grammar school inspector in 1864, Young made a series of annual reports in which he pointed out defects in the existing system and suggested necessary changes. The main targets at which Young took aim were the classical nature of the curriculum and the continuing low level of instruction. Both these factors were abetted by the government's grant system set forth in the Act of 1865. In his visits to schools, Young was everywhere appalled at the students' lack of knowledge of English and appreciation of history and literature.

"The time has come", he reported in 1867, "for the organization of a different sort of school from either the existing Grammar School or the existing Common School".[38] Young's influence on Ryerson's thinking is readily apparent in the Act of 1871 whereby the grammar school was in effect abolished and replaced by two institutions. One known as the "high school" was to enable boys and girls to receive an education in English, commercial subjects, and natural science, especially agriculture. The other known as the "collegiate institute" retained a good deal of the former prestige and status of the grammar school. It was intended primarily for boys studying Latin and Greek and those hoping to enter university. Incentive payments amounting to $750 per annum were available to collegiate institutes having a staff of at least four master teachers and sixty boys learning Latin and Greek. This special status accorded the classical languages, a feature on which Ryerson insisted, was slow to die in the secondary schools of Ontario.

Young was also responsible for another practice that had a carry-over effect. In a sincere effort to raise sagging scholastic standards in the secondary schools, he advocated adopting an English practice known a "payment by results". Examination results in each high school and collegiate were to be used as a basis for distributing legislative grants (in addition to average attendance and the length of time the school was open each year). This scheme, introduced in 1875, increased pressure on students and teachers alike, and reliance on cramming and drilling. "The exam's the thing" became the watchword of Ontario's high schools. "Payment by results" was discontinued in 1882, but the type of learning it encouraged was still apparent in the schools almost 100 years later according to the Hall-Dennis Report. (See chapter twenty-one).

The Act of 1871 did not provide for "free" and compulsory secondary education. The fee system was allowed to continue and as late as 1905, 60 per cent of Ontario high schools still required fees of their students.[39] Although the act made attendance compulsory for four months of the year for children ages seven to twelve, the modern school-leaving age of sixteen years was not attained until 1919. The need for compulsory attendance was rendered imperative as grading and class teaching replaced the gradeless one-room schoolhouse.

University Development: 1843-1868
Background to 1843

If anyone is to be called the father of university education in Upper Canada, it is John Graves Simcoe, the colony's first Lieutenant-Governor. He tried to persuade the British government to establish a university in the colony's capital, arguing such an institution was essential if the country's leaders were to be properly educated. Not only would such an institution set a tone of loyalty to the mother country and the Church of England, but it would also lessen the danger of young men going for their higher education to the United States where they might become corrupted by the "pernicious influences" of republicanism and democracy. For Simcoe the university was to play an important formative role in colonial society. He failed to get his university, but his efforts were partially rewarded by the land grant of 1798 which set aside 540,000 acres of land for the support of grammar schools and a university. Of this figure, 250,000 acres were allotted to the future university.

No more is heard of the university until the 1820's when John Strachan put his mind to opening an Anglican-controlled university at York called King's College. Although the Royal Charter was obtained in 1827, the doors of the college did not open until 1843. (The story of King's College to this point is traced in the previous chapter). By this date there were three other universities in operation, all denominational: the Roman Catholic Regiopolis College at Kingston, the Methodist Victoria College at Cobourg with Ryerson as its principal and the Presbyterian Queen's College at Kingston. Although denominationalism in university development was destined to increase rather than abate, the first serious attempt to establish a secularized university was made in 1843.

Struggle for Secularization: 1843-1853

The major views concerning university development in the 1840's can conveniently be associated with three of the main protagonists. John Strachan, the founder of King's College, expected it to grow into prominence and its constitution to remain unaltered. Egerton Ryerson, the principal of Victoria College before becoming Superintendent of Education for the province, objected to the Anglican domination of King's and to its monopoly of the land endowment. He wanted to retain "non-sectarian" religious and secular education in the same institution, ideally a University of Upper Canada. Robert Baldwin, the Reform politician, stood for a purely secular provincial university with no religious instruction.

In 1843 Baldwin introduced a bill to create a University of Toronto which was to be the only degree-granting institution in Upper Canada. The time was propitious since no earned B.A. degree had yet been granted in the province. Regiopolis, Queen's, Victoria, and King's were to become constituent colleges teaching divinity. The university was to take over the King's College endowment and the colleges were to be supported by funds from the Clergy Reserves pending amendment of the Imperial statute. The bill had distinct advantages since it gave something to everyone and settled the Clergy Reserve question as well. It had the support of Queen's and Victoria, but, as might have been expected, was strenuously opposed by Strachan and the King's College Council. In any case the Government resigned in late 1843 before the bill could be passed.

In 1845 W.H. Draper, leader of the Tory government that followed, introduced a similar bill. His university at Toronto was to be called the University of Upper Canada and students were to attend the constituent college of their denomination. Despite the fact that this bill gave more privileges to the Church of England, Strachan and his Anglican supporters did not want to see the King's endowment tampered with. Their opposition helped to kill the bill, which was withdrawn after second reading. At this time a further complication was added by the 1843 schism in the Kirk of Scotland which led to the secession of the Free Church and the founding in Toronto of Knox College.

A final attempt at compromise was made by John A. Macdonald in 1847. His bill dropped the idea of setting up one central university. King's would be allowed to retain its lands in Toronto, but the annual proceeds of the remaining King's endowment were to be divided among the four existing universities (excluding Knox) with King's receiving twice as much as each of the others. Although the bill managed to gain the support of some Anglican members of the Assembly, and Egerton Ryerson and the Wesleyan clergy, Strachan and other Anglicans still maintained that the Church of England had the sole right to control the endowment. The Free Church Presbyterians and those who wanted secular university education also opposed the bill and it was eventually withdrawn. Macdonald's proposal was the antithesis of a strong provincial university scheme; it would have perpetuated denominational control of higher education.

Finally in 1849 the second Baldwin-LaFontaine Government passed an act creating the non-denomination University of Toronto with faculties of arts, law, and medicine. The main features of this act were secularization and government control. No clergyman could be chancellor; neither religious tests nor denominational forms of worship were permitted. There were to be no teaching posts in divinity; affiliated denominational colleges could become divinity schools if they relinquished all their degree powers except in divinity. The government was to appoint most of the Senate and all the faculty, and to have exclusive control of the endowment.

This act marked the high point of the secularization struggle. Complaints were immediate and loud against the "godless institution". For most citizens were convinced that an important role remained to be played by the denominational college. The centralization of university education in Toronto also aroused concern. Consequently Queen's, Victoria, and Regiopolis held aloof.

Bishop Strachan was furious over developments. With amazing energy he gathered almost 12,000 signatures on a petition to have the act annulled. Although unsuccessful in this regard he did see an act of incorporation for a new Anglican university named Trinity College passed by the Legislature in 1851 and the following year a Royal Charter issued. Here was a clear indication of the failure of the government's policy of attracting the other three denominational colleges into the University of Toronto fold, for extending a provincial charter to Trinity College was in no way assisting the attainment of one provincial university. Opened in January, 1852, Trinity remained a monument to the indefatigable energy of the "fighting bishop". The same year, Bishop de Charbonnel, the Roman Catholic prelate of Toronto, began St. Michael's College as the Roman Catholic answer to the new university.

The 1849 act remained in force for only four years until a modified statute was passed under the premiership of Francis Hincks. This 1853 bill introduced some features that still characterize the University. The University became solely an examining body, and teaching in the arts was assigned to a new college — University College. Provision was made for the various colleges to affiliate, indicating a swing back towards denominationalism. But since Queen's and Victoria never sent any candidates up for examination, the affiliation scheme became dormant and University College became in reality the University of Toronto. The endowment was left undivided; any revenue left over after defraying the expenses of the University and University College was to go to the affiliated colleges. There never was any surplus, however; the building of University College took care of that. As Macdonald commented: "Even Methodists can't steal bricks and mortar".[40] John Langton, Provincial Auditor and Vice-Chancellor of the University, summed up the new settlement by saying, "This was all very well in theory, but in practice it has been worse than Baldwin's measure . . . none of the colleges got any share of the spoils which was all they cared for".[41] The settlement lasted until the Federation Act of 1887.

An interesting sidelight might be mentioned. In the search for professors for University College, an application for the position of science professor was received from the young Thomas Huxley, later to become world famous as an associate of Darwin. Huxley was, however, turned down despite support from Darwin himself, and the appointment went instead to Rev. William Hincks, "through the influence of his brother,"[42] the premier, demonstrating a weakness in the appointments' system that lasted until 1906.

Struggle for the Revenues: 1853-1868

While the University was given an opportunity to get established, the main concern of the denominational colleges over the next nine years was to get money from the endowment that they considered their due. The legislative grants they were receiving were so small that the colleges were to a large extent forced to rely on voluntary contributions. This situation was highly unsatisfactory since by 1858 University College had an annual expenditure of $40,000 compared to $10,000 each for Trinity, Victoria, and Queen's. While University College registered sixty-three students, Trinity had forty-one, and Victoria and Queen's thirty-three each.[43] The result was that various groups spearheaded by Egerton Ryerson and the Wesleyan Methodists demanded an investigation.

As a result of these pressures the Legislature set up two commissions, one in 1860 and the other in 1862. In his appearances before the Commissions Ryerson performed two roles: he was chief spokesman of the Methodist Conference and also, as Superintendent of Education for Canada West, a member of the University Senate. But by his charges Ryerson left no doubt which role he preferred: he was clearly stumping for the welfare of Victoria College. He charged the University with extravagance and deliberate waste of the endowment. The establishment of chairs in modern languages, English, history, agriculture, and meteorology he termed "an unnecessary extravagance."[44]

In the formation of the second commission Ryerson's hand was truly revealed. In return for a university commission weighted in favour of his views, Ryerson promised co-Premier John A. Macdonald to return the Wesleyan vote for the Conservatives in the election of 1861. In a letter to Ryerson, Macdonald wrote: "At present we have *both* bodies all right [Orangemen and Roman Catholics] and we only want the Wesleyans to carry Upper Canada — I think you might embrace the occasion, or rather find an opportunity of giving the country one or two slashing letters".[45] The election went well for the Conservatives, and the commission came up with a report which, if implemented, would have restored position and influence to the denominational colleges at the expense of the provincial university. Despite Ryerson's continued efforts to ensure the report's acceptance, it was never implemented thanks to the fall of the Cartier-John A. Macdonald government, and the pressure of a revived University Senate and of the graduates on the new John Sandfield Macdonald-Sicotte government. The University settled down to twenty-five years of quiet development before further controversy broke out.

Meanwhile the various denominational colleges struggled to maintain their existence. Provincial grants had been extended to Victoria from 1842 reaching $5,000 per annum in 1860; to Queen's from 1845; to Regiopolis from 1847; Bytown College (University of Ottawa), from 1852; St. Michael's College (Toronto), from 1855; Trinity College received its first provincial grant in 1864. Despite financing difficulties, denominationalism in higher education increased. In 1857 the Baptists, late because of their opposition to an educated ministry, began the Canadian Literary Institute in Woodstock. The interests of the Institute were closely connected with its principal, Rev. Robert Fyfe, and later a generous patron, William McMaster. This college was united in 1887 with the Toronto Baptist College to form McMaster University that stood for many years on the fringe of the University of Toronto campus before moving to its present site in Hamilton. Three other colleges were founded during these years. The Methodist Episcopal Church began Belleville College which became Albert College, and the Evangelical group of the Church of England found Huron College in London in 1963 (the genesis of Western University founded by charter in 1878), and Wycliffe College in Toronto in 1877. The last two were opened in response to High Church Trinity College.

While the University of Toronto remained the sole beneficiary of the endowment of 225,000 acres authorized in 1798, most of these denominational colleges had to be satisfied with legislative grants and private subscriptions. In 1867 control of such grants passed to the provinces by the B.N.A. Act, and the new Ontario government announced that all grants to denominational institutions would be cut off after 1868. This action produced such financial difficulties that the colleges were eventually forced to consider seriously the federation proposals of the 1880's

Adult Education

Prior to 1868 the government also made substantial grants to literary and scientific societies, thus acknowledging their important work in the area of what is today called adult education. The Canadian Institutes in Toronto and Ottawa as well as the athenaeums of those two cities received substantial support.

In working class education the mechanics' institutes played their role. Beginning with the first in York in 1830, a number of such institutes sprang up throughout Upper Canada in both large and small urban centres. Like their counterparts in Great Britain, they were intended to provide for "mechanics", which meant clerks, tradesmen, and workingmen in general, lectures on all manner of subjects and to make available reading material. The lofty goals of the institutes are set forth in the following address which serves to underline the liberal humanitarian aims held out for education in the mid-nineteenth century.

To the young mechanic the advantages of connecting himself with the Institute are great, not only as a means of acquiring a more perfect knowledge of Arts and Sciences, but also as a means of securing him against the temptations to which the youth of our city are exposed, by opening to him the way to rational enjoyment, which cannot fail to strengthen his virtue while it mingles instruction with amusement.[46]

By 1892 there were 268 mechanics' institutes in Ontario. Three years later a provincial act converted them into either free municipal public libraries or association libraries under fee-paying private control.

Another important means of adult education was the weekly newspaper which incorporated in its pages many features of the modern magazine and even television. In addition to news of purely local interest, most newspapers carried some international news largely concerning the British Empire and the United States, as well as book reviews and books published in instalments. In this way newspapers provided a means of mass adult education.

Separate School Question
Various Categories

Although the term "separate school" is usually used exclusively in reference to Roman Catholic schools in receipt of public funds for their support, there were three kinds of "separate schools" in Canada West at the time of Confederation. These "public schools of a special nature" (defining public school as supported in part by legislative grants), were for special linguistic groups (French, German, Gaelic, Algonkian), special racial groups (Negroes, Indians) and special "denominational" groups (Roman Catholic and Protestant).[47] The first and third categories were and still are often confused. Thus a Catholic separate school in Canada West might also be a French or Gaelic school.

Special linguistic schools much predated the Ryerson period. In fact the first teaching done in Ontario was conducted in French and Indian dialect by the Jesuit missionaries in Huronia (1639-1649). The first school opened in the colony was a French school at Fort Frontenac (Kingston) in 1676. The matter of instruction in French did not become an issue until 1851 when seventeen French Canadians in Essex County made a request to the District Board of Education for the right to have their children taught in English since the current teacher could speak only French. The Board requested a ruling from the Council of Public Instruction which replied that a knowledge of French and German might be substituted for a knowledge of English. This regulation was reaffirmed in 1858 and 1871. Thus at this stage there was no idea that English was the exclusive language of Ontario's schools.

The use of Gaelic and various Indian languages in early common schools has also been recorded. The first Gaelic schools in Upper Canada were sponsored by Father (later Bishop) Alexander Macdonell, often called the father of English Catholic education in the province. His efforts to foster Catholic schools in Glengarry County in the first decades of the nineteenth century coincided with his concern that the recently arrived Scottish Highlanders should be educated in their own tongue, for they understood "neither french [sic] nor English".[48] The first known Indian school using English was opened at Fairfield on the Thames River by David Zeisberger in 1793. Both English and Delaware were taught and books in both languages were read including Zeisberger's Delaware Indian and English Spelling Book. Among the Six Nation Indians on the Grand River a school was established by 1805. The education of Indians was later encouraged by Ryerson who served as missionary to the Missassaugas on the Credit River in 1826, by Lieutenant-Governor Sir John Colborne, and by Thaddeus Osgood, an Englishman, and his Central Auxiliary Society for Promoting Education and Industry in Canada.

German, too, was used in the common schools in those areas of the province, such as Waterloo County, where German-speaking settlers had congregated. Eventually, however, the German population became assimilated, and as this occurred parents saw their children's need to be fluent in English. Thus by the early 1890's English was generally used as the medium of instruction in these schools.

Ryerson himself was responsible for establishing Negro separate schools. Petitions had been received from Negroes in Hamilton in 1838 and St. Catharines in 1842 and the Wilberforce settlement north of London in the same year requesting separate schools for their children. In the Hamilton and St. Catharines cases the grounds were simply the rejection or ejection of Negro children from the common schools with the result that these children were receiving no formal education. When asked his advice by the authorities, John Strachan opposed the idea of separating Negro children from white, citing the happy integration of coloured children at the Upper Canada Central School and the case of a "coloured young man [who] is distinguishing himself at the highest form of Upper Canada College". Instead of segregation he urged endorsement of the law which "made no distinction & recognizes no preference".[49]

But the complaints of Negro parents continued especially from the western end of the province. Consequently Ryerson saw fit in clause XIX of the Common School Act of 1850 to authorize the establishment of separate schools not only for Protestants and Roman Catholics but also for "Coloured People". This provision led to the opening of several coloured schools in the western end of the province. In 1891 the school in Chatham closed, followed by Sandwich (1893), Harrow (1907), and Amherstburg (1917). Clause XIX, however, remained on the statute books of Ontario until a law student wrote a condemnatory article in 1963.[50] The offending legislation which made school segregation legal in Ontario long after it had been declared illegal in the United States was finally repealed the following year. The last *de facto* segregated school in North Colchester closed in 1965.

Special Denominational Schools

As outlined in the previous chapter, the School Act of 1841 created in effect the "separate schools" of Canada West and the "dissentient schools" of Canada East, to use the terms current today. In this and subsequent acts, although the legislators used the terms "denominational" schools and "classes of persons", they distinguished only between Roman Catholics and Protestants, and hence really advocated a "dual confessional", not a "denominational" school system such as exists in Newfoundland today. At this juncture there was little controversy over separate schools since it was considered the duty of parents and church rather than of the state, to see that children were educated. Moreover, the principle of publicly supported, non-sectarian schools was not generally accepted. In the forties controversy raged more over free state schools than over separate schools.

Separate schools had been legally sanctioned for five years when Ryerson was named Superintendent of Schools for Canada West in 1846. On numerous occasions he made known his opposition to separate schools in principle because of the challenge they presented to the common schools. However, as he stated in his report of 1847, "I was not prepared to condemn what had been unanimously sanctioned by two successive parliaments".[51] Consequently, in the Common School Act of 1846 there were no changes in the previous separate school legislation. Ryerson was himself convinced that, given time, separate schools would "die out, not by force of legislative enactment, but under the influence of increasingly enlightened and enlarged view of Christian relations, rights and duties between different classes of the community".[52]

Throughout the separate school controversy of the next decade, Ryerson clung tenaciously to three principles. First, he believed the freedom of individual Roman Catholics to support the common schools must be ensured. To this end he continually opposed any suggestion that Catholics should be obliged to support separate schools. This illustrates his belief in the individual right of the parent to choose the type of education he wished his child to have within the limits set by the community. A second principle, the centralized control of curriculum and textbooks, resulted from his opposition to the development of two separate and distinct systems of education such as had occurred in Canada East. His third principle was equal public grants for all schools both common and separate in return for common inspection, which, Ryerson believed, would insure a modicum of uniformity in all schools.

The Common School Act of 1843, which applied only to Canada West, had established the right to set up a "separate school" provided the teacher of the local common school was of a different religious persuasion and ten or more resident householders of a school district applied. The separate school could be either Protestant or Catholic. The Common School Act of 1850 stated that twelve heads of family of either religion were necessary in order to establish a separate school. Coloured people, regardless of their religious affiliation, were also granted the right to establish separate schools while still retaining the "right" to send their children to common schools — if public opinion permitted. Separate school supporters, while obliged to acquire and maintain their school, still had to pay local common school rates. A share of the School Fund amounting to a government grant toward teachers' salaries was allowed each school.

Prior to 1852, the separate school question had not been a hot issue. John Moir speaks of the period from 1841 to 1851 as a negative period in the growth of separate schools, as a period in which separate schools were conceded as a "protection from insult".[53] The only voice demanding separate schools as a right was Bishop Strachan. He wanted a national system of education under Church of England control. Ryerson had continually pointed to the limited demands for separate schools, a demand he was certain would fade into insignificance as the benefits derived from his system of common schools became apparent. The desire for separate schools among Roman Catholics, he maintained, was common only in communities where friction between Irish Protestants and Irish Catholics had been transferred from the homeland, a contention which seems to be borne out by separate school figures for the period. By the late forties the number of both Catholic and Protestant separate schools was actually in decline. There were forty-one in 1847, while the next year there were only thirty-two.

Ryerson himself considered the year 1852 to be the significant turning-point. He reported to the Legislature that "until 1852, separate schools were never advocated as a theory, much less a doctrine, and still less an article of faith".[54] He often associated the change with the arrival in Canada West of Bishop Armand de Charbonnel, who succeeded Michael Power (1841-1847) as Roman Catholic Bishop of Toronto (1850-1860). Born in France, de Charbonnel was an austere count, ultramontane, and firm opponent of everything connected examination of the role played by Bishop Power is first required.

Power was the first chairman of the newly-created provincial Board of Education (later called the Council of Public Instruction), and is usually considered to have co-operated closely with Ryerson in helping to establish the province's common school system. This co-operation did not prevent Power's favouring the extension of Roman Catholic separate schools, however. In one pastoral he exhorted Catholics to send their children to schools where teachers were inculcating "those principles of religion and morality which will enable them to become not only faithful adherents of the true Church, but useful members of society".[55] Further, in June, 1844, he wrote to a priest in Waterloo asserting the right to a separate school.[56] Although de Charbonnel initiated new and bolder tactics to promote separate schools, fundamentally both he and Power accepted the need for Catholic children to be instructed in a sympathetic environment.[57] While in Ryerson's opinion de Charbonnel was responsible for the alteration of Roman Catholic attitudes towards separate schools, it is probably closer to the truth that the attitude remained unchanged but pressure mounted.

"War of Total Separation" (1852-1867)

In the period from 1852 to 1867, designated by Moir as "the war of total separation", the separate school question developed into a raging controversy. A combination of external and internal factors contributed to change the situation. Underlying the external causes was the great Catholic and Evangelical revival of the nineteenth century which began in England in the thirties and eventually spread to the Continent and North America. This revival is an important element in understanding the politics and education of mid-nineteenth century Upper Canada which, as J.M.S. Careless has pointed out, was in many ways a cultural colony of England.[58]

Of the external factors, the first was the strong stand taken by Pope Pius IX against the new currents of thought — liberalism and socialism — of nineteenth-century Europe. Frightened by the revolutions of 1848, not the least because he was forced to flee from Rome, Pius, when restored, strengthened the Church's adherence to tradition and strongly upheld ultramontane views in church-state relations. It is conceivable that de Charbonnel's appointment as Bishop of Toronto was influenced by his pronounced ultramontane views. A second external factor was the so-called "Papal Aggression" that broke out in England in 1850. In October of that year, N.P.S. Wiseman was named Cardinal Archbishop of Westminister, in a papal brief from Pius IX creating a Roman Catholic hierarchy in England complete with territorial titles and boundaries for the first time since the Protestant Reformation. The high-sounding phrases of the papal brief convinced many English Protestants that this was an unwarranted intrusion by the Pope in the secular affairs of the country. Protestant outrage in England was soon duplicated in Canada West, and precipitated one of the most important internal causes of the dispute.

Although not the first editor to comment on the question, George Brown of the *Globe* was responsible for sparking the tinder box. Dared into publishing "Dr. Wiseman's Manifesto", Brown attacked the mounting papal pretensions to secular power and made an eloquent plea for the application of the voluntary principle both in Britain and in Canada. Brown was the leading spokesman in Canada of voluntaryism, the principle that no church or sect should receive state aid in any form but should be supported solely by voluntary contributions. This was a typical Non-Conformist, Victorian liberal view and flew in the face of the traditional Catholic and Church of England attitude towards church-state co-operation. In his editorial Brown felt obliged to become specific: "In our country — in Upper Canada — do not popery and churchism combine to destroy our national common school system?"[59]

Thus ignited, the controversy raged into the next year. Brown was now solidly committed to voluntaryism and a national system of public education. His enemies were quick to label him a fanatical anti-Catholic, and while he spared no quarter in condemning separate schools, his main objective was to preserve and nourish a national system of free, non-denominational secular schools. A watchword became "Common schools for all or nor common schools at all".[60]

Brown's cry of "no popery in education" aroused public opinion in Canada West. The Catholic press and hierarchy valiantly defended their position against Brownite supporters who, included not only Grits but also traditional conservatives, such as members of the Orange Order. Any incident that sharpened cultural antagonisms between French and English, Protestant and Catholic was bound to strengthen Brown's hand. One such incident was the riots in Quebec and Montreal occasioned by the visit of the Italian apostate, Father Alessandro Gavazzi, fresh from a very successful speaking tour of Canada West. Speaking on an anti-papal theme to Protestant audiences, Gavazzi barely escaped unscathed in the resulting melee. News of the riots reached Canada West in no time and aroused calls of "Protestant union" in retaliation.[61]

A second incident was the Corrigan murder trials in Quebec in 1856. Edward Corrigan, an Irish Protestant, had been beaten to death. The dying Corrigan had identified his chief assailant, and the conviction of his seven Irish Roman Catholic attackers seemed a foregone conclusion. However, the French-Canadian Roman Catholic judge delivered his final charge to the Roman Catholic jury in such a way as to invite acquittal, and acquittal was what he got. The uproar was immediate. One Upper Canadian newspaper saw in Corrigan's murder the predictable results of sectarian education. At precisely this time Bishop de Charbonnel had issued a pastoral declaring that Upper Canadian Catholics who did not use their votes in support of separate schools were guilty of mortal sin.

Therefore de Charbonnel, Ryerson, and Brown all figure prominently in any discussion of the internal factors contributing to the separate school controversy in the fifties. Each represented a different view point. Bishop de Charbonnel and the Catholic hierarchy in general thought that separate schools ought to exist as a right and have every advantage afforded the common schools, including state support. Ryerson, John A. Macdonald, and the Liberal-Conservatives generally, including, for political reasons, some prominent Orangemen, accepted the existence of separate schools, but held that the state support for their extension after a certain point involved the granting of unwarranted privileges. Probably the majority of Upper Canadians followed George Brown in completely opposing the existence of separate schools.

Another important factor was the influx of Irish immigrants. Driven from Ireland by the potato famine of the late forties, tens of thousands of poor and unskilled Irish Roman Catholics flocked to the cities and towns of Canada West looking for work. Because of their numbers their presence could not be overlooked. In the period from 1842 to 1851, their numbers grew from 65,203 to 167,695, an increase of 157 per cent.[62] Moreover, Irish internal disputes between the Orange and the Green were effectively transferred across the Atlantic. Thus while some prominent Orangemen, for political reasons, conceded separate schools, many rank and file members found the anti-Catholic arguments and "French domination" charges of George Brown very appealing.

Separate School Legislation (1853-1863)

The expansion of separate school privileges began with the School Act of 1853. The provisions of the act brought the separate schools more in line in financial terms with the common schools. Separate school supporters were relieved of paying common school taxes, bringing to an end double taxation. Each separate school was allowed to share in the provincial grant although not in the municipal one. Separate school trustees were granted corporate status and allowed to collect their own rates or fees. The act of 1853 was an important milestone on the road to the attainment of Roman Catholic goals in education.

Bishop de Charbonnel, however, remained unsatisfied. He launched a campaign to attain for the Catholic minority of Canada West the same educational advantages enjoyed by the Protestant minority in Canada East. In vain Ryerson tried to point out the differences between the school systems of the two sections: Canada East possessed a dual confessional system whereas the western section had a national system of which denominational separate schools were a part. In response to pressures exerted by the bishops of Toronto, Kingston, and Bytown (Ottawa), another bill was proposed in 1855. It was introduced into the Legislative Council, not the Assembly, by Étienne Taché, Receiver-General of Lower Canada, although the bill applied only to Upper Canada. After much debate and some amendments the bill was put to the vote so late in the session that most of the members from Canada West had left Quebec for home believing all serious legislative business was over. Over Brown's violent objection the vote was pressed in the Assembly by John A. Maconald. Of the fifty-seven members present in the House, forty-six voted for the bill and eleven against. Eight Upper Canadian members voted with the government as did every Lower Canadian member present. To many Upper Canadians the charge of "French domination" seemed to ring true. George Brown's principle of representation by population gained new strength from the passage of the Taché Act.

The act itself further strengthened the position of separate schools in Canada West. Now ten resident Roman Catholic freeholders could set up a separate school by electing three trustees and notifying the municipal authorities of their action. It was no longer necessary for the common school teacher in the area to be a Protestant. From this point the number of separate schools increased, and because of the restrictive terms of the Taché Act they were confined almost exclusively to Roman Catholics. In 1855 there were forty-one separate schools, five years later 115 and by Confederation 161. By contrast the number of Protestant separate schools declined markedly. In 1896 there were ten, In 1938 four and 1967 only two. By the latter date there were 1,380

Roman Catholic schools in Ontario receiving 28 per cent of elementary school-age children.[63]

A final pre-Conferation separate school bill was enacted in 1863. This was the famous Scott Act proposed by R.W. Scott, the Roman Catholic member for Ottawa, who is perhaps better remembered for another statute, the Canada Temperance Act of 1878. Scott presented his bill each year for four years before it was finally passed, again because of the solid Lower Canadian vote. Although its terms were not particularly radical, the Upper Canadian Protestant majority, with the exception of Conservative government supporters, stood flatly opposed to it. In the vote which favoured the bill seventy-six to thirty-one, the Upper Canadians showed their opposition thirty-one to twenty-one.

The act marked a further consolidation of the separate school position in Canada West. Separate schools could receive a share of municipal as well as provincial grants. Facilities for establishing separate schools were extended to rural areas. In return for these concessions, separate schools had to accept inspection by provincial inspectors, centralized control of curriculum and textbooks, and government control of all teacher training. This act was considered by many to constitute the final settlement of the separate school question. In the course of events it has proved the basis of Ontario's separate school system, for no major change has been made in the Separate School Act since 1863.

In a flurry of activity prior to Confederation Protestants in Lower Canada and Roman Catholics in Upper Canada tried to improve their respective positions. Each side's efforts tended to cancel out the other's, and new school legislation that had been introduced in the last session of the United Legislature in 1866 was withdrawn. It was decided instead that the settlement of 1863 should be embodied in the new federal constitution of the Canadian provinces. Thus Section 93 of the British North America Act stated that nothing in any law relating to denominational schools "shall prejudicially affect any right or privilege . . . which any class of persons have by law in the province at the Union".

Conclusion

"The chief outlines of the [Upper Canadian] system are identical with those in other countries, but in its adaptation to the wants of the country and the genius of the people, it is essentially Canadian".[64] If this were so, it was due to Ryerson's ability to apply foreign ideas and practices to the service of local needs. His accomplishments included the attainment of free and universal elementary education and the beginning of a uniform system of secondary education which would eventually become free and compulsory to age sixteen. He never achieved a "national" system such as proposed by George Brown.

To Brown, Ryerson's system was marred by the inclusion within it of a system of "separate schools" intended primarily for the Roman Catholic minority.

In pursuit of his goals Ryerson acquired many enemies. Repeated changes in the school laws angered superintendents; pressure on teachers to become better trained and utilize new methodological techniques perturbed them; ratepayers accepted grudgingly the increased cost of education necessitated by the new system; and Ryerson's impatience and paternalism were generally disliked. By the seventies politicans were after his scalp. In the van was Edward Blake, Liberal premier of Ontario (1871-1872), who charged that the irresponsible nature of Ryerson's position as Chief Superintendent and also of the Council of Public Instruction was not compatible with responsible government. Ryerson tried valiantly to defend the validity of the non-political nature of his office, and to answer his persistent critics.

In 1872 Oliver Mowat succeeded Blake as provincial Liberal leader and premier. Ryerson found Mowat much easier to get along with than Blake. "The Government is very cordial", he said, " and doing all I could desire in regard to myself personally and the Education Department".[65] But Ryerson was already contemplating retirement. As early as 1868 he had addressed a formal letter of resignation to the Provincial Secretary. By 1873 and his seventieth birthday his years were beginning to tell. Moreover, he has the writing of his history of Loyalists in America to consider. His resignation finally came in 1876 and was followed by the creation of a Department of Education with Adam Crooks, the Provincial Treasurer, as the first minister.

Thus ended the career of a sincere educational reformer and a consummate politician. His success at achieving his educational goals had far outstripped the attainments of John Strachan before him. Paradoxically, while he extolled the benefits of a non-political Superintendent of Education, he was himself closely attuned to the political realities of his day. So whether his educational ideas were original or imitative is of little consequence since his primary goal was to see them implemented. This desire obliged him to enter into associations with certain politicians. In this regard his closest political associate seems to have been John A. Macdonald. Rightly praised by historians for his efforts at forging the new Dominion, Macdonald's role in educational developments during the period of the United Canadas was determined solely by political expediency. His hand was particularly noticeable in the intricacies of the university question and the separate school question.

Egerton Ryerson's influence continued long after his death in 1882. In 1908 the author of the first history of Ontario education concluded: "So complete is the system, so carefully is every contingency provided for, that the observer . . . is apt to feel that its completeness is perhaps its greatest defect".[66] Sixty years later the Hall-Dennis Report came to the same conclusion.

Notes

[1] The chief biographies of Ryerson are by J.G. Hodgins, J.H. Putnam, Nathanael Burwash, C.B. Sissons, and most recently, Clara Thomas.

[2] William Boyd, *The History of Western Education*, (8th ed.) (London: A. & C. Black, 1966), p. 382.

[3] Susan E. Houston, "Politics, Schools and Social Change in Upper Canada Between 1836 and 1846" (M.A. thesis, University of Toronto, 1967).

[4] David B. Tyack, ed., *Turning Points in American Educational History* (Waltham, Mass.: Blaisdell Publishing Company, 1967), p. 121.

[5] J.G. Hodgins, ed., *The Story of My Life. Egerton Ryerson* (Toronto: William Briggs, 1883), p. 349.

[6] Egerton Ryerson, *Report on a System of Public Elementary Instruction for Upper Canada* (Montreal: Lovell and Gibson, 1847), p. 7.

[7] *Christian Guardian*, April 23, 1831.

[8] *Journal of Education for Upper Canada*, I(1848), I.

[9] Sylvia Carlton, "Egerton Ryerson and Education in Ontario, 1844-1877" (Ph.D. thesis, Pennsylvania, 1950), p. 65.

[10] Egerton Ryerson, 1841 address, Ryerson Letters, 1840-1846, Victoria College Archives.

[11] *Christian Guardian*, November 24, 1841.

[12] For further details, see A.J. Madill, *History of Agricultural Education in Ontario* (Toronto: University of Toronto Press, 1937).

[13] J.H. Putnam, *Egerton Ryerson and Education in Upper Canada* (Toronto: William Briggs, 1912), p. 146.

[14] W.E. Macpherson, "The Ontario Grammar Schools", *Bulletin of the Departments of History and Political and Economic Science at Queen's University*, October 1916, p. 12.

[15] Robin S. Harris, *Quiet Evolution: A Study of the Educational System of Ontario* (Toronto: University of Toronto Press, 1967), p. 40.

[16] A circular sent out in 1847 listed the following as being used in the schools of Canada West: 13 spelling books, 107 reading books, 35 arithmetic books, 21 history books, 16 grammar books and 53 miscellaneous books. *Annual Report, 1857* (Montreal: Lovell and Gibson, 1849), p. 12.

[17] Ryerson to Superintendent of Common Schools for Brock District (Oxford County), February 1, 1847. J.G. Hodgins, *Documentary History of Education in Upper Canada 1792-1876*, VI, 283-234.

[18] The adoption and retention of the Irish National Series was a particularly sore point with George Brown of the *Globe* who thought they should be replaced by Canadian textbooks. In reply, Ryerson accused Brown of trying to get a monopoly of school books for his brother-in-law, Thomas Nelson, of Nelson & Sons Limited.

[19] V.E. Parvin, *Authorization of Textbooks for the Schools of Ontario* (Toronto: University of Toronto Press, 1965), p. 31.

[20] This goal was not quite achieved in the Act of 1846 since the superintendents held office at the pleasure of the District Councils.

[21] Quoted in W. Pakenham, "The Public School System", in *Canada and Its Provinces*, ed. A. Shortt and A.G. Doughty (Toronto: Glasgow, Brook and Company, 1914), XVIII, 305.

[22]Egerton Ryerson, *Report on a System of Public Elementary Instruction for Upper Canada*, pp. 179-180.

[23]He also found time to make four trips to Europe during his superintendency.

[24]See G.T. Stubbs, "The Role of Egerton Ryerson in the Development of Public Library Service in Ontario". (M.A. thesis, University of British Columbia, 1865). Published as *Occasional Paper No. 51*, by Canadian Library Association, 1966.

[25]Quoted in C.E. Phillips, *The Development of Education in Canada* (Toronto: W.J. Gage, 1957), p. 284.

[26]Richard B. Splane, *Social Welfare in Ontario 1791-1893* (Toronto: University of Toronto Press, 1965), p. 284.

[27]Ryerson to W.H. Draper, April 20, 1846, as quoted in C.B. Sissons, *Egerton Ryerson: His Life and Letters* (Toronto: Clarke, Irwin & Company Limited, 1947), II, 101.

[28]Draft Bill of 1846, in Hodgins, *Documentary History*, VI, p. 76.

[29]M.J. Duncan, "American Influences on Ontario's Elementary School Legislation, 1836-1850" (M.A. thesis, University of Rochester, 1964), p. 234.

[30]*The Preston Reporter* in its July 19, 1967 edition, erroneously reported in its heading that Preston was the "birthplace of free schooling in Upper Canada".

[31]Hodgins, *Documentary History*, VIII, p. 70.

[32]Letter to Editor, *Globe*, January 31, 1852.

[33]Quoted in W.L. Smith, *The Pioneers of Old Ontario* (Toronto: Morang, 1923), p. 114.

[34]Letter to Editor, *Globe*, February 5, 1852.

[35]Quoted in Sissons, *Egerton Ryerson*, II, 223.

[36]*Recensement des Canadas 1851-2* (Quebec: 1853), I, 66. Also J. Spelt, *The Urban Development of South-Central Ontario* (Assen, Netherlands: Van Gorcum, 1955), p. 81.

[37]Macpherson, "Ontario Grammar Schools", p. 13.

[38]Hodgins, *Documentary History*, XX, 116.

[39]*Report of Minister of Education for 1905*, II, 39.

[40]W.S. Wallace, *A History of the University of Toronto: 1827-1927* (Toronto: University of Toronto Press, 1929), p. 72.

[41]Letter from John Langton to William Langton, November 12, 1856, *Canadian Historical Review*, V (1924), 132,145.

[42]W.S. Wallace, ed., *Royal Canadian Institute Centennial Volume 1849-1949* (Toronto: Royal Canadian Institute, 1949), p. 197.

[43]N. Burwash, "A Review of the Founding and Development of the University of Toronto as a Provincial Institution", in *Transactions of the Royal Society of Canada*, XI, ser. II, 40.

[44]Wallace, *A History of the University of Toronto*, p. 81.

[45]Quoted in Sissons, *Egerton Ryerson*, II, 429.

[46]Toronto Public Library, "Address of the Mechanics Institute of Montreal to the Mechanics of this City . . ." (Montreal, 1846). For a full history of the York Mechanics' Institute, see Foster Vernon, "The Development of Adult Education in Ontario, 1790-1900" (D.Ed. thesis, University of Toronto, 1969.

[47]Categories borrowed from C.J. Jaenen, "French Public Education in Manitoba", Revue de l'Université d'Ottawa, XXXVIII, No. 1 (1968), p. 20.

[48]Macdonell to Prevost, Montreal, December 1814, Upper Canada Sundries, item 9181, Public Archives of Canada.

[49]Strachan to John Macaulay, August 9, 1838, Educational Papers, V, item 597, Public Archives of Canada.

[50]H.W. Arthurs, "Civil Liberties — Public Schools — Segregation of Negro Students", *Canadian Bar Review*, XLI (1963),, 453-457.

[51]Hodgins, *Documentary History*, VII, 178.

[52]Quoted in C.B. Sissons, *Church and State in Canadian Education* (Toronto: Ryerson Press, 1959), p. 20.

[53]John S. Moir, *Church and State in Canada West* (Toronto: University of Toronto Press, 1959), pp. 129-149.

[54]Appendix (No. 43), *Journals, Legislative Assembly*, 1858, XVI, No. 7.

[55]Quoted in Minority Report of *The Royal Commission on Education in Ontario, 1950*, p. 823.

[56]"Catholics have a right to a school of their own and this ought to be the case where practicable. The trustees must be in every case Catholics chosen according to law and the School Master a member of the Catholic Church". Franklin A.. Walker, *Catholic Education and Politics in Upper Canada* (Toronto: J.M. Dent & Sons Limited, 1955), p. 54.

[57]The Roman Catholic view on education remains essentially unchanged. For a precise statement, see Pius XI's encyclical *Rappresentanti in terra*, December 31, 1929. For example, "And first of all education belongs pre-eminently to the Church . . . Again it is the inalienable right as well as the indispensable duty of the Church to watch over the entire education of her children".

[58]J.M.S. Careless, *Brown of the Globe: The Voice of Upper Canada* (Toronto: Macmillan Company of Canada Limited, 1959).

[59]Quoted in *Ibid.*, p. 127.

[60]*Globe*, November 4, 1851.

[61]For a definitve study of Gavazzi, see Robert Sylvain, *Alessandro Gavazzi, 1809-1899* (Quebec: Centre Pédagogique, 1962).

[62]Moir, *Church and State*, p. 148.

[63]*Report of the Minister of Education for Ontario, 1967*, pp. 32, 33, 97.

[64]J.G. Hodgins, "The History and System of Education in Upper Canada, 1855", Paper before the American Association for the Advancement of Education, New York, 1855.

[65]Ryerson to his daughter, December 15, 1872, as quoted in *My Dearest Sophie*, ed. C.B. Sissons (Toronto: Ryerson Press, 1955), p. 235.

[66]H.T.J. Coleman, *Public Education in Upper Canada* (New York: Brandon Printing Company, 1907), p. 105.

Canadianization and the Curriculum:
Setting the Stage, 1867 - 1890*

Neil McDonald

The federation of the British-American colonies raised a number of critical questions for nineteenth century schoolmen. Among the most important was the orientation of the loyalties of youth to "the new nationality". Although the discussion of "Canadianization" in educational historiography usually focusses on the ethnic immigrant, it is in the wider context of the political socialization of youth that the issue must be analyzed. Essential to accepting this broader framework is the knowledge that the belief in the power of the school to politically socialize youth was as firmly held as it was promoted in nineteenth century Canada. Indeed, by 1867, the belief that early political learning influenced adult behaviour was conventional wisdom. Politicians and educators alike consistently supported policies whose underlying assumption was that the political beliefs, attitudes, and knowledge of youth would mirror and shape the future of the country. "Education", wrote Ontario's Superintendent of Education, Egerton Ryerson, "is the chief element in forming the mind and heart of an individual, or a Nation" (Ryerson, 1868:221). It was also the belief that prompted John A. Macdonald to confide to Ryerson his regret that education had not become a responsibility of the federal government (Macdonald to Ryerson, March 25, 1872; Sissons, II, 1947:601).

This belief in the efficacy of the school was not confined to early Ontario. From Winnipeg, the Normal School Principal, W.A. McIntyre, could take comfort in the knowledge that "the schoolmistress is abroad in the land" in spite of the long list of serious political problems facing the country (McIntyre, 1912:98). The Superintendent of Schools for the North-West Territories, David Goggin, gravely concerned about the waves of new immigrants coming to the West, could confidently report from Regina that "A common school and a common language will produce that homogeneous citizenship so necessary in the development of that greater Canada lying West of the Lakes" (Goggin, 1906:200). And, it was Alexander McKay, Superintendent of Education for Nova Scotia, who presented the original motion in support of Empire Day at the Halifax meeting of the Dominion Educational Association in 1898 (Sheehen, 1974:264). Indeed, at MacKay's urging, Nova Scotia was the first province to adopt the Empire Day motion.

---

*Reprinted from *The Curriculum in Canada in Historical Perspective* CSSE Yearbook 1979, with permission of the editor.

The public statements of educators and other citizens were not mere rhetoric. Interlaced throughout the early decades of educational development since Confederation is the evidence of overt attempts, with public support, to translate those beliefs into school policy and, therefore, into classroom practice. It is the efforts to effect curricula appropriate to the designs of those concerned with socializing our youth to their concept of Canada that is the subject of this paper.

This interest in the political socialization of youth is not surprising. Canada, as A.R.M. Lower has noted, was a carpentering, not a smelting. In the original coming together of the British North American colonies, there was no great desire to consolidate a common bond. The complexity of loyalties was well described by Christopher Dunkin, the Harvard educated lawyer and Assembly representative who was chief critic of the Quebec Resolutions:

> We have a large class whose national feelings turn towards London, whose very heart is there; another large class whose sympathies centre here in Quebec, or in a sentimental way may have some reference to Paris; another large class whose memories are of the Emerald Isle; and yet another whose comparisons are rather with Washington; but have we any class who are attached, or whose feelings are going to be directed with any earnestness, to the city of Ottawa, the centre of the new nationality to be created (*Parliamentary Debates. . . Cook, 1969:19*).

Aside from these extra-territorial loyalties, there were intense local loyalties, especially in the new Maritime Provinces, which found their expression in resistance to the federal concept. The realization of these problems caused great concern among those who were responsible for making the new political arrangements work. The immediate goal was not only to build a sense of community in those who made up the "new nationality", D'Arcy McGee's now familiar reassuring phrase describing the fledgling union. Also in the minds of those who had helped promote public schools since the 1840's, there still remained concern with building support for those levels of the political system David Easton has labelled the regime and the authorities (Easton, 1965). In the 1860's, bitter, clear memories survived of events associated with Durham's Report, the Metcalfe affair, responsible government, the Rebellion Losses Bill, the Annexation Manifesto, the Gavazzi riots, the Clergy Reserves, separate schools, and political deadlock. The apparent political failure of the union of the Canadas was compounded by the American Civil War, the misguided Fenian raids, and the ominous pronouncements of the American continentalists. All of these events and movements were grim reminders that acceptance of constitutional order and loyalty to political authorities still could not be taken for granted. Macdonald's solution was expressed in his well known preference for a system of federalism that called for a "strong central government". Based on his frustrating experiences governing under the Act of Union and his avowed abhorrence to the principle of states' rights as practised in the

United States (Pope, 1930), he claimed that in the proposed design for Canada:

> We thereby strengthen the Central government and make Confederation one people and one government, instead of five peoples and five governments, one united province with the local governments and legislatures subordinate to the General Government and Legislature (Williams, 1956).

This concern for unity was at the root of Macdonald's desire to have education designated as one of the central powers. The Prime Minister, like his friend and advisor Ryerson, believed that the importance of central control of education lay in its potential to build support for the new political community. In the interests of national unity, the schools could be instrumental in helping replace local loyalties with national loyalties. Indeed, it was this concern that motivated the inclusion of Section 93 in the British North America Act drawn up by Macdonald and Cartier on December 6, 1866. Since federal control of education was not possible, this section was intended to safeguard majority infringement of specific minority rights which had proved to be such divisive issues in the United Province. Clearly, this provision was intended to preserve national unity in the event that subsequent legislation by a predatory provincial government would endanger the fragile union. Ironically, the provision became the focus of such bitter political debate that within three decades it contributed heavily to the demise of Macdonald conservatism and, as well, severely strained the tenuous bond that held together the various units of the new Dominion (Clark, 1961).

The confusion and contradiction that prevailed during this period were painfully evident to Canadian educators. At one level a virtual political war was being waged by the linguistic and religious minorities over the educational issue, while at another level a sustained attempt was being made to make the classroom an instrument for national unity by demanding that it accept as one of its primary roles the making of future citizens who were loyal and committed to the new political reality. These perverse problems did not daunt schoolmen, although their responses varied depending on the period, issue, and place. If there is a common thread that runs throughout their responses, however, it is the unquestioned belief that solutions lay in adjustments to the school curriculum. The political socialization or the Canadianization of Canada's youth is a striking example.

As noted above, the assumption underlying the concern of several publics about provincial control of education was that a centrally controlled educational system could play a significant role in developing national loyalties. Educators who shared this assumption responded with two complementary strategies. First, since federal control was not possible, the provincial systems adopted the manifest characteristics of 'national' schools; i.e., a government education ministry managed by an elected official with cabinet rank, or a superintendency reporting to a designated ministry, which centrally controlled the curriculum and entrance to teacher training institutions, teacher certification, the prescription and supervision of approved textbooks, examinations, attendance, regulations with respect to local administration, and a network of inspectors to ensure compliance. Second, numerous attempts were made to organize national associations and projects that would compensate for the perceived divisiveness encouraged by this ill-advised but inevitable diversity in the educational systems of the country. The Dominion Educational Association, Empire Day, the National History Contest, and the League of the Empire were but a few early examples that illustrate the concern. As Superintendent Goggin reminded the members of the Dominion Educational Association at a national gathering, the provinces should take their cue from the Empire and work for the welfare of the whole rather than their own particular interests. This kind of thinking he called "the imperial spirit" (Goggin, 1901:44). Similarly, George Bryce, in his 1910 presidential address to the Royal Society of Canada, called on the public school to become "the great national unifier" because it was the proper "agency for building up an united and powerful state" (Bruce, 1911:LI-LVII). The curriculum, of course, was singled out as a special area of concern in these strategies.

In Upper Canada, there had long been an interest in "Canadianizing" the curriculum. By the 1860's, however, there was a notable acceleration of this interest among educators. Several factors account for this concern. Amid the tensions of political deadlock, the economic uncertainties created by the failure of reciprocity, fears of inadequate provisions for defense fed by the American Civil War and the subsequent Fenian raids, discussions with the other British American colonies on the possibility of union, and the expectation of North West expansion, there crystallized a new awareness and concern for things Canadian. In 1861, for example, "The Teacher's Association of Canada West" was founded (Hardy, 1938:8). The preamble to its constitution, outlined the objectives of the Association. Not surprisingly, the second objective read: "To secure the improvement of textbooks, or the adoption of others more suitable to the wants of the country" (Hardy:8-9). This concern about "Canadian" content in textbooks was soon turned into a a campaign by the new Association, openly encouraged by a powerful booksellers' lobby (Parvin:1965). The primary focus of this attack was the firmly entrenched Irish National Series of Readers, the first ever textbooks to receive formal authorization. Many teachers claimed that the series was "not sufficiently Canadian in sentiment to justify their continued authorization" (Marling, 1890:7). An original member, Robert W. Doan, recalled that at the 1864 gathering:

> The most important business was the consideration of the fitness of the Irish National Series of textbooks for the requirements of the Canadian schools. After a lengthy and exhaustive discussion the following resolution was carried: "That the Council of Public Instruction would confer a public benefit by offering prizes for the most approved emendation of the Com-

mon Schools Series of Text Books" (Ontario Educational Association, 1911:54).

In the following year, at a session attended by Ryerson, this issue was again vigorously debated. According to Doan, "a resolution was *unanimously* passed strongly urging the necessity of having a series of reading books introduced, better adapted to the requirements of our Canadian schools than are the Irish National Series" (*Ibid.*) In 1867 the Association decided that in spite of the heavy promotion of a variety of Readers by the booksellers "only one series be used in the schools" (*Ibid:*55). Although Ryerson long resisted a substitute for the Irish Readers, by now he was ready to concede that "a strong and general desire was evinced that an improved and strictly Canadian Series of Text-books should be prepared". Indeed, he acknowledged that the demand was so strong it "could not longer be resisted, without injury to our School System" (DHE, XX:134). Thus, in the year of Confederation, a series of Readers was commissioned by the Council of Public Instruction (Marling:7). On January 4, 1868, the Canadian National Series of Readers was formally authorized and according to Ryerson, it was:

> . . . founded upon the same principles as the Irish National Readers here-tofore used, but greatly improved and Canadianized, and printed in the best style, and of the best materials (DHE, XX:134).

The Teachers' Association was especially pleased and, in Doan's words, the uniform series of Canadian Readers owed its adoption "to the persistent discussion of these subjects at our annual conventions". In the early 1930's, the former Princeton classics professor and then president of the University of Western Ontario, William Sherwood Fox, described the Canadian Readers as the first attempt to introduce nationalist ideas to Canadian youth, and for that reason were "the first authorized Readers which even remotely deserve the name Canadian" (Fox, 1932:700). Fox went on to observe that his research showed there was a clearly perceived need for Canadian materials among "leaders of Canadian thought during the period just prior to Confederation". He continued:

> In one of his addresses, Thomas D'Arcy McGee said with deep feeling "When I can hear our young men say as proudly . . . 'our country' . . . as the young men of other countries do . . . I shall have less apprehension for the result of whatever threats may be in store for us". These words show that all the time they were uttered, the idea of Canadian nationality did not exist except in the most germinal form. Ryerson perceived that the common school was the most powerful and promising agency for fostering the idea (700).

Although this latter interpretation by Fox has recently been challenged, there is no doubt that Ryerson believed strongly in the socializing power of the school. As indicated above, however, there were also other influences at work to meld Ryerson's beliefs with the cultural demands of Confederation.

National readers were not the only curricular concerns at this critical point in Canadian history. Educators, for example, had taken the opportunity to edit and publish Canadian versions of arithmetic and other mathematics texts with the introduction of the decimal system of currency in the late 1850's. Moreover, in the standard address that Ryerson gave at teachers' conventions throughout Canada West in 1866, in keeping with the growing nationalist mood of the country, he said that "Canada should not only have her own school laws and her own teachers, but that we should have every article required for our schools manufactured in our own country" (Journal of Education, March, 1866:37). Indeed, stepping beyond his role as superintendent, he went on to add that, "Not only should our school system and our school architecture be Canadian, but Canadian skill and enterprize should produce or manufacture everything the country requires". The momentum of this new spirit did not fade. The following year, the Superintendent predicted that within a year or two all textbooks, including those used in the Grammar Schools, would be "printed, as well as edited in Canada, and wholly adapted to Canadian schools" (DHE, XX:134). The new Canadian geographies were cited as a case in point:

> It was very generally known that our American neighbours, perhaps with pardonable pride, had represented themselves and their country, in their own geographies, as the greatest people and country in the world; and as many of these geographies were in use in Canadian schools, it was at once felt that it would be an advantage to replace them by works more strictly national in their character. This was now done . . . Thus, in our endeavours to prepare Canadian Geographies, we have made ourselves and sister Provinces a good deal more respectable in size than we have hitherto been made to appear (Journal of Education, March, 1866:37).

By the end of the decade, the Chief Superintendent could report that not only textbooks but "the maps and globes, and most other apparatus used in schools are now manufactured in Canada . . ." (Annual Report, 1870:9).

The emphasis on things Canadian, however, must not be interpreted to mean that the sole orientation of the curriculum was toward specific Canadian content. During those early years one objective of schooling was clearly and consistently articulated and it seemed to subsume all other declared objectives of education. There is overwhelming evidence to show that character training was believed to be the primary objective of schooling. With near missionary zeal and insignificant resistance, it was urged that what Canada needed most was "good" citizens who lived morally upright lives according to the norms of an assumed Christian standard; a standard that was self-evident to those properly socialized. In the words of one teacher to his colleagues at a local association meeting, in the interests of good citizenship, the primary objective of schooling should be to give the student knowledge that will form "the religious, rightly-governed will" (Rogers, 1880:542). George Ross, editor-owner of the Ontario Teacher and future Minister of Education and Premier of the province, expressed similar sentiments. In 1876 he cautioned that concerns with Canada's material resources, territorial expansion, and communications network must not overshadow "the great moral interests of this country" (Ross, 1876:5). Canadians, he explained, must give serious attention to the "social forces which really determine our power". The real threat to Canadian nationhood was not the politically uninvolved or disinterested citizen, but the immoral and unethical citizen. He continued:

> The true basis of national power, and the true bond of union between the various parts of a nation are more subtle than those ordinarily recognized by political economists and legislated for by Ministers of Finance. What avails it, if wealth should increase and political boundaries should be extended, while vice revels in our streets and ignorance is undermining the foundations of the State. Let us grapple with the evil — let every teacher . . . bestir himself to diffuse . . . a spirit of refinement and progress, and thus check in the most effectual manner those evils which our Public Schools are admitted on all hands to be a most effectual corrective (*Ibid.*).

Later in that same year, Adam Crooks, Ryerson's successor and Ontario's first Minister of Education, warned in a series of public addresses to local teachers' associations that teachers were not to promote the "intellectual culture" of youth at the expense of "moral culture" (Crooks, 1876:8). On another occasion he claimed that "The County School House offers a greater antidote to crime than all our Gaols and Houses of Refuge" (*Ibid:3*). In the same tone the provincial teachers were warned that if unity and loyalty were to be the result of the Canadian experiment their first concern must be the citizen who has "self-reverence, self-knowledge and self-control" (MacVicar, 1879:69). Like so many of their contemporaries, Ross and Crooks at this point believed that Canadianizing youth was a matter of producing law-respecting and law-abiding citizens.

Critical to understanding this approach to nation-building was the tendency of educators in the immediate post-Confederation period to stress the potential of the future rather than dwell on the seemingly intractable issues associated with Canada's past. In their view it was more important to transmit to youth an image of political harmony and consensus than one of conflict (The Nation, May 14, 1875:224). It was similar to the thinking associated with the Canada Firsters who, according to Professor Berger, believed that the emphasis on party struggles and divisions impeded national unity. Partyism and nationalism were incompatible because parties "institutionalized and perpetuated the very sectional and racial differences which made a general Canadian sentiment impossible" (Berger, 1970:68-9). Ryerson, too, vigorously promoted this belief. On the eve of Confederation he warned his fellow citizens that party was at the root of "most of our civil disorders and executive abuses". "Partyism", he added, "is a *clog* in the machinery of civil government, as in that of the school or municipal government" (Ryerson, 1867:4).

The consequences of this thinking were clearly evident in the curriculum. In their haste to forget the difficult past, educators preferred to link Canada's past with an idealistic interpretation of Britain's past. For example, in 1878 the president of the Ontario Teachers' Association, J.A. McLellan, presented a vision to the membership of Canada's future. The president stressed that Canada's future greatness was assured because "the rich heritage of Britain's history is ours". Britain's glory, he claimed, "is reflected in our national escutcheon". In his vision of the future, McLellan could "hear the tread of the uncounted millions coming up to the possession of this great Canadian zone" where there was a common culture, a common language, limitless prosperity, an enlightened populace and "pure laws and high intelligence and refined manners, and truth, and justice and honour and patriotism and divine benevolence, everywhere prevail" (McLellan, 1878:35, 37). Buoyed by this utopian view, educators tended to project a glorious future for Canada without the crippling liability of its own troublesome past. The School, therefore, was not asked to heal past wounds because those wounds were now not there. It was not Canada's authentic past that was to be continued or celebrated, but an idealized version linked intimately to the past, present and future triumphs of the mother country. The recent criticism of the "bland consensus version of history" taught in Canadian schools (Hodgetts, 1968) has a long tradition.

In terms of Canadian content, therefore, the real concern with the curriculum in the post Confederation period must not be interpreted in precisely the same sense as it is understood in contemporary literature. For example, the educators who were concerned with the Irish Readers were not immediately perturbed that their replacement, the so-called "Ryerson" Readers, were largely a carbon copy of the former. It was more important that the Readers be produced in Canada but, for reasons related to socialization, they must maintain their strong moral emphasis. Whether the teachers influenced the change in Readers more than the publishers is a moot point. Moreover, as far as the policymakers were concerned another important principle had to be preserved, namely uniformity and standardization of textbooks to assure content control. The years when the uncontrolled proliferation of texts was the norm, especially those originating from the United States, must not be permitted to return. It was firmly believed that uniformity in textbooks would strengthen social and political harmony. The school, in organization and classroom practice, must be a model of the society it hoped to help build.

Under Ryerson, complete standardization of textbooks, although much desired, was not totally achieved. The Superintendent, however, managed to get accepted the vital notion of formal textbook authorization. This recognition was a critical first step to complete standardization. Even under Ryerson's successor, Adam Crooks, who was influenced by the Reform philosophy of local control, the Department permitted only authorized texts. Crooks' strategy was to allow individual teachers and local school boards a choice of textbooks, but to keep control of content with the Department. He announced in the Assembly:

> My proposal was to take control of every textbook in these esssential points, namely, as to its need, as to its educational merits, as to its mechanical execution, and as to its reasonableness in cost . . . My principle was that no newly authorized textbook should be used or placed in any school unless upon the combined consent and sanction of the Trustees and Public School Inspector (Crooks, 1879:20).

With the arrival of George Ross to succeed the ailing Crooks, authorization and standardization soon became synonymous.

Long in sympathy with the centralization characteristic of the Ryerson years, Ross sought to continue this trend. The opportunity to resume the continuity was given him immediately on coming to office. One year prior to resignation, Crooks had decided to give boards and teachers a wider selection of authorized Readers. Consequently, the new Minister was faced with the possibility of four sets of authorized Readers. Failing to reconcile the publishing interests, he cancelled all commitments to them and started afresh. Under the new arrangements, he went even further than previous policies. Now, the Department not only controlled Reader authorization but also made all the decisions with respect to content. Publishers could no longer submit texts in the hope of gaining official approval. The Department appointed educators to select appropriate materials for textbooks and held the copyright. In Ross' words:

> I regard it as of primary importance that persons responsible for the publication of textbooks should have the fullest control over them, and I sincerely trust that before long every textbook in use in our public schools will be similarly controlled by the Department (Ross, 1885:11).

Eventually his objective was, in the main, achieved, but it was a long and bitter fight with the publishers (Parvin, 1965).

Ross also went beyond his predecessors on another important issue. To ensure that trustees and teachers complied with Department directives on approved textbooks, he tied the legislative school grant to their use (Parvin, 1965:62). Earlier visits by inspectors, external examinations and teacher integrity were the principal means to ensure compliance. Thus, by the 1890's a distinct pattern had emerged in the development of curriculum for Ontario schools. The Department had established the orientation, and the control, at least in theory, to effect it.

As noted above, in Eastonian terms, the curriculum during these early years of Ontario educational history was directed towards generating support for the political system by emphasizing the authorities and the regime. In this sense, Confederation did not bring drastic changes to the curriculum. With Ryerson as its chief policymaker, continuity with past practice was maintained. Grim memories of the social and political unrest of the 30's and 40's as well as more recent events were clear proof that priorities must remain as originally understood (Houston: 1975). As Ross and his contemporaries were so fond of repeating, the best protection against a return to those days of dissent and discord was to raise a nation of upright moral citizens. Indeed, this assumption was firmly embedded in educational literature from the beginning of the public school movement in Canada. In his special report on a system of public education for Upper Canada in 1836, for example, the Reform politician, Charles Duncombe, argued that the most important justification for such a system was to ensure "the welfare and safety of government" (Houston, 1975:33). Similarly, the Ryerson of the 1840's who was so determined to design a school system that would be "the indirect but powerful instrument of British Constitutional Government" could confidently report in 1867 that:

> In Canada it is notorious that the attachment of the people to the monarchial system of government and British connection is far stronger now than it was twenty years ago (Ryerson, 1867:6).

Two decades later, writing on Canadian national character, the editor of The Week would claim that, "We have made our educational system one of the finest in the world. Our people are law-abiding, church-going, and thrifty" (The Week, August 11, 1888:596).

In spite of the early emphasis on Canadian textbooks, however, there was not a sustained effort among educators to become concerned about the third level of the Eastonian analysis, the political community, namely Canada, until the 1880's. The series of events usually associated with the second Riel affair had a profound effect on educators as it did on others in Canadian society. The realization that the deep religious, ethnic, and political divisions in the country could so readily come to the surface was a shock to those who believed that the socializing impact of the school would result in social stability and harmony. It was a disturbing outcome for public school advocates who had long argued that a schooled populace would be more inclined to engage in reasoned debate and to hold enlightened attitudes.

The result of this perceived internal threat to social harmony was that the two major ethnic groups closed their respective ranks. Instead of seeking accommodation for each other's linguistic and cultural differences, there was an increased vigilance to assure that this adjustment did not occur. In Ontario, Manitoba, and the North-West Territories there was a determined effort to foster the notion of a distinct Canadian identity. For the dominant, English-speaking, Protestant majority of these political regions this identity was defined in terms particularly appropriate to the preservation of their ethnic dominance. The school was early seen to be a major institution in the achievement of this objective. The province of Manitoba and the North-West became the locus of this new thrust. There, during the 1880's English-speaking, Protestants, for the most part Ontario-born, had gained numerical dominance over the French-speaking Roman Catholics. Still smarting from their earlier defeat at the hands of Riel, they would not be denied a second time. With their increased strength and sensing the dominant mood of the country, they attempted to redesign the school systems on the Ontario model. The existing models were based on the dual denominational system of the Province of Quebec. Their preference is not surprising when it is realized that the overwhelming majority of policymakers were products of Ontario schools. Although Thomas Greenway, Joseph Martin, George Bryce, William McIntyre, Frederick Haultain, David Goggin, and James Calder were among the better known, the number of administrators and teachers from Ontario was legion. The ensuing political wrangle which was underlined by uncompromising cultural animosities became a *cause célèbre* in Canadian historical development. Perhaps the majority mood that underlined the thrust to redirect the prairie educational system was aptly represented by the editor of the Edmonton Bulletin. The French, he warned, must remain content with the rights accorded them in Quebec, and attempts to extend those "privileges" outside her borders may result in serious losses, even "in her own stronghold". Defiantly he concluded, "This is an English colony until it is something else" (August 15, 1892).

By the time the parties to the school question reached a workable solution, it was painfully clear that the Canadian federation was severely strained. Aside from the Riel affair and the schools question, there were other indications that Canadians were becoming concerned about developments in the country. One example was the growing influence of an idea prompted by a seemingly innocuous association formed in 1884, the Imperial Federation League. Events both within and without Canada were responsible for the gradual emergence of Canadian imperialism, a curious strand of nationalism that became, for a time, a dominant feature of Canadian political development. As the years progressed the imperialist impulse was quickened by the threat of continental union, Queen Victoria's Diamond Jubilee, the Spanish American War as well as by a coterie of Canadian propagandists who rarely missed an opportunity to promote the imperial ideal among their countrymen (Berger, 1970). Schoolmen, led by the newly appointed, articulate Minister of Education for Ontario, George Ross, were no mere observers of these developments. As in the wider society, a myriad of associations, conferences, projects, leagues, special events, scholarships, textbooks, regulations, institutes, exchange programmes and the like, with our emphasis on encouraging a sense of Canadian identity, virtually mushroomed throughout the various school systems. Gone was the relaxed, lassez-faire approach to Canadian content as mere character training. It is true, that the the heavy moral emphasis persisted. As one teacher expressed it, "No one can be a true patriot without being patriotic" (Cameron, 1895:326). The relationship between morality and the "good" citizen, however, was now considered as being too general. A new attempt was made to broaden the concept of patriotism as it related to citizenship. The "new" patriotism would include an emphasis on specific Canadian content with a view to inculcating "national" loyalty. As noted earlier, up to this point loyalty to a government and its representatives was stressed. Now, the political community was to take priority, with all the complexity introduced into the definition of that community by the imperialist nationalists.

The critical lesson soon to become obvious from this period was that the stage was now set for later developments. Just as the young country was emerging from this decade of intense and bitter debate centered on the whole question of cultural accommodation, the first great numbers of continental European immigrants began to arrive in Canada. Significantly, as noted, the major events that precipitated and prolonged this controversy took place in the West where most of these new immigrants settled. Given the political and social climate of the country, the reception of these newcomers in terms of concessions by the schools to their ethnicity might be predicted. As early as 1898, the Chief Superintendent of Schools for the North-West Territories, David James Goggin, warned:

> It would be criminal to shut our eyes to the fact this rapid increase of a foreign and relatively ignorant population is at once a challenge and invitation to our institutions. . . To assimilate these different races, to secure the cooperation of these alien forces, are problems demanding for their solution, patience, tact and tolerant but firm legislation . . . If these children are to grow up as Canadian citizens they must be led to adopt our viewpoint and speak our speech . . . A common school and a common tongue are essential if we are to have a homogeneous citizenship. (Report of the Council of Public Instruction, 1898:11).

The early note sounded by the Ontario born, Ryerson trained, Goggin, soon became a veritable battle cry to an already well practiced Anglo-Celtic nativism in the West. The thinking also indicated that "Canadianization" was now being seen in the context of the political community. It was a concern that most schoolmen were anxious to accommodate (McDonald, 1971; Tomkins, 1977; Barber, 1978; Huel, 1978; Jaenen, 1978).

Notes

D.H.E. in this paper refers to: John George Hodgins (ed.) *Documentary History of Education in Upper Canada from the Passing of the Constitution Act of 1791 to the Close of Dr. Ryerson's Administration of the Education Department in 1876.* (Toronto, 1894-1910) 28 vols.

Barber, Marilyn, "Canadianization Through the Schools of the Prairie Provinces Before World War I: The Attitudes and Aims of the English-Speaking Majority" in M.L. Kovacs (ed.) *Ethnic Canadians: Culture and Education.* Regina: Canadian Plains Research Centre, 1978.

Berger, Carl, *The Sense of Power: Studies in the Ideas of Canadian Imperialism 1867-1914.* Toronto: University of Toronto Press, 1970.

Bryce, George, "The Canadianization of Western Canada." Toronto: *Proceedings and Transactions of the Royal Society of Canada,* 1911.

Cameron, Bertha, "The Best Method of Teaching Patriotism in the Schools." *Canadian Educational Monthly,* XVII, 1895.

Clark, Lowell, "The Conservative Party in 1890's", *CHAS,* 58-74, 1961.

Cook, Ramsay, *Provincial Autonomy, Minority Rights and the Compact Theory, 1867-1921.* Ottawa: Queen's Printer, 1969.

Cornell, Paul G. et al., *Canada: Unity in Diversity.* Toronto: Holt, Rinehart and Winston of Canada Ltd., 1967.

Crooks, Adam, "Public Address to Teachers' Association of Countries of Lennox and Addington" September 9, in *D.H.E.* 28, 1876.

Crooks, Adam, "Public Address to Teachers' Association of East Middlesex" in *D.H.E.* 28, 1876.

Crooks, Adam, *Speeches in the Legislative Assembly of Ontario.* Toronto: C. Blackett Robinson, 1879.

Easton, David, *A Framework for Political Analysis.* Englewood Cliffs: Prentice-Hall, 1965.

Fox, Sherwood, "School Readers as an Educational Force: A Study of A Century of Upper Canada", *Queen's Quarterly,* XXXIX, 1932, 688-703, 1932.

Goggin, David, "Reply to the Addresses of Welcome", *Proceedings of the Dominion Educational Association.* Toronto: Murray Publishing, 1901.

Goggin, D.J., "North-West Autonomy", *Empire Club Speeches 1905-6,* Toronto, 1906.

Hardy, John H., "Teachers' Organizations in Ontario", unpublished D. Paed. thesis, University of Toronto, 1938.

Hodgetts, A.B. and P. Gallagher, *Teaching Canada for the 80's.* Toronto: Ontario Institute for Studies in Education, 1978.

Houston, Susan, "Politics, Schools and Social Change in Upper Canada" in Michael B. Katz and Paul H.. Mattingly (eds.), *Education and Social Change: Themes from Ontario's Past.* New York: N.Y.U.P., 1975.

Huel, Raymond, "The Public School As A Guardian of Anglo-Saxon Traditions: The Saskatchewan Experience, 1913-1918", in M.L. Kovacs (ed.), *op. cit.,* 1978.

Journal of Education for Upper Canada, March, XIX, 1866.

MacVicar, D.H., "Moral Culture in Public Education", *Proceedings of the Ontario Teachers' Association.* Toronto, 1879.

Marling, Alexander, *A Brief History of Public and High School Textbooks Authorized for the Province of Ontario, 1846-1889.* Toronto: Warwick and Sons, 1890.

McDonald, Neil, "Egerton Ryerson and the School as an Agent of Political Socialization", in Neil McDonald and Alf Chaiton, *Egerton Ryerson and His Times.* Toronto: Macmillan, 1978.

McIntyre, W.A., "Dr. McIntyre's Address", *Proceedings of the Ontario Educational Association,* 1912.

McLellan, J.A., "President's Address", *Proceedings of the Ontario Teachers' Association.* Toronto, 1878.

Ontario Educational Association Proceedings. Jubilee Volume. Toronto: Ontario Educational Association, 1911.

Parvin, Viola, *Authorization of Textbooks for the Schools of Ontario.* Toronto: University of Toronto Press, 1965.

Pope, Joseph, *Memories of the Right Honourable Sir John Macdonald, G.C.B., First Prime Minister of the Dominion of Canada.* Toronto, 1930.

Rogers, W.M., "Some Thoughts Upon Education and National Prosperity." *Canadian Educational Monthly* December, II, 1880.

Ross, George, "Illiteracy in the United States and Canada." *Ontario Teacher* January, 1876.

Ross, George, *Speech on the Motion to Consider the Agreement Respecting the Publication of a New Set of Readers.* Toronto: "Grip" Publishing, 1885.

Ryerson, Egerton, "A Canadian's Reply to Mr. Goldwin Smith on the Colonies", Toronto: Lovell and Gibson, 1867.

Ryerson, Egerton, *The New Canadian Dominion: Dangers and Duties of the People in Regard to Their Government.* Toronto: Lovell and Gibson, 1867.

Ryerson, Egerton, "The True Principles Upon Which A Comprehensive System of National Education Should be Founded", *DHE,* XX, 1868.

Sheehan, N.M., "Alexander H. MacKay: Social and Educational Reformer", in R.S. Patterson, et al., (eds.), *Profiles of Canadian Educators.* Toronto: Heath, 1973.

The Nation, "Nationality", May 14, 1875.

Tomkins, George, "Canadian Education and the Development of a National Consciousness: Historical and Contemporary Perspectives", in Neil McDonald and Alf Chaiton (eds.), *Canadian Schools and Canadian Identity.* Toronto: Gage, 1977.

Williams, John R., *The Conservative Party in Canada.* Durham, N.C.: Duke University, 1956.

Education
and the Clash of Cultures
in the West

The western prairies were Canada's great frontier during the nineteenth century. In fact the annexation of that vast region had been one of the objectives of the founders of the Dominion. Title to the land was held by the Hudson's Bay Company through its charter from Charles II in 1670. By the time of Confederation the only significant white presence in the region was Company employees. Of course, there was also the Red River settlement — a curious amalgam of French-speaking and English-speaking half-breeds, missionaries and the descendants of the Selkirk settlers. Canadian jurisdiction in the West was established in 1869 in a financial settlement worked out with the Company. The prairies and the northern lands as far as the Arctic Ocean were to be administered as the Northwest Territories by a lieutenant governor and council appointed by Ottawa.

This arrangement was viewed with alarm by the French-speaking settlers at Red River, who feared that an influx of Ontarians would threaten their language, their Catholic religion and their land titles. It was this fear that prompted Louis Riel to set up his provisional government in the settlement late in 1869. This action was an attempt to gain recognition of the special status of Red River. In the negotiations that followed with Ottawa this was conceded and the settlement entered Confederation in 1870 as the province of Manitoba. In the Manitoba Act that brought this about official status was granted to both the French and English languages and the continued existence of denominational Catholic and Protestant schools was guaranteed. Though Riel's regime was short-lived, he had apparently succeeded in securing French and Catholic educational rights in the province for perpetuity.

But as W.L. Morton points out in his article "Manitoba Schools and Canadian Nationality, 1890-1923", these rights rested not just on the clauses written into the BNA Act and the Manitoba Act, but also on the continued demographic balance of English and French speakers in the province. And this was not to be. Heavy migration from Ontario and the British Isles determined that the English-speaking Protestant element rapidly outnumbered the French-speaking Catholics. It meant the creation of new political elite — English-speaking, Protestant and mostly Ontario-born. And it had little sympathy with the concepts of 'dual nationality' and the denominationalism in education. The school system was, therefore, restructured largely in accordance with the principles of the Ryersonian model as developed in Ontario. The schools were under state control and English became the sole language of instruction.

The French, of course, were not the only victims in this course of events. Shortly after its inception Manitoba experienced an influx of immigrants who were neither English or French — Mennonites and Ukrainians, for instance — and it was deemed vital that they be assimilated into the dominant Anglo-Canadian culture. A uniform educational experience in the English language was to be the major instrument to this end.

The rest of the prairies — that vast area that was to become the provinces of Alberta and Saskatchewan in 1905 — was organized as the Northwest Territories in 1875 with a federally appointed governor and council. The white inhabitants of the region worked from the beginning to achieve provincial status and major steps on this road were the creation of a completely elective assembly in 1888 and formal acceptance of responsible government in 1897. However, this transition was not a smooth and trauma-free process.

When the Territories were first organized in 1875 its white population was insignificant indeed. Yet the native Indian population was already virtually crushed by a combination of starvation, disease and warfare. This demoralization, brought about by the destruction of the buffalo herds and the ravages of whiskey traders, made the natives dependent on the whiteman's largesse for very survival and forced them to sign away their claims to the land.

This was hardly an auspicious beginning. The return of Louis Riel and his rebellion of 1885 showed how fragile the Dominion's authority was in the area. However, the defeat of the Metis and their Indian allies secured the Northwest permanently for Anglo-Canadians. The ethnic and relgious animosities aroused by these events meant that the principle of toleration for cultural diversity could not find fertile soil.

Neil McDonald's article, "Canadian Nationalism and North West Schools, 1884-1905", shows that the "numerical and political ascendancy of English-speaking Protestants" resulted in the abrogation of French language rights in education and the imposition of a stultifying cultural uniformity through the schools. Men like Haultain and Goggin held a preconceived notion of Anglo-Canadian identity and the school system was designed to fit all minorities into this mold. Not only was "Anglo-conformity" to be imposed on French-speakers, but also on those other minorities — Hungarians, Mennonites, Poles, etc. — who began to arrive in the Northwest in the 1890's. Catholic separate schools were reluctantly tolerated only because it was constitutionally impossible to abolish them. Yet the Ontario-born establishment ensured that these schools were virtually identical to those in the public system in terms of curriculum and teacher certification requirements.

In retrospect, the educational developments in Manitoba and the Northwest were remarkably similar. Both areas found themselves controlled by an Ontario-born elite who saw the school as the key institution in ensuring the English cultural character of the new society — and consequently the key to their continued ascendancy. It illustrates that the metropolitan influence of Ontario had a profound effect on the shaping of society in the West.

Manitoba Schools and Canadian Nationality
1890-1923*

W.L. Morton

I

Prior to the entry of the Red River Colony into the Canadian federation, the population and schools of the colony had been English and French, Protestant and Catholic. The duality of nationality and education was given formal , recognition in the Manitoba Act in 1870 which granted official status to the French and English languages and to denominational schools. In the course of time, however, the duality of language and education was challenged by the growth of a British-Ontario majority and by the immigration of people who were neither English nor French; and during the period with which this paper is concerned the principle of duality was abandoned.[1] This process was finally completed by the enactment of the School Act of 1916 which established English as the sole official language and created a secular public school system.[2]

II

The precarious balance of English and Protestant, French and Catholic, elements in the West rested, not only on the constitutional safeguards of the British North America Act 1867 and the Manitoba Act 1870, but also upon the numerical equality of the two groups. This equality, however, soon disappeared in the face of the comparatively large and rapid inflow of settlers from Ontario and the British Isles. "Le nombre va nous faire défaut" wrote Taché sadly, "et comme sous notre système constitutionel les nombres sont la force, nous allons nous trouver à la merci de ceux qui ne nous aiment pas".[3] The Roman Catholic clergy fought to preserve the language and culture of Old Quebec in the West, and with aid from Quebec and from France, they encouraged the foundation of compact French-speaking parishes both in Manitoba and the North West Territories.

---

*From Canadian Historical Association *Report,* 1951. Reprinted with permission.

It was, however, a losing battle, and in 1890 the defences of French culture were breached when Manitoba became a province of municipalities rather than a province of parishes.⁴ The agents of commercial civilization, the railway and the grain trade, had swept away the old order. In that year the legislature of Manitoba, controlled by the Liberal party under Premier Thomas Greenway, abolished both the official use of the French language in the province and the dual system of separate denominational schools.

For these drastic acts, carried out after nineteen years of comparative satisfaction with the separate school system and two official languages,⁵ there were, in the main, two particular and two general causes. The anti-Catholic agitation which D'Alton McCarthy led in Ontario, in reaction against the Jesuits Estates Act of 1888 and inspired by the fear of *political Catholicism,* was carried to Manitoba in August of 1889. There it awakened a sympathetic response in the new English and Protestant settlements west of the Red River Valley. The agitation neatly coincided with the political embarrassment of the provincial Liberal party, which after the agitation against the railway "monopoly" of the Canadian Pacific Railway, had failed to procure a lowering of freight rates in a contract with the Northern Pacific Railway. To divert attention from their failure, the Liberals had already determined to take up the amendment of the separate school system. "Fighting Joe" Martin's famous outburst on the platform with McCarthy at Portage la Prairie committed the Government to going much farther along the same road, to establish a system of secular public schools and to abolish the official use of the French language.⁶

These two particular causes brought into play two general causes which had been shaping beneath the surface of politics as the settlement of the West proceeded. One was the difficulty and cost of organizing and maintaining municipal and educational institutions on the frontier at the speed competitive settlement required. The burden of local taxes for local improvements and schools was heavy on settlers engaged in making farms in new territory.⁷ The dual system of schools threatened to increase this burden — threatened rather than did, because, as the English and French settlers in Manitoba were segregated, few school districts had in fact to provide separate schools.⁸ Related to the question of cost and also related to the question of duality, was the growing feeling that a country of heterogeneous population, as Manitoba had become with the formation of Mennonite and Icelandic colonies within its borders, should develop a uniform nationality through the agency of a "national" school system.⁹ It was this immigration, neither English nor French, and either Protestant or Catholic, which began to complicate the working of the principle of duality in Manitoba. It was used, by those who questioned the principle itself and feared the political power of the Catholic Church, to justify the abolition of the dual system of education and the denial of the concept of dual nationality.

With the events of the litigation and political controversy caused by the school question from 1890 to 1896 this paper need not be concerned. Suffice it to say that the result was the Laurier-Greenway Compromise of 1896 as an amendment to the School Act of 1890. By the amendment religious teaching, in defined circumstances, was permitted in the public schools from 3:30 to 4 p.m., with a conscience clause which permitted parents to have their children excused from such teaching. The amendment also provided that when ten or more pupils spoke French (or any language other than English) instruction should be "in French (or such other language) and English upon the bi-lingual system". The bi-lingual clause was not directed to circumstances in Manitoba, where the new immigration was just beginning, but to political circumstances in Ontario and Quebec. The concession of teaching in French was designed to please Quebec, the concession of teaching in a language other than French was designed to prevent criticism in Ontario of a grant of equality to the French language alone.[10] It is also to be noted that the amendment of 1897 did nothing to repair the omission from the Act of 1890 of any clause providing for compulsory attendance.[11] The public school system of Manitoba in 1897 was one in which, because of the right of Catholics to separate schools, attendance was voluntary.

III

The passage of the Compromise of 1897 was followed in 1899 by the defeat of the Liberal Party in the provincial election of that year, a defeat in which the Compromise played some part. The accession to power of the Conservative party did not lead to the repeal or amendment of the Compromise. However the administration of the school law now lay with men who were not wholly sympathetic with its terms.[12] The Roblin Government maintained the "national school" system intact in principle and fact, yet in its administration made all possible concessions to the French and Catholics. In rural French parishes the results were satisfactory to the French; only in Winnipeg and St. Boniface did Catholics suffer actual hardship from the operation of the School Act.

Grave and growing difficulties, however, were encountered in the administration of the public school system in the newly settled districts along the northern and eastern frontiers of Manitoba. These were the years of the great immigration into the West, a great part of which came from east central Europe. In 1897 the three language groups of Manitoba were English, French and German; a fourth, the Icelandic, accepted public education in English while maintaining the mother tongue in the home and Icelandic press. By 1911, many other groups had been added, of which two, the Polish and the Ukrainian, were devoted to the maintenance of their native languages.[13] Moreover, of these groups the Poles and many of the Germans were Roman Catholics and to them the ministrations of the church, led by Archbishop

Langevin of St. Boniface, were naturally extended. The Ukrainians were mainly Greek Catholics. They had come without their native clergy and they therefore invited evangelisation by both the Protestant churches and the Church of Rome.

The great immigration, and the still active resentment of the Catholic clergy and of the lay leaders of the Manitoban French towards the school law, led to an increased emphasis on the bi-lingual provision of the school law. They also perpetuated the denominational hostility which had done so much to provoke the School Act of 1890. The French of course insisted on their right to instruction in the mother tongue; the Germans, both the Old Colony Mennonites and the newcomers did so too; the Poles and Ukrainians soon learned, from the politicians not least, to do the same. The result was to demonstrate that, under the new conditions, the bi-lingual system of 1897 was unworkable.[14]

As if these difficulties were not sufficiently harmful, there was also the lack of a school-attendance law. The lack had engaged the attention of the Roblin Government in 1900. It then and later, on legal advice, accepted the view that a compulsory attendance law would violate the constitutional rights of Catholics to separate private schools and re-open the school question. Accordingly, the administration decided to achieve its object by way of police legislation, rather than by altering the school law. In 1909 it amended the Children's Act.[15] The defects of this legislation were that delinquency had to be proved before children could be compelled to attend school. When the Act was tightened in 1914, however, and the Department of Education directed enforcement through its own truancy officers, the average school attendance in the Province began to rise. The advantages of central administration overcame the defects of the law.

Because of these difficulties and deficiencies, the school administration of the Roblin Government came under ever sharpening criticism, and the Liberal opposition made the most of the Government's embarrassment. The criticism from English Protestants was intensified by the passage of the ambiguous Coldwell amendments of 1912. These amendments, which seemed to permit the separation of Protestant and Catholic children in the larger schools, had coincided with the extension of Manitoba's boundaries, and with them of the jurisdiction of the School Act. Whatever the meaning of the amendments, they aroused strong resentment among the Orangemen of Manitoba.[16] The provincial Liberals, who had campaigned for reform of the school system in 1910, in 1914 included in their platform pledges to maintain unimpaired the national school system of 1897. They proposed to provide educational facilities for all children in the Province and to make adequate teaching of English obligatory in all public schools. In a carefully drawn plank the party undertook "to provide for a measure of compulsory education, which, while respecting the personal rights and religious convictions of the individual, shall make it obligatory on parents and guardians of all children that such children shall receive a proper elementary education, *either by attendance at the public schools, or by such substitute within the choice of the parents as shall attain this end"*. The party also pledged itself to increase the provincial grants to rural schools, and repeal the Coldwell amendments. They thus undertook to make the system of 1897 work, and at the same time they hoped to evade the constitutional difficulty with respect to compulsory attendance by allowing parents a substitute acceptable to the Department of Education.[17] The religious rights of Catholic parents were to be respected; but there was no suggestion of compromise on the principal of duality.

IV

The Liberal party failed to win the election of 1914, but came to power in 1915 when the Roblin Goverment fell for reasons unconnected with the administration of education. The new government of Premier T.C. Norris was emphatically a reform administration and in the Minister of Education, Dr. R.S. Thornton, possessed an administrator of clear purpose and unflinching will. A school-attendance act, correcting the existing anomalous situation, was carried through the legislature in the session of 1916 without opposition.[18] The bill to repeal the bi-lingual section, No. 258, of the Public School Act, however, provoked bitter opposition from the French-speaking members, and the only Ukrainian member, of the Legislature. It was, in fact, the only measure introduced by the government during the session which led to a division in the legislature. The bitterness expressed by the French members was natural enough. The Liberal Party, in its platform of 1914 and during the election campaigns had committed itself only to the enforcement of adequate instruction in English thereby implying the retention of the principle of the bi-lingual system and the use of administrative methods to improve English language teaching. Now the party proposed to do away with the whole principle of bi-lingual instruction.

In moving the deletion of the bi-lingual clause from the School Act the Minister of Education explained that until the autumn of 1915, he had hoped to achieve the purpose of the government, that is, to enforce adequate instruction in English, by administrative means. That hope had been defeated by the mandatory character of the legislation of 1897, the conditions revealed by a special report on the bi-lingual schools, and by an increase in the petitions for bi-lingual teaching. The problem had ceased to be, as in 1897, a peripheral one; one quarter of the schools with one sixth of the enrolment were bi-lingual in 1915. The Deputy-Minister, Robert Fletcher, had reported that the situation was nearly out of hand. In short, it had been proved to the Minister's satisfaction that adequate instruction in English could be provided only by making English the sole language of instruction.[19]

Over and above these administrative considerations, it is to be noted, there were the mounting racial sentiment of the war years and the effect of the powerful and sustained campaign by the *Manitoba Free Press* against the bi-lingual system. And it is to be remembered that the dispute in Ontario over Regulation 17 was at its height, that Bourassa had forced Laurier to take up the cause of nationalism in Quebec, and that the conscription issue was loom-ing.

The Minister convinced his colleagues of the need for legislation but to convince the caucus of his party was more difficult. The meeting which con-sidered the proposed change of policy lasted until the small hours. Influential leaders sought to preserve for the French language a status similar to that which it possessed in Saskatchewan. It was reported that the French members refused to accept the concession of instruction in French as well as English, but demanded the re-establishment of separate schools as of 1889. Compro-mise was impossible, and Thornton's proposal was adopted.[20] The two French Liberal members, P.A. Talbot and J.P. Dumas, then broke with the Liberal party.

The grounds of opposition were manifest and were debated at length in the Legislature. The French members of the Legislature, both Liberal and Conservative, declared that the rights of the French had been betrayed by the Liberal party. That party had pledged itself to maintain the compromise of 1897. In office it spurned its public and unequivocal undertakings. The Pre-mier himself, it was charged, had given pledges, both in writing and in speech, that the rights of the French would be respected. The charges were met fairly by Norris and Thornton, but the bitter sense of betrayal felt by the French members drove them on to assert the whole claim of their people, their histor-ical, moral and constitutional right to have denominational schools and to have equality of the French language with English; to assert, in short, the principle of duality. "If any single member expects the English to assimilate the French in this Dominion", said Talbot, "I might give them the friendly advice to disabuse themselves [*sic*.] The French are a distinctive race, and we will not be assimilated, whether you like it or not. The sooner you know it the better. We have been given our rights as a separate nationality and we will hold them".[21] The bill, the French members declared, was a violation of the "pact",, or "treaty" of Confederation, which had recognized the equal and distinct status of the French in Canada. "The French and Catholic population of Manitoba", declared a protest prepared by a committee of the Manitoban French and tabled in the Legislature "have by natural law, by the title of first occupancy, by solemn treaties, by the B.N.A. Act, by the pact solemnly entered into by the Delegates of the Territory of Assiniboia and the North-West Ter-ritories with the Dominion of Canada, by the Manitoba Act and subsequent legislation, rights and privileges which have been violated by the Legislature of Manitoba".[22] To the embittered and bewildered French, the bill was "an attempt on our national life".[23]

The reply of the government was that the French language had no consti-tutional standing in Manitoba. The religious rights of Roman Catholics were not touched, were indeed not involved. Some members, and the local press, admitted the special status, on historical and moral grounds, of the French language. But there was no obligation, it was asserted, to respect that status, as the French had neither accepted the Compromise of 1897 nor an offer of special treatment.[24] By standing out for their whole claim, based on natural law and the constitution, and for the retention of the bi-lingual system of 1897, they had identified themselves with the other language groups, the Germans, Ukrainians and Poles and menaced the Legislature with the re-opening of the school question in its entirety. By their refusal to compromise, the French of Manitoba had brought down on their cause the fate preparing for the other non-English languages.[25] As. J.D. Baskerville reminded the Legislature, "the battle at Babel had broken the contract".[26] The reply of the government and its supporters was made, not unsympathetically but very firmly; for the general conviction in the Legislature was that the operation of the bi-lingual clause had threatened the very foundations of Canadian nationality in Manitoba. It was imperative that the danger be removed, "if a common citizenship were to be built up in Canada".[27]

Immigration into the West had introduced a third element into the crucible, a third element which by 1916 had affected both the distinct and formed nationalities of 1870. Because the newcomers were assimilated to the English group, the influx reduced the French to a minority and led to the loss of the rights held by them from 1870 to 1890. It also affected the English group by the insistence of many of the immigrants both on assimilation to the English group in public life and on the retention of their mother tongue and culture in private life. In this trend the Icelandic and Scandinavian peoples led. Both the Icelandic members of the Legislature in 1916 supported the abolition of bi-lingual teaching and one of them, Hon. T.H. Johnson, declared: "We admit, and we all must admit, that there is only one nationality possible in the future, a Canadian nationality, and we claim the privilege of becoming merged in that, and the privilege of contributing towards that, whatever national characteristics we may possess".[28] While rejecting the principle of duality, Manitoba, out of the confusion created by the bi-lingual clause and the great immigration, was groping towards a combination of political uniformity with cultural plurality.

In the end the abolition of the bi-lingual system was carried by thirty-eight votes to eight. The opposition was made up of two dissident French Liberals, one Ukrainian member, and the Conservative Opposition of five, of whom two were French speaking. The decisive character of the vote settled the issue. Although opposition flared up briefly in 1917 when the Government proposed to make the University of Manitoba a state university, the year 1916 witnessed the end of political controversy over the school question in the province of Manitoba.

V

The legislation of 1916 was enforced with both firmness and tact.[29] But the Liberal party of Manitoba had to pay the penalty for its courage in grasping the nettle. In 1920 it lost its majority to candidates of the United Farmers and to opponents of the school legislation of 1916.[30] In 1922 its defeat was completed by the same forces. The fusion of the United Farmers with the opponents of the school legislation did not lead to any change in the school system. The Liberal leader might argue that the combination was a revenge for 1916, but Premier John Bracken made it clear that no one had ever suggested to him any change in the school system as the price of support.[31] Bracken's statement was never challenged in the debates. It seems clear that once the personalities of 1916 were removed from public office, the school question was a closed issue as far as the political parties of Manitoba were concerned.

Notes

[1]See Noël Bernier, *Fannystelle (Publié sous les auspices de la Société Historique de Saint-Boniface,* Manitoba, n.d. [1939]) p. 162.

[2]See Pamphlets, Hon. R.S. Thornton, *Bi-Lingual Schools: An Address in the Legislature on January 12th, 1916.* (Department of Education Winnipeg, 1916) p. 11.

[3]Dom Benoit, *Vie de Monseigneur Taché,* (Montreal, 1904) II, 195-196. Taché wrote to Sir George Cartier in 1869, "J'ai toujours redouté l'entrée du Nord-Ouest dans la Conféderation parce que j'ai toujours cru que l'élément français catholique serait sacrifié . . ." *Ibid.,* II, 17.

[4]See C.B. Sissons, *Egerton Ryerson, His Life and Letters,* (Toronto, 1947) II, 270.

[5]While there was an outburst in 1875 following the first Ontario immigration after 1870, against the school system and the official use of French, there was in fact little public criticism of either until the late summer of 1889. The point is exhaustively established by A.E. Clague in "The Manitoba School Question, 1890-1896". (Unpublished M.A. thesis, University of Manitoba, 1939) chaps. I-III.

[6]P.A.M., Greenway Papers, Joseph Martin to Thomas Greenway, August 6, 1889; also J.S. Willison, *Sir Wilfred Laurier and the Liberal Party,* (Toronto, 1903) II, 202.

[7]This point is too easily lost sight of in the controversy over principles. See John S. Ewart, *The Manitoba School Question,* (Toronto, 1894) 246-247; also *Canada, House of Commons Debates,* 1897, I, 371-374. The later phases of the school question in Manitoba and the events leading to the formation of the United Church of Canada enforce the point.

[8]Ewart, *Manitoba School Question,* 63; address before Governor-General in Council, January 21, 1893.

⁹P.A.M., Manitoba School Case (clippings from contemporary press) I, 90. Resolution of Grand Lodge (Orange) of Western Ontario; ". . . separate schools . . . perpetuate an improper union between church and state; . . . they do not teach that the duty of every good citizen is to give his first loyalty to the nation in which he lives . . ."; *Gladstone Age,* April 17, 1895, J.W. Armstrong at public meeting on school question: "Where we have so many different nationalities, it is necessary to have some time to bind them together and blend all their characteristics in one common nationality"; *Winnipeg Tribune,* (clipping) 1895, "Is Manitoba Right?": "If public education has been found necessary in a country like Britain, the necessity is greatly emphasized in a new community like Manitoba, with its heterogeneous and polyglot population, and the great diversity of intelligence and ideas which characterizes its yet unassimilated elements".

For a direct challenge to the principle of duality, see F.C. Wade, *The Manitoba School Question,* (Winnipeg, 1895) 51; "It cannot be conducive to our national welfare to bring up the two great sections of our population apart from each other". The view of John S. Ewart and James Fisher, that a school system at once "national" and "separate" was possible, commanded little sympathy on either side of the controversy.

¹⁰P.A.M., *Manitoba Debates,* (F.P.) 1916, 8; J.W. Dafoe, *Clifford Sifton in Relation to His Times* (Toronto, 1931) 98.

¹¹The explanation of the omission of clauses providing for enforcement of attendance given by Premier R.P. Roblin in the Legislature in 1914 and 1915 may be accepted. Roblin was an independent member of the Legislature in 1890, and the bill of 1890 as amended in committee is in the files of the Legislature of Manitoba, with the attendance section struck out and initialled "C.S.", just as Roblin described it in 1914 and 1915. (See P.A.M., *Manitoba Debates,* (F.P.) 1914, 28-30, and *Manitoba Debates* (Trib.), 1915, 72). Roblin said that Attorney-General Martin, who drew up the bill, had included clauses providing for attendance. On advice from D'Alton McCarthy, however, he had them struck out in committee. The chairman of that committee was Clifford Sifton. It was feared that compulsion would destroy the constitutional ground on which the bill was based, namely that the Catholics had a right to private and voluntary denominational schools, but not to separate schools supported by public funds. To compel the children of Catholic parents to attend the public schools would violate this right.

¹²The provincial premier after 1900, R.P. Roblin, had opposed both the School Act of 1890 and the amendment of 1897; the Conservative platform of 1899 had called for the freeing of the school systems "from party politics by the establishment of an independent board of education"; P.A.M., Pamphlets, *Record of the Roblin Government,* 1900-1909, 5.

¹³The composition of the population of Manitoba in 1911 was as follows: British, 266,415; French, 30,944; German, 34,530; Austro-Hungarian, 39,665; Polish, 12,310; Scandinavian, 16,419; and smaller groups, to a total of 55,311; *Canada Year Book* 1912, 24.

¹⁴For an informed contemporary description of the operation of the bi-lingual section, see C.B. Sissons, *Bi-lingual Schools in Canada* (Toronto, 1917) pp. 116-155. See also R. Fletcher, "The Language Problem in Manitoba Schools", *papers read before Historical and Scientific Society of Manitoba* III (6) (Winnipeg, 1851) 55-56. Dr. Fletcher was a member of the Department of Education from 1903, and Deputy-Minister of Education, 1908-1939.

[15]This account is based on the defence of the government policy by Premier Roblin and the Minister of Education, Hon. George Coldwell, in moving amendments of the Truancy Act in 1914; P.A.M., *Manitoba Debates,* 1915 (T.) 72.

[16]*Canada, H. of C. Debates,* 1911-12, III, 4839-4925 and 4934-4973. No direct connection between the boundary extension of 1912 and the amendments has, to the writer's knowledge, ever been established. But that the amendments were a fumbling attempt to conciliate Catholic feeling without arousing Protestant resentment seems probable; see A.G. Morice, *Vie de Monseigneur Langevin,* pp. 284-285. In further confirmation of this assumption, it is of interest to know that the amendments were drafted outside the Province of Manitoba.

[17]P.A.M., Pamphlets, *Liberal Platform of 1914.* (Saint-Boniface, 1919). The legal thought behind the substitute clause was later expounded by Attorney-General A.B. Hudson, subsequently a member of the Supreme Court of Canada, P.A.M., *Manitoba Debates,* (F.P.) 1916, 28.

[18]Much of the benefit of this act was, however, lost by placing its administration in the hands of local officials.

[19]P.A.M., *Manitoba Debates,* (F.P.) 1916, 5-7.

[20]The reports of this caucus are, as is usual, meagre, P.A.M., *Manitoba Debates,* (F.P.) 1916, pp. 44-45. The substance of the Reports is accepted here, because it is supported by the subsequent debates.

[21]P.A.M., *Manitoba Debates,* (F.P.) 1916, 31. Talbot was reproached in the debate with being a "nationalist" and a "separatist", but denied that he was a Nationalist of Bourassa's school. He was, in fact, at that time a Laurier Liberal.

[22]*Canadian Annual Review,* 1916, 673.

[23]*Ibid.,* 1921, 774.

[24]*Ibid.,* 8, 46-47, 49-51, 53-55; also *Manitoba Debates,* (F.P.) 1920, p. 46, in which A.B. Hudson reviewed the controversy; ". . . it seemed to him what had been done was the only thing that could be done".

[25]*Winnipeg Free Press Library,* Dafoe Papers, J.W. Dafoe to Thomas Coté, April 6, 1916.

[26]P.A.M., *Manitoba Debates, (F.P.) 1916, p. 53.*

[27]*Ibid.,* p. 48.

[28]*Ibid.,* p. 55.

[29]P.A.M., Pamphlets, *Addresses in the Legislature by Hon. R.S. Thornton 1917 to 1919.* (Department of Education, Winnipeg, 1917, 1918, 1919). See also P.A.M., *Manitoba Debates,* (F.P.) 1921 pp. 83-89; *Ibid.,* 1917, 9; *Ibid.,* 1920, 30. I am told on good authority that it was Dr. Thornton who coined the term, "New Canadian".

[30]Dafoe Papers, J.W. Dafoe to Clifford Sifton, December 29, 1920; *Canadian Annual Review,* 1921, 739; *Manitoba Free Press,* February 25, 1921, p. 13.

[31]The Farmers' Platform of 1922 merely called for stricter enforcement of attendance, but made no reference to language instruction.

Canadian Nationalism and North-West Schools, 1884-1905*

Neil McDonald

A study of the early development of the school system in the old North-West Territories reveals one of the most undisguised attempts in Canada to use formal education for nationalistic purposes. The basic structure of the system was shaped in the decade of national turmoil and disunity that followed the execution of Louis Riel at Regina; a period which, pertinently, coincided with the numerical and political ascendancy of English-speaking Protestants in the North-West. Acutely self-conscious of their new power, and Canada's problems in building a 'new' nationality, this group was determined to raise the North-West above colonial status and to mould it according to its perception of Canadian nationality. With the introduction of the principle of responsible government in 1891 the most important step toward both goals was realized. First, encouraged by this legislation, it was realized that full responsible government and eventual provincial autonomy was within reach; second, the North-West Assembly now possessed the legislative power to make laws with minimal federal intervention.

In the context of this study, the latter provision is most significant. According to the new Anglo majority there was an inherent contradiction in attempting to build a united Canada when the French language and separate schools were granted "privileged" status. Their ideal of a united Canada was a homogeneous nation founded on a common language and cultural background, an appreciation of British institutions, identification with the Empire, and pride in the so-called Anglo-Saxon race. Thus, with this ideal in mind, and armed with the 1891 legislation, as well as the knowledge of events in Manitoba and Eastern Canada, these self-styled nationalists deliberately organized the schools to legitimize the cultivation of their particular brand of Canadian nationalism. They succeeded in imposing their views because of their numerical superiority, and their domination of the media, churches, teaching profession, and the Legislative Assembly. Later, with the coming of European immigrants in significant numbers, the basis for their concern was dramatically reinforced, and, since the machinery was already in place, a wider application of the overall plan was easily effected. Indeed, it now became

*From *Canadian Schools and Canadian Identity* edited by Alf Chaiton and Neil McDonald. ©Gage Eductional Publishing Ltd., 1977. Reprinted with permission of Gage Publishing Ltd.

more urgent to champion the school as the most effective agency to "Canadianize" the youth of the country.

I

The initial legislation providing for formal schooling in the North-West was passed by the federally appointed North-West Council in 1884. Sensitive to an ethnic imbalance and denominational preference, as well as the separate school and language clauses of the North-West Territories Acts of 1875 and 1877, the councillors opted for a dual-confessional system of schools. Almost on cue, however, the Council underwent a collective change of mind and took firm steps to retrieve the controlling power it had so indulgently given the churches. Carried out on an annual basis, this gradual process of retrieval was dramatically quickened in 1892 when the North-West Assembly brought schools completely under central control. A series of constitutional, political, and social factors conspired to facilitate this final step.

Constitutionally, a most important amendment to the North-West Territories Act was passed by Parliament in 1891. It permitted the establishment of an Executive Committee of the North-West Territories to aid and advise in territorial government. In effect, the principle of responsible government was now introduced. In no small measure, this amendment reflected the changeover from the appointed Council of 1884 to an elected Assembly, whose 22 members more actively pursued the question of self-government. Socially, the ethnic balance, that in earlier years had favored French-speaking Roman Catholics, had shifted decidedly to favor the English-speaking Protestants. Representation in the Assembly clearly reflected the ascendancy of the new, articulate Anglo majority. Another important factor to consider in the context of this change in the management of educational affairs in the North-West is the intense controversy and cultural conflict triggered by the hanging of Louis Riel in 1885. Although the storm centre of this controversy was in Ontario and Quebec, the battleground soon embraced the West. D'Alton McCarthy, the leading spokesman for English-speaking opponents of French language privileges and separate schools, vigorously promoted this position on personal tours of Manitoba and the North-West. Describing French Canadians as a "bastard nationality", McCarthy declared, "This is a British country, and the sooner we take up our French Canadians and make them British, the less trouble will we leave for posterity".[1] The subsequent moves to abolish separate schools and to remove legislative protection for the French language in the West are telling indicators of the sympathy felt for the views articulated by McCarthy. This heightened consciousness, brought about by the growth of a strident and belligerent nationalism among the two major ethnic groups in Canada, was the political and social context in which the decision was made to effect a fundamental change in the organizational structure and orientation of North-West schools.. These factors alone, however, did not cause this basic restructuring. The final outcome was skilfully orchestrated by the Chairman of the North-West Executive Committee, Frederick William Gordon Haultain.

Born in 1857 near Woolwich, England, Haultain was only three years of age when his family moved to Canada. The father, a former army colonel, was elected member for Peterborough in the Legislative Assembly of the Province of Canada in 1864. Although identified as a Conservative he voted for more Liberal motions than his own party.[2] A supporter of the 1864 coalition, he participated in the Confederation debates,[3] and argued strongly for legislation "to protect the English speaking Protestants of Quebec from a recent papal encyclical denying immigrants to Catholic countries freedom of worship".[4]

The younger Haultain attended the common schools of the province, Montreal High School and Peterborough Collegiate Institute. In 1879, he graduated from the University of Toronto with first class honors in Classics, and three years later was called to the Ontario Bar. in 1884, despondent of career opportunities in Ontario, he moved to Fort Macleod, North-West Territories, to practise his profession. When the population of that area reached the mandatory 1,000 persons the Macleod electoral district was created. At the age of thirty Haultain was chosen to represent the new district. In 1891, he was elected chairman of the Executive Committee, and, in 1901, Commissioner of Education. Recognized by all as 'premier' of the Territories, Haultain continued to hold the Macleod seat until 1905 when the provinces of Alberta and Saskatchewan were created. In that year, as a result of his public opposition to the separate school clauses of the Autonomy Bill, a controversial Haultain was passed over in favor of Walter Scott, a Liberal, to form the first Saskatchewan government. Undaunted, he formed the Provincial Rights Party. Although his new party was never able to elect sufficient members to form the government, it did command widespread support from the electorate and remained the official Opposition while Haultain was its leader. He resigned the leadership in 1912 to become Chief Justice of the Supreme Court of Saskatchewan. In 1938 he retired from the bench, and moved to Montreal, where he died on January 30, 1942. He was twice married, but there were no children from either union.

As the above record indicates, from his early years in the North-West Council, and, later, Legislative Assembly, Haultain demonstrated a distinct capacity for political leadership. In spite of his youth and lack of legislative experience, he quickly became recognized as one of the best debaters and most able parliamentarians among the members. The assessment of Walter Scott, then owner of the *Regina Leader,* was typical. Scott wrote:

> Imperturbable always, with a well trained legal mind, and having a good grasp of the principles of law and of British institutions, Mr. Haultain, almost from the moment of his entrance was looked to as a leader in the

House and in the stirring, exciting, and at times bitter events which marked all of the sessions . . . he became the chief spokesman and acknowledged leader, who championed the cause of democracy against the tenacity of bureaucracy.[5]

This verdict was shared not only by contemporaries, but in historical studies by Lingard[6] and Thomas[7], Haultain emerges as the most influential politician in the two major constitutional developments in the North-West during the Territorial period, namely responsible government and provincial autonomy. A more recent work by Lupul[8] identifies Haultain as the most visible political figure associated with Territorial educational developments.

In spite of later events, in Territorial politics Haultain was a non-party man, although he generally supported the Conservatives at the federal level. He made his position clear in a letter to the editor of the *Regina Leader* at the height of the autonomy crisis in August, 1905. Uncannily in the spirit of the future farmers' parties, he stated out-right that he stood for "non-party government regardless of what any political party or both sides may declare"; he argued that his eighteen years in public life stood as unquestionable evidence that "the welfare and interests" of the North-West "always have been more important than the success or convenience of any political party".[9] He believed that, in practice, party politics were divisive, and often cited the experience of the older provinces as evidence. His stand in this matter was consistent with his position on separate schools.

In the North-West, as in other parts of Canada, separate schools was an issue that went hand-in-hand with the French language question, and it is difficult to discuss them separately. Even before election to the North-West Council, Haultain made known his opposition to a confessional school system.[10] Early in his public career his name became linked to both issues. Within a few months of his first election the French-speaking Roman Catholic minority identified him as an antagonist.[11] Haultain, however, did not hide his views. Openly declaring his intentions, a Haultain campaign speech in early 1891 was reported in the *Macleod Gazette* as follows:

> We now have two systems. Under our present constitution a Protestant or Roman Catholic minority have the right to establish separate schools. He [Haultain] was thoroughly opposed to such a system. He did not wish to interfere with religious belief, but religious training was not necessary in the school. We did not need to introduce religious teaching. We got that at home, at the churches and in the Sunday Schools. There was no reason why Protestants should not go to school with Catholics. His position with regard to the separate school question was that he would work and vote against it as hard as possible.[12]

The following year the *Regina Standard* noted that Haultain drew "loud cheers" from a Yorkton audience when he asked their assistance to abolish

"Protestant and Catholic antagonism in politics, education and social life".[13] With their support he claimed that it was possible to unite the people of the North-West "in one bond of national ideas". Since, in his view, "the function and mission of schools was to mould and assimilate all families making the prairies their home", a system of national schools was the most effective means to effect this end.[14] Therefore, he claimed on still another occasion, national schools were *essential* to a great nation. In the United States their value was recognized early and, there, "separate schools are regarded as national evils".[15] Similarly with the French language, he was adamant that legislative grounds for the cultural and linguistic wars, so sharply dividing the central provinces, should not find constitutional support in the Territories.

In Haultain's view, the North-West was intended to be an "English-speaking country" and he articulated and actively campaigned for policies that advanced this end.[16] Indeed, at the first opportunity after the federal Government granted the North-West Assembly the right to decide the language of its proceedings, Haultain moved that "the proceedings of the Legislative Assembly shall be recorded and published hereafter in the English language only".[17] The motion passed 24 to 4; a clear indication of the political support for these measures. Moreover, the indecent haste in which the Assembly acted indicates the pressing desire of the new majority to assert its political supremacy. The alacrity of the members did not go unnoticed by the minority. One member expressed his chagrin "that the first avowed act of the first responsible government of the Territories should be to attack the privileges of the French people".[18] However, so confident was Haultain in the success of his policies that a few months later he could tell a Toronto newspaper reporter that he thought it only "inexpedient" that D'Alton McCarthy should agitate the school and language question at that particular time. It was not a question of fundamental disagreement with McCarthy but of timing. He reasoned, as usual, from a position of power:

> The English speaking people were now, and always would be, in the ascendancy in the North-West, and there was no danger that the separate school question would be engrafted on the Territories.[19]

In spite of charges of prejudice and bigotry leveled at him by his critics, particularly the Roman Catholic clergy, Haultain maintained his position. Later when the ethnic newcomers sought special consideration for their native languages he enforced similar policies. An example was the request made in 1901 for permission to use the German language schools. *The Standard* reported:

> Haultain took the ground that the average child's attendance as a rule was too short for even a satisfying grounding in English. He objected therefore to curtailing the time already at disposal for this purpose enabling parents to employ any competent person to teach in a foreign tongue after the

English curriculum has been disposed of; remuneration of this teacher to be paid by the parents whose children benefited by it.[20]

This solution was considered typical of Haultain because:

In this way, if there is any strong desire for teaching to be given in the native tongue of native children, the desire could be gratified without interfering with the existing school system.[21]

Politically, Haultain had found a way to defuse a potentially explosive issue, but, in practice, he did little for the petitioners. Few immigrants were in a position to take advantage of the legislation. In any case, he was not about to reverse his long held views. A few months before this decision, in response to a French-speaking member of the Assembly concerning minority rights to representation in autonomy discussions, Haultain replied; "Our rights are not our rights as Englishmen, Scotchmen or Irishmen, or as Doukhobors or Galicians or anything of that kind but as citizens of a common country".[22] Rhetoric aside, his actions left little doubt about which group should determine those "rights".

It is difficult to underestimate the intensity with which Haultain believed, and pursued his objectives. In 1904, when the Autonomy Bill threatened to undo much of the legislation that he had supported, he campaigned around the country against its provisions. He told a *Toronto Globe* reporter, "If I were made a dictator tomorrow, I would not change it".[23] Clearly aware that it would jeopardize his political career, he nonetheless took the risk. Undoubtedly, the loss of the Saskatchewan premiership was related to this issue; as was the lack of success of his Provincial Rights Party in which the first plank was the right of the province to decide the schools question. The verdict by the Conservative editor of the *Toronto News,* however politically biased, gives an insight into what Haultain may have perceived as the stakes to be lost:

The schools of the North-West are the best in Canada. . . . As educating agencies, politics apart, they are unexcelled. As political instruments for the fusing together of diverse nationalities they are exceedingly efficient. The North-West certainly is fortunate in having a system which on the one hand ensures a particularly sound education to the children who in a few years will control its destinies, and, on the other hand, supplies a powerful engine for the welding of extremely heterogeneous elements into a common citizenship.
The present excellence of the school system must be laid to the credit of Frederick Haultain. He had at his back the enlightened desire of the men of the West for education and unity; he supplied the means.[24]

Underlying Haultain's approach to the language and schools question in the North-West was a fundamental, but convenient, political article of faith, namely unity, both national and regional. In speeches and public statements on these vital issues rarely did he fail to make this argument the basis of his position. Like the Anglo-conformists of his time, he firmly believed that the future stability and development of the North-West depended on the unity and cohesion of its people. In his view the tragic example of the central provinces was a clear indication of the chaos created by diversity. If the North-West did not act decisively it would fall heir to similar intractable problems. As the years advanced and the North-West became the settling ground for thousands of European immigrants, Haultain became more convinced of the wisdom of his position. At the regional level, unity was seen as essential to the two fundamental political problems facing the Territories, the achievement of responsible government and eventual provincial status. Unless the federal Government could be convinced that the elected Assembly represented the legitimate aspirations of the people, further political development would be frozen in the hands of a remote, unsympathetic central government. Closely related to federal neglect was the widely held belief of Territorial residents that Eastern Canada, particularly Ontario, viewed the North-West as little more than a colonial possession. To cope with the attitudes and practices that stemmed from this mind-set Haultain again needed to project the image of a determined, independent, and united people. On one other ground, too, he considered unity an important issue in the North-West. It served as an antidote to counter the influence of a giant neighbor to the south — a familiar theme in the Canadian experience, but nonetheless a real concern to a thinly populated and relatively isolated North-West.[25]

However desirable unity was to the development of the country, it must be realized that Haultain and his supporters defined unity in terms that clearly strengthened their political hegemony over North-West affairs. For example, by insisting that unity implied cultural uniformity and, therefore, an important key to national and Territorial strength, by inference, those who were opposed, or even culturally different, were looked on as either permanent obstructionists, or temporary impediments, in an otherwise clear path to national progress. To the dominant group all the signs suggested that, by a kind of historical necessity, cultural uniformity was essential to Canada's future and this group was determined to hasten its arrival.

II

In part, the vehicle that the Assembly provided to accomplish the objectives described above was the legislation passed in the early nineties. On the other hand, legislative provisions are effective only insofar as they are administered efficiently. For this task Haultain personally chose David James Goggin, a capable administrator whose beliefs, sympathies, and goals were remarkably similar to his own. Goggin was soon to become a central figure in the development of North-West education.

Born in Cartwright Township, Durham County, Canada West, of Irish Protestant stock, in 1849, Goggin began his formal education in the common schools of Canada West and continued at the Universities of Toronto and Manitoba. Recognized by his peers as an outstanding teacher, headmaster and Model School principal, he came to the West in 1884 as principal of the Manitoba Normal School on the strength of exceptional recommendations by such noted Ontario educators as James L. Hughes, J.J. Tilley, and James A. McLellan.[26] Meeting with comparable success in Manitoba, in April of 1893, on Haultain's invitation he came to Regina as Director of Normal Schools and Teacher Institutes; within a few months he was appointed Superintendent of Education, a position he held for nine years. In 1902, he returned to Toronto to become literary manager of the Canada Publishing Company. The death of his wife and the care of two teenage children were important factors in this decision. In 1909, he was appointed Textbook Commissioner, and three years later became General Editor of Textbooks, for the province of Ontario. Subsequently he succeeded J.C. Hodgins as provincial historiographer and ended his active career as editor-in-chief of the Macmillan Company of Canada. He died in Toronto on December 18, 1935.

Except for some disapproval of his annual salary, which exceeded Haultain's, and objections from the Catholic clergy, Goggin's appointment was generally well accepted throughout the North-West.[27] An active and articulate member of provincial and local teachers' associations in Ontario and Manitoba, he had been a frequent guest and invited speaker at several North-West teachers' conventions.[28] By the time he resigned the Superintendency his work as an educator not only attracted attention at home but received notice from educators throughout the Empire and the United States.[29] The author of several textbooks, journal and newspaper articles, as well as numerous public addresses, Goggin was an active member of many prominent organizations, associations, and clubs, especially in his later years. An examination of these writings, speeches, and activities reveal important insights into the ideas and beliefs that motivated the new Superintendent.

Prior to his arrival in the Territories, Goggin had attracted the attention of the Roman Catholic hierarchy. First, by his active support of the attempt to make the University of Manitoba a teaching institution. As a member of the University Council, Goggin was in a position to advance his views. This proposal was vigorously resisted by Archbishop Taché of St. Boniface who saw it as a direct violation of the original agreement under which he permitted St. Boniface College to become an integral part of the university.[30] Second, by the activities associated with his position as provincial grand-master of the Masonic society.[31] Taché, an ultramontane cleric, failed to discriminate between the virulent anti-clericalism of European Freemasonry and its various manifestations in North America. He was particularly incensed when Goggin took official precedence over the minister of education at a cornerstone laying ceremony in Virden, Manitoba.[32] Third, on several occasions he had made clear his position on the separate schools question. Significantly, one such occasion was a speech to the Regina and Central Assiniboia teachers' convention at Qu'Appelle in November 1891, in which, incidentally, he practically predicted coming events in the North-West. He declared:

> While the church was in the ascendant, education was modelled in accordance with religious needs. Now that the state is the ascendant we may expect education to be moulded more in accordance with political — I mean the word in the best sense — needs. The church to do its share in educating the child must adapt itself to the changed order of things.[33]

To Taché, in the midst of his campaign to have the 1890 School Law disallowed, the implications of Goggin's appointment for this "changed order" were painfully evident. To the Roman Catholic clergy in the North-West, the selection of Goggin as Chief Administrator of educational affairs confirmed their worst fears. Three years later Father Leduc, the education critic whose views often represented those of the less articulate Bishop Grandin, could write that Goggin had come "not brutally to abolish catholic schools as Messrs. Martin and Greenway have done in Manitoba, but to attain the same end by cleverer and more astute means".[34] In Leduc's estimation, the early fears were well justified.

Like Haultain, Goggin argued that separate schools and language diversity presented a very real threat to national unity. A Canadian nationalist imperialist, he strongly identified with the conservative WASP community of his time. Lay secretary to the Anglican Synod of Rupert's Land, Masonic grand-master for Manitoba and the North-West, and a Conservative, he also held office as secretary of the Canadian Club of Toronto, and membership in the National and Albany Clubs. The latter three were noted for their nationalist and imperialist views. Indeed, the National was a direct descendant of the Canada First Movement, and the Albany Club was the successor to the United Empire Club. Almost from its beginnings, Goggin was a member of the Empire Club of Toronto, whose primary object was "the advancement of the interests of Canada and a United Empire".[35] In 1908 he was elected president. A later president and former Conservative premier of Ontario, G. Howard Ferguson, described Goggin as "a great Canadian and British patriot" who was very active in the Empire Club and did a great deal to promote its spirit.[36] Goggin's son, Victor, in a talk to the club, confirmed this view:

> The Empire Club was part of home to my father. His many friends in the Empire Club were part of the best in life to him. The accomplishments of the Empire Club were his pride and served as part recompense for a long life devoted to public service.[37]

In the early 1890's Goggin was associated with a group of Canadian educators concerned with the ultimate implications of provincial control of education for national unity. The group sought to counter the potential for divisive and uncoordinated solutions to common educational problems by forming a national organization to serve as a forum for discussion of these problems. The Dominion Educational Association was the result. Goggin, who served as its president from 1901 to 1904, and secretary for three more years,[38] stated the case for the group at the 1904 Convention:

> Education within the Provinces tends to become parochial in spirit, and narrow in view, while the type of education which it is the function of the school to build up, should have a national rather than a provincial outlook. It was mainly because of this that years ago a number of us felt the need of some organization that would bring together in conference the leading educationists of the Provinces, so that those engaged in the calling should understand each other's aims and plans.[39]

Thus, in concert with other Canadian educators, Goggin made constant use of the Association's biennial meetings as a forum to advance the view that their colleagues in the teaching profession should think "nationally" rather than in narrow provincial terms. Indeed, he frequently urged his associates to look to the organization of the Empire as a model. There, one could see a prime example of commitment to the welfare of the whole, and not to mere selfish particularist interests. This type of united action he characterised as "the imperial spirit".[40]

During his years in the North-West, perhaps the most public recognition of Goggin's imperialist sympathies came in 1897, Queen Victoria's Diamond Jubilee year. Throughout Canada it was occasion for elaborate celebrations; sentiments of loyalty and devotion to Queen and Empire became the stock-in-trade of guest speakers at uncounted public gatherings and private clubs. The Territories was no exception. At Regina, the day was climaxed with a large public gathering in the "market square where a pavilion had been erected and a large platform seated".[41] Goggin was chosen to deliver the major address. Considering the importance attached to the event, and the list of public officials available, including Lieutenant-Governor Mackintosh, Haultain, and Mayor Eddy of Regina, his selection was significant. But just as the choice implied public recognition of his views, by the same token, their expression by the Superintendent confirmed the public perception. His address, replete with appropriate imperialist sentiment, asked his listeners to "take stock" of the growth of the Empire since Victoria's accession to the throne. This stock-taking included a united Canada, the impending union of Australia's states, an Indian Empire "of 300 millions of subjects", one-third of Africa, and Egypt, where "we have restored order out of chaos". With a note of triumph, he noted:

> Today the British flag floats free over one-fifth of the world's area. Today the little Englander is mute. This day the grown-up sons, our Premiers, are

at home [i.e. England] and they stand shoulder to shoulder steady and ready, the Greater Britain looms larger and the note of Imperialism is dominant.[42]

The constant emphasis on Victoria's person and reign in which were embodied all the great ideas and advances of the age was the common theme: the progress in science, literature, the arts, religion, education, as well as giant strides in exploration, wealth, culture, and the development of free institutions. The language was hardly sufficient to describe the remarkable heights to which civilization had reached under British inspiration. Goggin's address, in fact, had a near religious tone. He began by noting that:

> . . . sixty years ago the official representatives of the temporal and spiritual powers of England on bended knee kissed the hand of Victoria, hailing her as Queen, and today millions of loyal subjects, embracing one-fifth of the world's population, with grateful hearts circle the earth with the cry of 'honor, honor, eternal honor to her name'.[43]

He closed by asking his audience "to halt and thank God for an Empire, the most splendid possession ever entrusted to any people".[44]

When the 1892 School Law was passed by the Assembly the French-speaking minority was perceived as the main obstacle to Anglo dominance. The main thrust of the legislation, therefore, was directed at undermining their constitutional position in the North-West. Within a few years, however, other ethnic groups begin to arrive in the Territories in great numbers. These new immigrants came with their distinctive cultural and linguistic heritage, and greatly added to the socio-cultural "mix" of a once thinly populated North-West. As the French before them, these peoples were seen immediately by the dominant group as a potential challenge to its now entrenched position of power. Once again, as with the French, the argument was advanced that the social and political stability of the country was the issue, and national unity demanded that these "foreigners" be assimilated. Goggin aggressively promoted this argument.

As early as 1898, in his second *Report* as Superintendent, he considered the block settlement of "so many foreign nationalities . . . as one of the most serious and pressing educational problems" in the North-West. He argued that "it would be criminal to shut our eyes" to the challenge that this "foreign and relatively ignorant population" offered to Territorial institutions.[45] The solution he proposed was predictable:

> Only through our schools getting an early hold of these settlers can we hope to train them to live according to our social system and to understand and appreciate the institutions of the country which they are to form an integral part of. If in these respects we can place these people two generations hence where their Anglo-Saxon neighbours now are we shall have done well.

> . . . If these children are to grow up as Canadian citizens they must be led to adopt our viewpoint and speak our speech. . . . A common school and a common tongue are essential if we are to have a homogeneous citizenship.[46]

Interestingly, Goggin's particular concern was the "block or 'colony' system" of settlement. He assumed that where there are mixed or town settlement the likelihood of assimilation was increased due to the everyday demands of communication and the English-based schools. Where the "colony" system prevailed, however, the situation was reversed and called for immediate action to counter the danger of mutual support and consequent group solidarity encouraging members to maintain their indigenous cultural and linguistic heritage. Interesting, too, that the "exclusively French speaking districts in Saskatchewan" were included with the "colonies of Swedes, Finns, Bohemians, Hungarians, Jews, Australians, Germans, Russians, Icelanders, Mennonites, Galicians and Doukhobors".[47] Although not categorized as "foreign", Goggin also considered it essential that the French attend "a common school" and speak "a common tongue" to become part of this "homogeneous citizenship" that, in his view, defined Canadian citizenship.

Pleading not only the desirabiltiy, but the necessity, of providing the conditions for developing a "homogeneous citizenship", in the interests of national unity, soon became a familiar theme with Goggin. In an address to the Dominion Educational Association in 1901, for example, the Superintendent hoped that all members were inspired by a common zeal in pursuit of a common aim, namely the moulding of children of "different races and creeds into that homogeneous product, the Canadian Youth" who, as citizens, were responsible for building up a great Canadian nation. He proclaimed a pride in Canadian citizenship but warned that with this privilege came the responsibility to ensure that Canada would achieve its ultimate greatness. Her unlimited possibilities could only be realized if her immigrants, differing in race, creed, customs, tradtions, and political instincts could be made homogeneous. "The unifying influence of the schools", he acknowledged, was already working toward this end but the aid of press and statesman must also be enlisted.[48] At the 1904 convention he reminded members that their primary concern should be the same now as it was when the organization was founded. Again his concern was the role of the school in the development of a "homogeneous citizenship". The members were to aid "in the development of Canadian sentiment of a national rather than a provincial spirit", and, thus, prepare themselves "to think imperially".[49]

Goggin's commitment to a policy of cultural uniformity for the Territories was particularly evident in his fervid opposition to the education clauses of the 1905 Autonomy Bill. In a much publicized speech to the Empire Club he declared that the "only truly successful way" to achieve assimilation was:

. . to gather the children of different races, creeds, and customs into the common school, and 'Canadianize' them. . . . Though they may enter as Galicians, Doukhobors, or Icelanders, they will come out as Canadians. . . . In the West we have asked for no school that divides us on the basis of our creeds, or that separates us at all, but we do need schools that unite us. A common school and a common language will produce that homogeneous citizenship so necessary in the development of that greater Canada lying West of the Lakes.[50]

During this period, strongly urged by Haultain, Goggin actively campaigned against the government's position. It was his first and only foray into platform politics.

Given Goggin's sympathies and commitment it was not surprising that Haultain should have chosen him to implement the 1892 legislation. Their close friendship continued long years after Goggin left the North-West.[51] Haultain's papers contain the rough draft of an address obviously intended for delivery at a farewell function for the Superintendent.[52] In those notes Haultain wrote that, in his view, there were two essential problems requiring urgent attention when he hired Goggin, namely the courses of study and the training of teachers. Although he recognized there were a "110" other "technical" problems, he was not interested in a mere technician. "It was necessary", he wrote, "to lay down courses of study and methods of instruction best suited to the *development* and *instruction* of the boys and girls of the country". The "*incompetent*" and "*untrained*" were not to be permitted in North-West classrooms, and it was within Goggin's terms of reference to prevent their entrance. Summing up Goggin's contribution Haultain noted:

> For 9 or 10 years I had Dr. G[oggin] as a principal technical advisor and no man ever had a better or more competent guide, counsellor, philosopher, and [,] may I add [,] friend. Through him and with his advice and assistance the foundations were laid — you know what the superstructure is. It is quite impossible to attempt to say how much we owe to Dr. G[oggin]'s knowledge skill, executive ability and supreme gift of tact.[53]

This view of Goggin's central place in the educational affairs of the North-West was shared by his supporters and detractors. A former student from the Winnipeg Normal School, James Calder, who was his closest professional associate, and eventual successor, claimed that Goggin "was the guiding spirit in the educational development of Western Canada".[54] While recognizing that Goggin was not party to the "political moulding" of the system, the editor of the *Regina Leader* declared that the Superintendent was the "prime factor in its making".[55] The most vocal criticism of his activities was voiced by the French-speaking Roman Catholic clergy. They, too, acknowledged his central position. Father Leduc referred to Goggin as "The Tzar of Education"[56] in the North-West. He wrote:

> I am well aware and fully convinced that it is he who steers the bark and guides the helm, not by right, but in fact, so that the captain [i.e. Haultain] and sailors may take a rest.[57]

To emphasize Goggin's position in the North-West is not to deprecate Haultain's influence. On the contrary, Goggin held his appointment at Haultain's pleasure and there is every indication that mutual consultation preceded initiatives in educational activities. Indeed, Haultain and Goggin were so inextricably linked to educational developments in the Territories that it is difficult to assess them separately. It was as though each compensated for the authority and knowledge which the other lacked. In any case, continuity was maintained when Goggin resigned because Haultain remained as Commissioner of Education with Calder serving as his assistant.

III

Goggin's activities in the North-West and his ready-made solution reflected the arrogant assumptions of a dominant élite, not just those of a Superintendent of Education. As indicated above, these views were supported by Premier Haultain, and an overwhelming majority in the Legislative Assembly who were, for the most part, Ontario-born, Protestant, and English-speaking. This support, however, was much more widely based. It is evidenced most clearly in the voting patterns of the North-West citizenry.[58] But consideration must also be given to press and pulpit. These two agencies heartily concurred in creating a favorable socio-political climate in the North-West that made these objectives not merely acceptable, but highly desirable; an observation that was often made by early British visitors to the North-West.[59]

The North-West press was a highly visible phenomenon of the social and political scene. Every community with claim to a stable population usually had at least one newspaper. The limitations enforced by poor communications, expensive paper, inexperienced writers, and small circulation often accounted for economy of space, bluntness of style, and limited coverage. Compensation for these apparent deficiencies was made with adequate coverage of local issues, outspoken partisanship, and verbal sparring with rival journals. Partisan mien and political bias notwithstanding, a sampling of the major newspapers shows a certain unanimity and common response to a number of separate, but in the context of the times, interrelated concerns. These include: immigration, imperial sentiment, the superiority of the Anglo-Saxon, and national schools.

The schools issue became a lively topic of discussion in the press after public reaction was aroused by developments in Manitoba. It had always been of some concern but certainly not to the degree that it reached after the late summer of 1889 when McCarthy brought his "Equal Rights" campaign to the West. Interesting, too, was the shift in emphasis of the argument for national schools. An editorial in the *Edmonton Bulletin* was typical:

> If we desire to build up a strong nation, having a national sentiment, that will be purely Canadian, the work must be done in our Public Schools. Associations are formed there that are more binding than any other, and a united people can only be found by one system of common schools, where the same course of study is pursued by all, and where every child, no matter whether white, black, or red; British, French or German, can meet on common ground, and feel that if nowhere else, in the school at least, the only line of division is that created by merit and ability. This is an impossibility in any community, when there are two sets of schools, in many of which the language used in one is not the same as that used in another. Looked at from a purely national, patriotic, point of view, there can be no question that it would infinitely help to create a national sentiment to have one set of schools, that would be purely national (sic.).[60]

A few years later the *Saskatchewan Times* cited developments in Manitoba as a "bright example" for the rest of the Dominion to follow. The editor considered that "foreign influence, religious or civil" should not be tolerated in a land where the "principles of government are hallowed by the highest and best form of civil and religious liberty" found anywhere in the world. He asked why Canadians should allow a system of education in their country that would "belittle these principles" and ultimately train disloyal citizens.[61] The French, warned the *Bulletin*, must be content with the rights accorded them in Quebec, and attempts to extend those "privileges" outside her borders may result in serious losses, even "in her own stronghold". The writer added, emphatically, "This is an English colony until it is something else".[62]

As indicated above, the chief concern of Anglo-conformists in the early 90's was the French. As the decade progressed and other ethnic groups came in large numbers it was a simple matter to broaden their argument to embrace the new arrivals. By this time the educational machinery was well in place to begin the difficult task of Canadianization. Given the expressed attitudes of Anglo superiority, there was no hint that the approach should be otherwise.

The reaction of the North-West press to Canada's official position on sending troops to South Africa accented these attitudes. The *Calgary Herald* provides a vivid example. Reporting on Major General Hutton's visit to that city soliciting volunteers for his proposed mounted rifle corps, the editor hoped that the response would demonstrate characteristic Anglo-Saxon loyalty and spirit, and prove to others the real depth of feeling for the Empire.[63] Later, when the government altered its position and became more responsive to the demands of English-speaking Canadians, the *Herald* noted that "Premier Laurier and Mr. Tarte have at the 11th hour realized that it is dangerous to trifle with the natural sympathy of the Britons"[64] Tarte, Laurier's Minister of Public Works and owner of *La Patrie,* a French-Canadian journal opposed to

Canadian participation in the war, was pronounced "a disloyal subject of Her Gracious Majesty Queen Victoria, and as such has no right to a seat on any cabinet organized on British principles".[65] The objections of the Ancient Order of Hibernians to Canada's participation in the war were called "idiotic ravings" and "merely the expression of implacable hatred to Great Britain by traitors to whom this country has been but too lenient".[66] The eventual outcome of the war was never in doubt; the only question was when and how complete the victory would be in view of the intense nationalism of the Boers:

> Sixty thousand ignorant Boers are governing 200,000 more intelligent white people who are mainly British and American. It is high time this disgrace to civilization was wiped out. Kruger has chosen his own medicine and it will be rammed down his throat so effectively that in the near future the Transvaal will be a British colony and its people as free as the people of Canada.[67]

Conveniently, the editor failed to note that French refusal to support the war was based on a similar argument; freedom defined in terms of majority rule.

The superiority of the Anglo-Saxon race is intimated in the reference to "this disgrace to civilization". The press consistently associated the "race" with "enterprise", "energy", "high civilization", "free institutions", "self-government", "Christianity", and the like. Indeed, these particular racial characteristics were part of the Divine plan, and not an acquired superiority.[68] Consequently, the greatest boon to a people was to fall under British rule:

> Nothing better could be desired in the interests, not only of the native tribes of Africa, but of the civilized world as well, that British ideas and institutions should prevail in Equatorial Africa. . . . In short, all benefits that have occurred to India, Canada, to New Zealand, and Australia would be conferred on Central Africa by it passing into the hands of the British nation. . . . So long as there is any part of the world unsettled and unoccupied by civilized people, the expansion of the British Empire will go on.[69]

An extension of this argument, of course, was that those who came in contact with this superior culture were expected to model their behavior on its virtues.

The Protestant churches in the North-West also saw Canadianization as an essential part of their mission. As early as 1875, in a sermon given at the first Provincial Synod of Rupert's Land, the Episcopal Bishop of Minnesota warned Westerners of their civilizing mission in view of expected massive immigration. He claimed that, as proof of the Apostolic origins of the Church, God called the "Anglo-Saxon race . . . to receive into itself these diverse peoples, and to give them its customs and traditions and laws".[70] There is much evidence to indicate that Bishop Whipples' call was accepted, as the Anglican church in the North-West was prominent in promoting the mission he described.[71] Linking the Church with "British ideals, British institutions,

British justice, British love of fair play" was common in the Anglican literature of the day. In Canada, the bearers of these gifts, in the first instance,
were "the 60,000 United Empire Loyalists who left all their earthly posses-
sions, endured cruel persecutions and untold hardships" to lay the foundations
of the nation.[72] In the West the Hudson's Bay Company was the means of
"maintaining British influence" and holding the whole region for Britain.[73]
According to the General Secretary of the Missionary Society of the Church
of England in Canada, Canon L. Norman Tucker, this represented "a
remarkable illustration of the capability of the English race to play the important part in the world's affairs to which it has been called".[74] Now that the
land was won for the Empire, the task of the Church was twofold: first, to
consolidate its position by claiming the immigrant from the mother-country;
and second, to win for church and country the immigrants from other lands.[75]

Archbishop Machray, the first Bishop of Rupert's Land, Canon Tucker,
Dean Kuhring of Wycliffe College, Toronto, and others made constant reference to the potential influence that the church could have on Canadian national
life if it could but "claim our own" among the immigrants.[76] The Anglo-
Saxon, by the mere fact of his presence and witness, would make a worthwhile
contribution to the tradition of loyalty to the Crown and devotion to the historic church of *the* race. Thus, the immigrant from the mother-country was
courted by the church, and reminded of his mission in the new land. For
example, a card given Church of England immigrants contained the following
message:

Don't Forget —
a) God in your eagerness to get on
b) The Old Country in the New Land
c) The Mother Church in its new surroundings

Remember —
a) You are now a Canadian
b) That Canada was part of the Empire
c) That the work of the Church and yourself is to make it more and
more the Dominion of our Lord and of his Christ.[77]

The responsibility to "rescue" the new arrivals from Britain was considered a
grave one:

Taken in the mass, it will largely determine whether the Church of England
in Canada is to grow and develop, and whether Canada is to become
increasingly British in its ideals and aspirations.[78]

The mission to the non-Anglo-Saxon was considered not merely in the
context of spiritual conversion. Since the church was perceived as the instrument of the Anglo-Saxon race, there was a further duty to initiate converts

into the British traditions of freedom and government. Perhaps the motive was not altogether altruistic, because, as Kuhring noted, "If we don't Canadianize him and his, and do it nicely, he and his will ultimately, to coin an effective word, un-Canadianize us".[79]

The church, however, did not seek to accomplish her goals single-handedly. She sought help from home and school. Canon Tucker, in a speech to the Empire Club, told his audience that their national concerns must reach beyond material considerations to "the training of citizens, the training of men for the nation, for the Empire". Home and school, according to the Secretary, must work together "to train all that makes for the full development of citizens, or the highest type of citizen — what we call the 'English gentleman'".[80]

But among the Protestant churches the Anglicans did not stand alone in their desire to model the West along the lines described above. The two other major Protestant denominations, Methodist and Presbyterian, were also firmly committed in this direction. Their views were expressed with particular emphasis during the early years of massive immigration. Predictably, the Methodist Church, whose "general outlook" Goldwin French has characterized as "aggressively Canadian,"[81] was active in this context:

> Almost instinctively Methodists dealt with their problems in what they thought to be Canadian ways. Through their all-embracing organization they contributed to the growth of national unity, an end to which they were deeply committed.[82]

The "Canadian way" for the immigrant was immediate assimilation through the church, school and other socializing agencies in the community.

The declared aim of the Methodist Women's Missionary Society in Canada for example, was, "To secure an intelligent, moral, united people, ever loyal to Great Britain".[83] Those who campaigned for, or supported, language rights for immigrants were denounced as "babel-tower-builders" with "proud and selfish ambitions". The newcomer, it was argued, "must be prepared to accept our flag and to adopt our language". Compromise on this issue foreshadowed disaster:

> The Union Jack must fly over our territory and our thousands of new citizens must be prepared to learn, and have their children learn, the English tongue.[84]

In Strachan's view it was a question of unity and loyalty. One solution adopted in many Methodist schools was to forbid "native" language. Strachan quoted this example: "One little girl learned very rapidly to speak English, for talk she would, and Russian was forbidden".[85] The mission established among the "Galicians" in Alberta was designed "to teach them to be good Christians and good Canadians".[86]

The education and Canadianization of the immigrant was also a vital concern to J.S. Woodsworth, Superintendent of Missions for the West. In his well-known book, *Strangers Within Our Gates,* Woodsworth expressed his alarm at the social and political implications of the pattern of development if allowed to continue unchecked. He claimed that "language, nationality, race, temperament, training, and all dividing walls" between the "foreigner" and the Canadian must be broken down. Like Goggin and many of his contemporaries, Woodsworth argued that an important place to start was with the colony or block type of settlement which tended to isolate large foreign communities from the mainstream of Canadian Life.[87] The public school, according to Woodsworth, must accept a major responsibility for breaking down those walls. In view of the importance and enormity of the task, he lamented the presence of separate schools in the provinces, particularly in those areas where the unity implicit in a system of national schools was such an obvious prerequisite to the life of this mission.

The story of the Presbyterian Church in the North-West is closely identified with James Robertson, Superintendent of the North-West Home Missions from 1881 to 1902. Taking an active interest in educational affairs from the first years of his ministry, he later tied this work to the church missions among the immigrants. His biographer claimed that Robertson "saw clearly that for the future unity and homogeneity of the nation, the great agencies were the Church and the public schools"..[88] For these reasons he became a powerful advocate of national schools and took the position that state funds should only be used to support non-sectarian institutions. He supported the 1890 Manitoba school legislation claiming, "The dead hand has too long hampered the freedom of the living".[89] Like his counterpart Woodsworth, he argued that ethnic block settlement was a threat to national unity. His efforts to establish missions among the immigrants was not so much to make them Presbyterians, "but simply to Canadianize these peoples and to develop in them the Christian ideals held by the Canadian people".[90] To Robertson, it was a patriotic exercise as well as a legitimate form of missionary activity, to bring into line those who were viewed as in conflict with Canadian ideals.

The identification of Christianizing with Canadianizing was not peculiar to Robertson's thinking. Period church literature suggests that this notion was widely accepted by the membership.[91] There was also a strong imperialist nationalist sentiment pervading the church in the decades preceding the first world war. Perhaps one of the most notable expressions of this view was made in a speech to the Toronto Empire Club in 1905 by the General Secretary of the Presbyterian Church in Canada, E.D. McLaren. Speaking on Canada's national aspirations, McLaren, in a manner not unlike his Anglican counterpart, Canon Tucker, reminded his audience that aside from Canada's vast natural resources there was a rich cultural heritage added to our greatness, "for let us not forget: We too are heirs of Runnymede".[92] He envisaged "slowly rising on this Western Hemisphere" a greater Britain which would be a worthy heir of "those principles and traditions that have made Britain's name a name of honor" among all the great nations of the world.[93] He claimed that "almost without exception" Canadians recognized "the desirable object of a confederation of all English-speaking peoples of the globe". This goal could "best be served by our maintaining our present position as an integral portion of the great British Empire". He concluded with the reminder that privileges bring responsibilities:

> . . . in every enlargement of our national life and power we must recognize a summons to bear a larger part of the white man's burden — to take a larger part in the moral evaluation and spiritual betterment of the whole human race.[94]

As with Robertson, other churchmen saw the school as a partner with the church in the task of immersing the "foreigner" in an "Anglo-Saxon atmosphere" and encouraging "a wholesome appreciation of British institutions",[95] Thomas Hart, Moderator of the Presbyterian Church in Manitoba and the North-West, writing in the *Queen's Quarterly* in 1905 discussed this question. Recognizing the difficulty of coping with such a variety of peoples, in Hart's view, merely served to underline the importance of "unifying these diverse races". Unity, to Hart, was equated with "making them intelligent citizens, English in speech, Canadian in sentiment, and British in their loyalty to the Empire".[96] The public school was the natural ally of the church in this most important task of making the newcomers fit.

IV

Taking into full account public recognition that the North-West school should be used in the nationalization process, as well as overt political support to facilitate this use, it is still important to examine the means devised to achieve the intended end.

The appropriate machinery to use the school for this purpose was set up in 1892. The Ordinance centralized the system, thus, granting state control of finances, curriculum, teacher certification, textbooks, and inspection. With this measure of control, authorities were virtually invulnerable. They could declare to administrators, trustees, teachers, students, and general public the direction and content of formal education. Armed with this power, under Haultain and Goggin, there was a systematic attempt in the North-West to prepare and implement policies designed to mould students according to a particular concept of Canadian identity directly related to the authorities' perception of the North-West's place in Canada's political, social and economic development. According to this view, the North-West was to be united in culture, language, and purpose, steadfastly loyal to the British connection and British institutions, and closely identified with the worldwide Empire.

Keenly aware that the North-West was a new land where institutions were gradually, but decisively, being formed, these authorities were determined that the mistakes and compromises made in the older provinces would not be repeated; a point Goggin made to a group of Ontario educators:

> We have benefited by your experiences and so have been able to avoid your mistakes. In a new country, unfettered by traditions and vested rights, it has been possible for us to advance more rapidly than the older provinces.[97]

The first and most obvious attempt to adjust the North-West to the ideal described above was with regard to language. As mentioned earlier, French was legislated out of the Assembly. It nearly suffered a similar fate in the schools. The language clause in the 1892 Ordinance read that, "It shall be permissible for the Trustees of any School to cause a primary course to be taught in the French language".[98] The intent was to reduce French from a language of instruction to a subject of instruction. Even this seemingly minor accommodation was permitted only after a long and bitter debate. Opponents argued that the diversity of peoples in the North-West demanded a strict English-only policy. It was believed that a true feeling of patriotism was contingent on everybody speaking the same language.[99] The clause immediately became the centre of controversy among French-speaking Roman Catholics, the federal Government, and the Territorial Assembly, but it stood as passed in 1892. The only change that took place before 1905, was the German request discussed earlier. In 1896, a suggestion that a multi-lingual inspector might be hired for the Whitewood district was greeted in the Assembly with laughter.[100]

In later years even greater emphasis was placed on English. For example, only English-speaking teachers were authorized to teach in "foreign settlement" schools. Through this arrangement it was hoped to discourage attempts by the various ethnic groups to preserve their indigenous languages. It was feared that a native teacher would retard the nationalization process. The 1898 *Report* noted that "the most effective work in such schools has been done by Canadian teachers practically unacquainted with the language of the colony".[101] In the same *Report,* Goggin, in an obvious reference to French-speaking Roman Catholics, railed against trustees who hired only those teachers who spoke "a certain modern language", and members "of a certain church".[102] A later *Report* indicated that Council policies had not changed. Inspectors in 1900 reported that progress made by "English-speaking teachers" in the "colony" schools was "most encouraging".[103]

This approach was supported by reports from the field. One principal wrote that, "The assimilation of this foreign element is pre-eminently the work of the educationist". In his view the school was "a potent equalizer and leveller", and "the channel through which national sentiment filters into a diverse population".[104] Many inspectors wrote in a similar vein. In reference to his area in Northern Alberta, T.E. Perrett claimed that, "The quickest and surest method of assimilating the foreign elements in our population is through our schools. Here is seen the ready adoption of dress, language, manners and customs".[105] A criterion often used in these reports to decide the quality of a school was the speed with which a particular group was being assimilated or, conversely, the overt resistance to learning English. On that dubious basis "Galicians", and later Doukhobors, were designated "poorest", with "Swedes" and Germans among the best.[106]

With this approach in mind a great deal of attention was given to teacher-training in the North-West. Again, there was an emphasis on culture and language. It was required that a high school principal hold a degree in Arts from a university within the Empire.[107] Moreover, exemptions were made from Normal School training only for those who held first or second class certificates from a Canadian province or from the British Isles. All others were required to attend regular sessions of the Normal School to receive and maintain certification. Mere teaching experience without formal training, even in Canada, was not sufficient guarantee that a Territorial teaching certificate would be granted; much to the ire of Roman Catholic teaching orders.[108]

This attempt to standardize certification gave central authorities the power to require all North-West teachers, regardless of religious or ethnic background, to attend Normal School in the Territories. Thus, non-conforming teachers who did not adjust their methods or ideas to North-West conditions were required to seek an official stamp of approval before obtaining permanent certification. This requirement, in Goggin's words, was "the people's safeguard against empiricism in the classroom".[109] It was a common complaint among teachers and inspectors that those teachers who did not "understand our conditions, ignorant of our school laws, fail to appreciate our aims" had more than ordinary difficulties interpreting the Programme of Studies. Inspectors were unanimous in recommending a session at the Normal School as a prerequisite to "receiving authority to teach". Significantly, those sessions were personally supervised by Goggin in his capacity as Director of Normal Schools. In each session given by an inspector, the Director delivered a series of lectures. Candidates for higher certificates were required to attend classes at Regina where Goggin was the instructor.[110] The value placed on uniformity and central control is evident in the regulation of the Council of Public Instruction that all prospective teachers, except for the "approved" minority, had to go through a uniform program under Goggin's direction. Haultain also viewed this policy as another step in the effort to unite the people of the Territories. Again, the North-West had avoided the "animosities arising from certain difficult and delicate questions" associated with Normal School policies in other provinces.[111] As with separate schools, he could boast that he had "administered all the separateness out of them".[112]

There is much evidence to suggest that Goggin gave high priority to this dimension of his work. A true believer in the proposition that schools should, and did, shape attitudes and character, the Superintendent regularly preached the influential role of the teacher in the classroom.[113] He wrote that the influence of the school in developing "correct thinking", "right action" in the student, "is far reaching". A skilful, motivated teacher who could lead "the child to control himself and perform his daily tasks will have a powerful influence in shaping his character".[114] It was a view shared by Haultain,[115] and by many of his colleagues.[116] Indeed, it was Goggin's preference that the school influence behavior rather than intellectual development if a choice was forced on the system.[117] In several public addresses he reiterated this belief. On one such occasion in Edmonton, speaking on "Morals in the Public School", he declared that he would "rather see a poorly educated but good mannered child, than a highly educated but poorly mannered one".[118] To guard against this unlikely combination Goggin insisted that teachers in his jurisdiction not only demonstrate professional competence but also possess a measure of culture. In his view, a teacher "must be cultured if he is to be an effective means of culture,"[119] because, "out of him goes forth virtue, from him radiates influences that shape character, that trains for manhood, citizenship and industrialization".[120] This thinking is manifestly clear in his statement of purpose for the Programme of Studies he introduced into the Territories. In 1898 he wrote:

> In the programme of studies provision is made for the teaching of those subjects a knowledge of which is helpful in the transaction of business, the duties of citizenship, the care of the body, the formation of moral character.[121]

Against this background must be reviewed the emphasis in the teacher-training program and school curriculum on those subjects that encouraged and quickened Canadianization, namely, British and Canadian History, English Literature, Grammar, Composition and Reading, and the Geography of the British Empire. In history, for example, the lives of great men were studied "to form moral notions in children" and "to teach patriotism and civic duty".[122] Thus, history, a compulsory subject from the second year of school, was seen as training in moral judgement and as a preparation for "intelligent citizenship". In the moral sphere the students, as early as the second and third standards, were introduced to the lives of "leading" Canadians and Englishmen and led to consider their public acts. Teachers then guided the students toward making judgements on the morality of these acts:

> This condemning of wrong deeds and approving of right deeds will tend to establish just ideas of right and wrong in the children's minds and these ideas must have their influence on conduct, must contribute to nobler living.[123]

The lessons were supplemented with the singing and recitation of patriotic songs and poems to foster feelings of patriotism. This approach to history was also strongly encouraged in one of the chief textbooks used in the teacher-training program, Sir Joshua Fitch's *Lectures on Teaching*.[124]

Much the same rationale applied to other subjects. The student who began in English Literature with an examination of ethical content was progressively introduced to character studies and the detailed study of selected authors so that he might "receive guidance and encouragement from the master minds".[125] Geography was intended to complement history in cultivating national and imperial sentiment by giving the student an intimate knowledge and appreciation of Canada and the Empire.[126] Other components of the curriculum such as music, manners and morals, temperance, and special patriotic exercises were also designed as aids to mould character and shape attitudes.[127]

During Diamond Jubilee celebrations in 1897 teachers were instructed to make "every effort to deepen the public's feelings of loyalty and respect for Her whose benificent reign, wisdom, and virtues Her grateful people are about to celebrate".[128] Victoria, or Empire, Day was planned to familiarize students "with the growth and development of the Empire and to encourage and foster patriotic and imperial sentiments".[129] In "Manners and Morals" teachers were to exercise their own "influence and example", to tell "suitable tales to awaken right feelings", to provide "gems embodying noble sentiments", as well as "maxims and proverbs containing rules of duty" for memorization so that students may be led "into a clear understanding and constant practice of every virtue".[130] The priority that these values and attitudes were intended to have in the North-West school system was underlined by Goggin when he wrote that "the cost of education is the premium paid on the policy that declares that the safety of the state depends on the character of its citizens".[131]

V

There can be little doubt that "the character of its citizens" was a primary concern of Territorial politicians, churchmen, media, citizens, and educators when their educational system was being developed. But the resolution of this concern hinged on absolute control of North-West political affairs. Having achieved this goal it became a relatively simple matter to adopt measures and to hire people to give the plan substance. The evidence is not yet in to measure the impact of these policies and programs on the development of the North-West or on the minds of individual children. In the absence of such evidence, however, one can speculate that with the majority having such power, control, support, and determination, pressure on the minorities to conform must have been intense. It must also have been a bewildering experience to feel the insensitivity and unyielding attitudes that threatened a most valued possession, namely one's culture.

Notes

[1]O.D. Skelton, *Life and Letters of Sir Wilfred Laurier* (Toronto: 1921), p. 398.

[2]P.G. Cornell, *The Alignment of Political Groups in Canada, 1841-1867* (Toronto: 1962), pp. 60 and 111.

[3]*Ibid.*

[4]M.R. Lupul, *The Roman Catholic Church and the North-West School Question* (Toronto: 1974), p. 82.

[5]*Regina Leader*, August 7, 1905. Scott did not change his view in later years. See L.H. Thomas, "The Political and Private Life of F.W.G. Haultain", *Saskatchewan History*.

[6]C. Cecil Lingard, *Territorial Government in Canada* (Toronto: 1946).

[7]L.H. Thomas, *The Struggle for Responsible Government in the North-West, 1870-1897* (Toronto: 1956).

[8]Lupul, *op. cit.*

[9]*Regina Leader,* August 7, 1905.

[10]Lupul, *op. cit.,* p. 82.

[11]*Ibid.,* p. 34.

[12]*Macleod Gazette,* February 12, 1891.

[13]*Regina Standard,* November 18, 1892.

[14]Castel Hopkins (ed.), *Canadian Annual Review, 1905* (Toronto: 1906), p. 251.

[15]*Regina Standard,* November 15, 1905.

[16]See *Edmonton Bulletin,* August 25, 1892; *Regina Standard,* January 22, 1892 and September 19, 1901; *Regina Leader,* August 14, 1901; and *Macleod Gazette,* October 3, 1902.

[17]*Journals of the North-West Assembly, 1891-1892 Session* (Regina: 1893).

[18]*Regina Standard,* January 29, 1892.

[19]*Winnipeg Tribune,* March 16, 1893.

[20]*Regina Standard,* September 19, 1901.

[21]*Ibid.*

[22]Lupul, *op. cit.,* p. 163.

[23]Lupul, *op. cit.,* p. 164.

[24]*Toronto News,* June 9, 1905.

[25]Robert Craig Brown and Ramsay Cook, *Canada 1896-1921* (Toronto: 1974), p. 62.

[26]*Winnipeg Free Press,* February 13, 1884.

[27]*Regina Standard,* March 10, 1893.

[28]*Regina Leader,* November 24, 1891 and November 7, 1892.

[29]*Annual Report of the Department of Education, 1901* (Regina: 1901), pp. 36 and 41; R. Balfour, "The System of Education in the North-West Territories", *Special Reports on Educational Subjects* (London: 1901), IV, 409-465.

[30]N.G. McDonald, "Alexandre A. Taché, Defender of the Old Regime", in R.S. Patterson, J.W. Chalmers, and J.W. Friesen (eds.), *Profiles of Canadian Educators* (Toronto: 1974), pp. 157-160.

[31] He held this position until June 13, 1894.

[32]Lupul, *op. cit.,* p. 83.

[33] *Regina Leader,* November 24, 1891.

[34] L.H. Leduc, *Hostility Unmasked* (Montreal: 1896), p. 7.

[35] See any published volume of *Empire Club Speeches.*

[36] *Empire Club Speeches, 1940-41* (Toronto: 1941), p. 129.

[37] Victor Goggin, "Yesterday and To-day in America", *Ibid.,* p. 130.

[38] Haultain also served as vice-president of the Association for two years while he was Commissioner of Education for the North-West.

[39] David James Goggin, "Reply to Address of Welcome", *Dominion Educational Association Proceedings* (Ottawa: 1904), pp. 34-35. See also George Ross, "Inaugural Address", *Dominion Educational Association Proceedings* (Montreal: 1892), pp. 50-51.

[40] David James Goggin, "Reply to Addresses of Welcome", *Dominion Educational Association* (Toronto: 1901), p. 45.

[41] *Regina Leader,* June 24, 1897.

[42] *Ibid.*

[43] *Ibid.*

[44] *Ibid.*

[45] *Report of the Council of Public Instruction, 1898* (Regina: 1898), p. 11. (Henceforth referred to as C.P.I.)

[46] *Ibid.*

[47] *Ibid.*

[48] D.J. Goggin, *op. cit.,* (1901), p. 44.

[49] D.J. Goggin, *op. cit.,* (1904), p. 35.

[50] D.J. Goggin, "North-West Autonomy", *Empire Club Speeches* (Toronto: 1906), pp. 212-213.

[51] Based on a conversation with Professor R.S. Patterson, Department of Educational Foundations, University of Alberta, Edmonton, who has done extensive research on the Haultain years.

[52] I am grateful to Professor Patterson for a copy of this material.

[53] *Ibid.*

[54] *Annual Report of the Department of Education, 1902* (Regina: 1902), p. 16.

[55] *Regina Leader,* October 9, 1902.

[56] Leduc, *op. cit.,* p. 7.

[57] *Ibid.,* p. 13.

[58] Thomas, *op. cit., passim* and Lingard, *op. cit., passim.*

[59] L.H. Thomas, "British Visitors Perceptions of the West, 1885-1914", in Anthony W. Rasporich, and Henry Klassen (eds.), *Prairie Perspectives* (Toronto: 1973), II, 193.

[60] *Edmonton Bulletin,* December 7, 1889.

[61] *Saskatchewan Times,* January 21, 1896.

[62] *Edmonton Bulletin,* August 15, 1892.

[63] *Calgary Herald,* October 12, 1899.

[64] *Ibid.*

[65] *Ibid.,* October 26, 1899.

[66] *Ibid.*

[67] *Ibid.,* November 20, 1899.

[68] *Regina Leader,* November 17, 1892.

[69] *Edmonton Bulletin,* December 28, 1889.

[70] Robert Machray, *The Life of Archbishop Machray* (Toronto: 1909), p. 256.

[71]G.A. Kuhring, *The Church and the Immigrant* (Toronto), *passim.*

[72]*Ibid.,* p. 19.

[73]L. Norman Tucker, *Western Canada* (London: 1908), p. 6.

[74]*Ibid.*

[75]*Ibid.;* see also Machray, *op. cit.,* p. 229.

[76]Tucker, *op. cit.,* pp. 156-157.

[77]Kuhring, *op. cit.,* pp. 54-55.

[78]*Ibid.,* p. 71.

[79]*Ibid.,* p. 67.

[80]L. Norman Tucker, "Canadian Patriotism", *Empire Club Speeches, 1910-11* (Toronto: 1911).

[81]Goldwin French, "The People Called Methodists", in John Webster Grant (ed.), *The Churches and the Canadian Experience* (Toronto: 1966), p. 80.

[82]*Ibid.*

[83]E.S. Strachan, *The Story of the Years* (Toronto: 1917), p. 41.

[84]*Ibid.,* pp. 67-68.

[85]*Ibid.,* p. 76.

[86]H.L. Platt, *The Story of the Years, 1881-1906* (Toronto: 1908), p. 123.

[87]J.S. Woodsworth, *Strangers Within Our Gates* (Toronto: 1908), pp. 279-280.

[88]Charles Gordon (Ralph Connor), *The Life of James Robertson* (Toronto: 1908), pp. 315-316.

[89]*Ibid.,* p. 316.

[90]*Ibid.*j

[91]See E. Henry, "Educating Prospective Citizens", in W.S. McTavish (ed.), *Harvests in Many Lands* (Toronto: 1908) and R.G. MacBeth, *Our Task in Canada* (Toronto: 1912).

[92]E.D. McLaren, "Our National Aspirations", *Empire Club Speeches, 1905-06* (Toronto: 1906), p. 133.

[93]*Ibid.,* pp. 133-134.

[94]*Ibid.*

[95]Henry, *op. cit.,* pp. 26-28 and MacBeth, *op. cit.,* pp. 44-45.

[96]Thomas Hart, "The Educational system of Manitoba", *Queen's Quarterly* (1905), XIV, 240.

[97]D.J. Goggin, "Reply to the Addresses of Welcome", *Dominion Educational Association Proceedings* (Ottawa: 1904), p. 35.

[98]*Ordinances of the North-West Territories, 1892* (Regina: 1893), Ch. 22.

[99]*Regina Leader,* August 8, 1892.

[100]*Regina Standard,* October 29, 1896.

[101]*Report of the Council of Public Instruction, 1898* (Regina: 1898), p. 12.

[102]*Ibid.,* p. 27.

[103]*Ibid.* (1901), p. 25.

[104]James McCaig, "Educational Problems in the North-West Territories", *Educational Monthly of Canada* (1903), XXVI, 157, 228.

[105]*Annual Report of the Department of Education, 1903* (Regina: 1904), p. 58.

[106]See *Annual Reports* (Inspectors Reports).

[107]D.J. Goggin, "The Educational System of the Territories", in J. Castell Hopkins (ed.), *Canada: An Encyclopedia of the Country* (Toronto: 1898), p. 248.

[108]*Globe* (Toronto), February 6, 1905; see also Lupul, "The Campaign for a French Catholic School Inspector in the North-West Territories, 1898-1903", in Craig Brown (ed.), *Minorities, Schools, and Politics* (Toronto: 1969), CHR, *passim.*

[109] *C.P.I.,* p. 15.

[110]*D.J. Goggin, op. cit.,* p. 248.

[111]*Regina Standard,* September 15, 1898.

[112]Unpublished interview with Haultain at the Assiniboia Club, Regina, August 8, 1931. Made available to the writer by Professor R.S. Patterson.

[113]*C.P.I.,* p. 15.

[114]*Ibid.,* pp. 28-29.

[115]F.W.G. Haultain, "Convocation Address by the Chancellor", (University of Saskatchewan, 1934). Made available to the writer by R.S. Patterson.

[116]James McCaig, *Canadian Citizenship* (Toronto: 1925), p. 228.

[117]D.J. Goggin, "Some Present Day Problems in Education", *Dominion Educational Association Proceedings* (Ottawa: 1904), p. 27.

[118]*Edmonton Bulletin,* May 22, 1893.

[119]*D.J. Goggin, op. cit.,* p. 41.

[120]*Ibid.,* pp. 38-39.

[121]D.J. Goggin, *"The Educational System of the Territories", loc. cit.,* p. 248.

[122]*Annual Report of the Department of Education, 1901* (Regina: 1902), p. 38.

[123]*C.P.I.,* pp. 22-23.

[124]J.G. Fitch, *Lectures on Teaching* (New York: 1881), p. 143, and *passim.*

[125]*C.P.I.,* p. 21.

[126]*Ibid.,* p. 21.

[127]*Ibid.,* p. 12.

[128]*Qu'Appelle Progress,* June 10, 1897.

[129]*Annual Report of the Department of Education, 1903* (Regina: 1904), p. 76.

[130]*C.P.I.,* p. 12.

[131]*Regina Leader,* June 24, 1896.

V

Educational Reform in Western Canada

The depression which enveloped Canadian society in the 1930's was far more than a period of material hardship. Following upon a decade of optimism and prosperity, it represented a loss of confidence, a loss of belief in inevitable progress. As such, it struck at the very soul of the nation. The general malaise forced people to examine critically the social, political and economic institutions which had evidently failed them. In the process radical solutions, which only a few years previously would have been dismissed as utopian, were given serious consideration.

This tendency was very much pronounced in the western provinces where the depression was felt most acutely. Not only did the price paid for agricultural products plunge to a disastrous low, but the farming community saw its livelihood further threatened by drought, dust storm and grasshopper. Here was fertile ground for radicalism in one form or another.

One manifestation of this search for drastic solutions was the emergence of Alberta's Social Credit Party. This was the creation of William Aberhart, a school principal and well-known radio evangelist. The Social Credit doctrine argued that the fundamental difficulty in the free enterprise economic system was the difference prevailing between the producing power of individuals and their purchasing power. If this gap were bridged, it was claimed, then the system would work well. This could be accomplished by the payment of a 'social dividend' to everyone. Aberhart estimated that a cash payment of $25 to all Albertans would be sufficient to restore prosperity, and his party came to power in the provincial election of 1935 on the strength of this somewhat bizarre promise. While federal control of currency and banking regulations frustrated attempts to implement Social Credit theory in its pure form, the party nevertheless remained in power in the province for decades, perhaps because it at least provided efficient administration and because ultimately its radicalism proved but skin deep.

A further manifestation of western radicalism in the 1930's was the formation of the Co-operative Commonwealth Federation (founding conventions were held in Calgary in 1932 and in Regina in 1933). This party's platform was frankly socialist — but it was the moderate socialism of the British Labour Party that it espoused. It advocated the nationalization of key industries and comprehensive social welfare legislation. The C.C.F. found its support among trade unionists and among farmers who strongly resented the economic domination of the west by eastern Canadian big business interests. It especially appealed to those who had been impoverished by unemployment and wage cuts at a time when relief measures were less than adequate. The party achieved its greatest popularity in Saskatchewan, although it did not form a government in that province until 1944.

Not only did westerners seek radical alternatives in the spheres of politics and economics; they sought them also in education. In the critical self-examination prompted by the depression, the school system too was seen as an institution that had somehow failed. A solution was sought in the doctrines of progressive education, at the time a vibrant reform movement in American education.

R.S. Patterson's article, "Hubert C. Newland: Theorist of Progressive Education", examines the pivotal role played by Newland in introducing progressive reforms in the west. Newland was not just an effective champion of teachers' rights, but an important educational innovator. While studying for a Ph.D. at the University of Chicago in the early 1930's he became thoroughly familiar with the principal doctrines of progressive education and came to believe that they offered a solution to the prevailing crisis in society. The new education would strengthen democracy by fostering free inquiry and a sense of social responsibility among the young and thus help lift society out of the depression. As Supervisor of Schools for Alberta during much of the 1930's he was in the fortunate position of being able to introduce progressive practices, with profound and long-lasting results.

American influence on Newland's thought was obviously crucial. And as Patterson points out in his article, "Progressive Education: Impetus to Educational Change in Alberta and Saskatchewan", it was of paramount importance in the adoption of progressive reform in those two provinces. American experts were invited to western Canada to share their expertise, while Canadian educators went south to attend graduate school, workshops and so forth.

In a sense, this was inevitable. Since the 1920's American movies, magazines and radio broadcasts had increasingly shaped Canadian popular culture while Canadian industry was coming to rely more and more on American investment and technology. In other words, the United States was becoming the major centre of metropolitan influence and control in Canadian life. It was natural, then for Canadians to look to their southern neighbour for leadership and expertise in education, as well as in other areas.

Hubert C. Newland
Theorist of Progressive Education*

R.S. Patterson

Biographical Sketch

Hubert Charles Newland was born in Fingal, Ontario in 1883. He was graduated from Fingal Public School where he was placed first among the students writing the Elgin County Public School Leaving Examination, and then entered the University of Toronto in 1900. Inadequate financial resources forced his withdrawal from the University and led to a family move to Saskatchewan. Following a year at the Regina Normal School under the tutelage of D.G. Goggin, he entered the teaching profession. Qu'Appelle, Little Red Deer and High River were the locations of the teaching assignments he completed prior to his return to the University of Toronto in 1909. Graduation with a Bachelor of Arts degree in Honours Philosophy came one year later for the young teacher. Armed with the first of the five academic degrees which he was eventually to earn, "Doc" returned West to serve as principal at Wildwood, then at Vegreville, before settling in Edmonton where he became a Latin teacher at Victoria High School. This assignment lasted from 1915 until 1928, when he became an instructor in psychology at the Edmonton Normal School.

The years in Edmonton were busy ones for Newland. A review of his activities during his professional life in Edmonton leaves no doubt as to his abilities, his eagerness for learning, his commitment to educational and social reform and his determination to see teaching elevated as a profession. In 1921 he received the LL.B. degree from the University of Alberta. His Master of Arts degree and his Bachelor of Education degree were both obtained from the same university in 1922 and 1928 respectively. Requirements for the degree of Doctor of Philosophy were completed at the University of Chicago in 1932.

During the period in which these last four degrees were being earned, Newland was doing more than teaching school and studying. In the years immediately following the First World War he was prominent as a leader of teachers in their struggle for recognition as professionals. He played an important role in the formative years of the Alberta Teachers' Alliance, holding a number of responsible leadership positions within the organization. Among

---

*From R.S. Patterson, J.W. Chalmers and J.W. Friesen (eds.), *Profiles of Canadian Educators* (Toronto: D.C. Heath, 1974). Reprinted with permission.

these were the following: President of the Edmonton High School Teachers' Alliance, teachers' representative on the Edmonton Public School Board, President of the Alberta Teachers' Alliance, Editor of *The ATA Magazine*, President and Managing Director of the Alberta Teachers' Alliance Bureau of Education and President of the Canadian Teachers' Federation. Conflict with J.W. Barnett, the General Secretary Treasurer of the Alberta Teachers' Alliance, resulted in Newland relinquishing in 1925 the positions of Editor of *The ATA Magazine* and Managing Director of the Bureau of Education.

Although Newland never again served as a leader within the professional organization of teachers, he did not cease playing an active part in encouraging and promoting educational organizations known as the Education Society of Edmonton and The Calgary Progress Club. These two small groups usually met every two weeks to discuss contemporary educational problems and relevant research and literature. Although their influence was never conspicuous to the public, these clubs did wield a great deal of power in educational circles. Their carefully selected members were excellent scholars, professional men and women concerned with education. Many of the members came to fill influential positions in the Department of Education, the university, the normal schools and the city school systems.

A number of the educators in these two clubs were singled out for rapid professional advancement. Newland was one of the ones who experienced a succession of promotions which carried him to the top levels of decision making in the Department of Education. He served in the normal school as an instructor of psychology for a period of four years. Upon his completion of his doctoral studies at Chicago in 1932, he became a high school inspector. Within three years he had served as Chief Inspector of Schools and was appointed Supervisor of Schools for Alberta. In this latter capacity, where he served for ten years, Newland directed a major curriculum revision for Alberta schools. Under his active and knowledgeable leadership Alberta became the foremost authority on progressive education in Canada.

Newland's professional career did not end in Alberta. Just three years prior to his retirement, differences between him and the Minister of Education caused him to resign his position and to join the Saskatchewan Department of Education as Director of Educational Research. Following his retirement and return to Edmonton, Newland commenced articling with a law firm in anticipation of filling his remaining active years with a legal career. This plan was abruptly ended by his death in 1948.

Teaching as a Profession

Throughout the thirty-year period following the end of World War I, many Canadians struggled to find satisfying solutions to the problems associated with industrialization, urbanization and the wider application of democratic principles. During this time H.C. Newland actively encouraged Canadian teachers to recognize education as one of the main factors in the creation of a new and better social order. His confidence in education as the means of successfully dealing with social problems was evident in his own avid pursuit of formal education, and in the way he dedicated his life to the improvement of educational provisions and resources. His faith in the creative and regenerative powers of education never waned. As a result, he relentlessly pursued educational and societal reforms throughout his professional career.

Newland functioned in a variety of leadership roles in a number of different areas of education but he maintained a consistent philosophy and approach throughout. In his earliest writings and speeches, as well as in his later pronouncements as Supervisor of Schools, there is evidence of his firm belief in the power and the importance of education in a democratic society. This conviction had as its corollary the acknowledgement that teachers, because of their prominent and significant place in the educational process, were essentially the guardians of the nation's welfare. Just as he was assured of the promise which education offered for the future, Newland was equally certain that this promise would go unfulfilled unless the personal and professional qualities of teachers were of the highest standard. It was imperative that teachers and public alike recognize the potential contribution available to society through a competent, dedicated teaching force.

Social betterment in a democracy, Newland acknowledged, required the intelligent and sustained efforts of many. However, he felt that more would be required of teachers than of any other group. If teachers were to help solve the pressing social problems of their time, then they needed to "become alert to the possibilities of education as the harbinger of a new and better social order".[1] They needed to be "apostles of progress and not reaction".[2]

There was no place where the call for progressive action was more apparent than within the teaching profession. Motivated by the deplorable conditions of teacher employment and by his unwavering conviction that education was central to the advancement of a nation, Newland vigorously addressed the problem of making teaching as a profession attractive. Working assiduously with others of similar conviction, he attempted to convince teachers that they deserved to be treated better than public slaves. He knew that until teachers believed in themselves there was little likelihood that they would be afforded the professional status and recognition which they deserved.

Newland's faith in teachers and education as precipitating forces in social change did not cloud his perception relative to the educational conditions prevailing in the early 1920's. Teachers were devoid of legal rights which served to guarantee the length of their service and the amount and the regularity of their remuneration. Dismissals without professional cause were sufficiently common to be of concern. Wages, hardly at a subsistence level, and the lack of professional security caused many teachers, often the more competent and well-educated, to enter other, more attractive occupations. The continual granting of permits to unqualified and poorly qualified teachers served to fill many classrooms, but also served to seriously undermine the quality of the educative experience. So deplorable were the conditions within the profession of teaching and within education generally, that Newland frequently expressed his belief that employment as a teacher was lower on the professional scale than employment as a labourer.

Like many other reformers of the period, both within educational circles and within the larger society, Newland recognized that organizational strength was essential if teachers were to gain the rights and recognition which they deserved. In 1921 Newland gave the Annual Report of the Alberta Teachers' Alliance to the Alberta Educational Association. He noted that "society today is organization, and the individual who doesn't belong to some kind of alert and functioning organization is helpless. . .

> In an editorial only a month before he had observed: Teachers cannot any longer resist exploitation if they remain unorganized, nor can they retain the respect of society. As individuals they are helpless. "No group in modern society", says Elihu Root, "can secure its just rights nor exert its due influence in the community without organization".[4]

Teachers were slow to sense the value of organization or to take full advantage of it. Common to many Canadians of the period was a distrust, even a fear of organizational strength and of the militant action which was becoming more frequently associated with it. These were the tools of labor groups and were not yet readily accepted and endorsed by most Canadians. The derogatory charges of trade-unionism which were levelled at the proponents and supporters of organizational power caused many teachers to postpone their affiliation with the A.T.A.

Newland was anxious to build a professional image for teachers rather than a trade-union image. He realized, however, as did other A.T.A. leaders, that refusal to employ all available reform tactics, even though some of them were tainted by an association with labour, would mean the prolongation of the slavelike conditions within teaching. Thus when school boards dealt unfairly with teachers, they were "blacklisted" and Newland, as editor of *The A.T.A. Magazine* encouraged teachers to avoid seeking employment in these districts.

On occasion Newland deemed even strike action necessary in order to ensure that the teachers' viewpoint was heard and properly considered.

The fledgling A.T.A. organization needed a means of communicating with members of the teaching force. In 1919 Newland presented a motion to the Annual General Meeting of the A.T.A. recommending the establishment of a press bureau and an official magazine.[5] The motion passed and under his editorship the first issue of *The A.T.A. Magazine* appeared in June, 1920. During his five years as editor, Newland utilized *The A.T.A. Magazine* to help formulate and mold a favorable view toward the professional recognition of teachers.

It was important to Newland that any educational reform be studied in conjunction with and related to the aims and philosophy of society. Himself an astute, informed and intelligent observer and critic of society, Newland wanted teachers to be concerned with more than the problems of the classroom. As a result, he purposely avoided giving the *Magazine* a narrow focus. It was not centred on the petty details of pedagogy. Instead it dealt with the more far reaching concerns of professionalism.

Newland's abilities and his own extensive education enabled him to serve in a variety of ways during the formative years of the teachers' organization. As a student of law, and after 1921 as a holder of an LL.B. degree, Newland played a conspicuous and important role in the many discussions of the A.T.A. relative to the establishment of legal rights for teachers. Of paramount importance was the obtaining of a standard contract for teachers which would include: a self-renewing clause, a salary schedule, provision for cumulative sick pay, a reduction in the school year from two hundred and ten days to two hundred days, and investigative procedure in cases of teacher dismissal. Newland and other leaders of the A.T.A. were persistent in negotiations with the obstinate Liberal Minister of Education, G.P. Smith, and then with the more compatible Perren Baker of the United Farmers of Alberta government. Their persistence resulted in a number of concessions being made during the years of the administration of the United Farmer's of Alberta.

As editor of *The A.T.A. Magazine* and as president of the A.T.A. and the Canadian Teachers' Federation, Newland campaigned vigorously for the improvement of teacher salaries. While some were pressing for a mere "living wage", Newland was agitating for more. This was in accordance with his belief that the salary of teachers should be in accord with the importance of their work. The right kinds of men and women would not be attracted to, nor retained in teaching, unless there was an appropriate remuneration available. It was his opinion that

> . . . if real professional standards are to be developed for teachers, the financial reward will have to be fixed at such a level as will hold the well-trained and capable, and will compete on equal ground with other professions for the most talented and the most efficient.[6]

Unfortunately, teachers were not above underbidding one another for positions of employment. Newland did not hesitate in condemning such behaviour. He also publicly abused those teachers who justified their refusal to fight for better salaries with claims of patriotic duty or self-sacrifice. Inasmuch as teachers, according to Newland, were as expert in their profession as were doctors and lawyers in theirs, they should receive comparable financial rewards. It was his belief that if teachers received remuneration and recognition commensurate with the importance of their service, there would be no problem with the quality of the service rendered in return.

In his endeavours to promote the professional advancement of teachers, Newland was concerned with more than economic or material gains. He worked as untiringly for the right of self-determination and professional autonomy, as he did for improved contracts and higher salaries. If educational policies were to benefit and to help improve society, then it was essential, Newland argued, that they should be dependent upon educational expertise rather than upon political expedience. Inasmuch as teachers bore the responsibility of implementing educational policies, they deserved to be consulted during the conceiving of the policies.

Newland's firm advocacy of professional participation in educational decision-making was motivated by his conviction that to act otherwise was to be autocratic and undemocratic. The importance of democracy cannot be overestimated as a governing principle in Newland's educational career and philosophy. Just as he determined to see the democratization of the decision-making process in education, he later encouraged curriculum and methodological reforms designed to transform classroom experience and to make the relationship between teacher and pupil more democratic. In his observations of the educational system, as well as of the larger society, Newland noted that force and compulsion were the dominant modes of operation rather than cooperation and harmony. Teachers, he observed, were no more than "mere cogs in the educational machine".[7] They were not consulted in those basic matters affecting their interests, rights and duties as teachers. If the schools were to be instrumental in the development of "free and self-controlled citizens" they "must be free as well as the students".[8] As a student of democratic theory Newland was without equal among professional educators. The reforms which he so actively pursued were, almost without exception, related to his conception of the ideal democratic society.

There were important changes which needed to occur in teachers if they were to be worthy of the professional gains which they were making. They needed to justify their claims for professional recognition and status by demonstrating a competence in which the public could place its trust. Newland believed that if the teacher was deserving of the same standing as doctors and lawyers, then it was important that the teacher be equally qualified in his special field of work. In the realm of professional preparation Newland was without peer. He obtained five academic degrees. It is not surprising that Newland frequently spoke out against those who endorsed inferior academic qualifications for teachers. The teacher's position and the quality of education were being undermined by inferior standards. It was on a motion from Newland in 1920 that the A.T.A. first went on record in opposition to the granting of permits to unqualified teachers, short normal school courses and the importation of teachers from other provinces.[9] During his tenure as President of the C.T.F., Newland voiced similar concerns about inferior teacher qualifications, permit teachers and the need for equalization of teacher qualification standards across Canada.

Included as a part of his program to raise teacher qualifications was the recommendation that teachers upgrade themselves through formal coursework. It was Newland's hope that the University of Alberta would offer advanced professional courses for teachers. He also encouraged the obtaining of a university degree by teachers. Such a recommendation was designed to discourage those prospective teachers who had neither the ability nor the commitment to succeed at university. Throughout the period prior to 1945, the year in which responsibility for teacher education was completely assumed by the University in Alberta, Newland was one of the most vocal supporters of such a move.

There were numerous ways in which Newland tried to encourage and provide for the upgrading of teacher qualifications. He advocated the utilization of leaves of absence for professional training and the provision of financial assistance to teachers willing to attend summer school. Within the teachers' organization he stimulated interest which led to the creation of the Bureau of Research and the Bureau of Education. When he spoke before the Annual General Meeting of the A.T.A. in 1920 in support of the motion to establish a Bureau of Research, he offered the following explanation of the intent behind the Bureau:

> The fundamental idea is this: If teachers are to occupy their position in the eyes of the public, of school boards, or of the Department of Education, they must justify their claim to higher salaries and administrative problems by showing that they are competent and efficient in every line of educational endeavor.[10]

The Bureau was to explore a variety of important educational questions such as taxation, school administration and any other matters affecting the aims and interests of the Alliance. Its findings were published monthly as a column in the *A.T.A. Magazine*. It was designed to assist teachers in becoming more expert in matters relating to all phases or concerns of education. According to Newland, the Bureau was organized, at least in part, to counter the criticism that the A.T.A. was interested in nothing but the question of raising salaries.[11] The Bureau was also an important publicity device because it provided an opportunity for the A.T.A. to cooperate with other organizations, interested laymen and other educators by sharing the results of its research on complex educational issues.

Encouragement for the formation of the Bureau of Education also came from Newland. Under his chairmanship the Law Committee of the A.T.A. recommended in 1922 that a Provincial Institute be established for the purpose of assisting teachers in improving their academic and/or professional qualifications.[12] To Newland went the responsibility of publicizing this organization and of drafting its terms of reference. Known as the Bureau of Education, this organizational service became Newland's special project. Its aims were fourfold. It was

(a) To assist members of the ATA to keep in touch with the scientific work in education.

(b) To assist members of the ATA to improve their professional training.

(c) To help mold public opinion in educational matters so as to make possible the putting into practice of the best educational knowledge.

(d) To assist teachers in the Province in bringing about a greater uniformity in the grading of pupils.[13]

The Bureau of Education with Newland as Managing Director, was another manifestation of the A.T.A.'s desire to demonstrate that professional competence and academic preparation were at least as important in the teachers' struggle for professional status, as were the material and legal gains which they sought. The Bureau served numerous teachers, but unfortunately, the value of its professional contributions was soon outweighed by the financial and administrative difficulties it presented to the A.T.A. executive. These difficulties were seized upon by J.W. Barnett, General Secretary Treasurer of the A.T.A., in his move to become the dominant power figure in the organization. When forced to choose between Barnett and Newland the executive of the A.T.A. chose in favour of Barnett. Both the position of Managing Director of the Bureau and Editor of the *Magazine* were taken from Newland and given to the General Secretary Treasurer.

With the ending of his prominent leadership role within the A.T.A. Newland did not cease his activity as an educational reformer. Instead after a short delay of approximately two years, another organization, the newly created Education Society of Edmonton, became a central interest in his life. From his involvement in the A.T.A. and C.T.F. Newland was convinced that a better informed and more able leadership had to be produced if education was to play the part it should in the development of the nation.[14] This, he believed, was possible, but only if a group of capable and interested persons came together regularly to study educational problems, to seek solutions and then unitedly attempt implementation of these solutions. Because of this belief Newland gathered a group of eleven teachers together in February, 1927, to discuss the formation of a private organization known as the Education Society of Edmonton. Admission to the Society was carefully regulated. Only those teachers holding a university degree and prepared to devote considerable energy to the study and to the reform of education were invited to join. The Society agreed to develop policies and to undertake actions which would elevate teaching to the level of other learned professions. Further, they accepted the challenge of becoming the leaders in education in Edmonton and in Alberta. Their preparation for this leadership role was accomplished through regular study, research and discussion.

Leader of Progressive Education

In 1929, only two years after the Society was organized and only one year after his appointment to the staff of the Edmonton Normal School, Newland spent the year at the University of Chicago. It was not uncommon during this period for Canadian teachers to undertake graduate study in education in the United States. When they did, Chicago and Columbia's Teachers' College were the two institutions most frequently selected. The Chicago experience, coming as it did for Newland at the outbreak of the Depression intensified his conviction that social philosophy and education were integrally related. In addition it afforded him the opportunity to explore more thoroughly the writings associated with progressive education, the educational movement which had captured the United States.

Before going to Chicago Newland had voiced views bearing strong resemblance to those of leading progressive educators. However, he did not clearly identify or distinguish himself as a supporter of this movement. In the early years of the 1930's and , particularly after 1932 when the final requirements for his Ph.D. degree were complete, Newland actively promoted the new education and encouraged his associates to study the writings and the philosophy of George S. Counts. Following his address to American teachers in 1932 which he entitled, "Dare the Schools Build a New Social Order?" Counts became one of the more well-known and popular exponents of the new education. The theme of his address and later writings was not new to Newland. He had utilized much the same message in the early 1920's as he campaigned for improved professional standing for teachers. Reinforced by the pronouncements of Counts, Newland continued to admonish teachers to be instigators of social reform. The time was ripe, he believed , for the introduction of a new philosophy of education and for an accompanying change in curriculum and methodology. In effect he wanted to introduce progressive education reforms in Alberta. Not unexpectedly, when Newland centered his attention on progressive education, many of those associated with him did so as well. With his encouragement and leadership the Education Society studied progressive education and the ideas of George S. Counts. In 1935 they went so far as to use one of Counts' book titles, *Social Foundations of Education* as the theme of their year's program.[15] Evidently, these ideas were persuasively presented and favorably received. Later that year, when the members were asked how many of them thought the new course in social studies should encourage the transition to a new and better social order, there was a unanimous positive response.[16]

The interest in progressive education shown by the Society during the 1930's was indicative of the mood of the country. Progressive education was finally gaining a foothold in Canada. In the United States these ideas and practices had been in vogue for at least a decade. The writings of John Dewey, William H. Kilpatrick, George S. Counts, Harold O. Rugg, Boyd Bode and numerous others had stimulated and effected a major reform in schooling. While best known for their contributions in educational reform, these men undertook more than the transformation of schooling. They argued in favor of a new conception of democracy which they felt was better suited to the rapidly changing conditions of twentieth century America.

Their popularity, however pronounced in the United States, was slow to develop in Canada. It was not until the 1930's that Canadian educators began giving serious and widespread consideration to these reformers. Once the interest started, it spread rapidly across the country. Conditions within education and society in general were ripe for change. Traditional values were under attack. Just as many Canadians were prepared to try new political parties and economic ideas, so they were ready to consider new approaches to schooling. Between 1929 and 1945 nearly every provincial jurisdiction in Canada attempted a major educational reform. All of these changes reflected the influence of the new educational ideas associated with progressive education.

A number of common elements characterized these various provincial reforms. Generally, they emphasized the uniqueness of the learner and attempted to provide more adequately for individual differences. Benefiting from the findings of psychologists and educational researchers, educators broadened the perspective of the school and made room for the whole child. Mental growth, once the central focus of the school was deemphasized as attention shifted to character development and citizenship. The acquisition of knowledge, while still important, was no longer revered as the ultimate purpose of schooling. Courses such as shop work, art, household science, physical education, health and mental hygiene became prominent in the curriculum, as educators attempted to cater to a wider range of abilities and interests in the learner. A change in the learning environment also occurred. Teachers and administrators accepted the claim that learning could be facilitated through the provision of a stimulating and attractive classroom. Even the traditional organizational pattern changed. Junior or intermediate schools were established in recognition of the unique needs of early adolescents. The most distinctive and universal aspect of the acceptance of progressive education was the introduction of activity programs. Learning by doing became the commonly acknowledged governing principle of the progressive school in Canada.[17]

The impact of progressive education was greater in Alberta than in any other Canadian province. This was attributable in large part to the leadership which Newland gave to the movement. As a senior official in the Department of Education, after his appointment as a high school inspector in 1932, he exerted considerable influence on the direction followed in education in Alberta. He was in fact the most important person in Alberta's move toward progressive education.

When it was decided within the Department of Education to undertake a major study of the curriculum and the philosophy of the schools, Newland was given the responsibility of providing leadership to those involved in the study. Elementary education was the first level of schooling to be scrutinized and changed. It was also at this level that the most sweeping changes in favor of progressive education were made. The bulk of the detail work of the revision was undertaken by a three-member committee consisting of Donalda Dickie and Olive Fisher, two normal school instructors, and William Hay, an inspector, but it was acknowledged by this threesome that Newland was the driving force in the reform.[18] Not only did he meet frequently with the Committee in its deliberations, but he directed both the experimentation with and the implementation of the new program.

Following a year of interviewing teachers, inspectors and normal school instructors, and of studying sample programs of study from other provinces and countries, the Committee prepared a new course of studies which was ready for trial in 1935. A group of approximately seventy-five teachers was selected to experiment with the new program. Newland was not above guaranteeing the outcome of the experiment in order to ensure the desired result. He selected as experimenters teachers of proven ability and those who had already shown an inclination toward the activity method. Their enthusiasm and success served to reinforce Newland's beliefs that the desirable reform had been found and that it was ready for implementation. After approximately two years in preparation the new enterprise approach was adopted for use beginning September, 1936.

There were a number of changes which occurred in Alberta schools in the period 1936 to 1942. One of the more important of these was the establishment of the intermediate school. The big news, though, was the enterprise. The name, drawn from the English Hadow Reports, embodied much the same meaning as the more commonly known project method. Also like the more familiar project it reflected the philosophy of progressive education. Students and teacher jointly selected a problem for study. They agreed on a plan for exploring the problem and then worked to accomplish their plan. The teacher ensured that there was ample student activity, relating of content to student interests and some integration of subject matter. The integration of subjects initially was limited to history and geography, but after 1940 a further revision extended the integration to include science and health education. In the course of the enterprise which lasted anywhere from four to eight weeks, children planned, organized ideas and materials, learned cooperation through group involvement, did both mental and manual work, practiced skill subjects and collected information. When Newland was speaking about the enterprise in 1940 before the Manitoba Education Association he offered the following definition:

> The new programme was a modified "activity" programme based on enterprises. The enterprise is a "series of purposeful activities arising out of the pupils' needs and interests and revolving around one central theme". The "enterprise" was . . . the " definite undertaking" which teachers and pupils agreed to carry out. It was chosen for its interest and value, carefully planned in advance, and brought to a definite conclusion according to plan, after which a careful evaluation of gains and achievements is made.[19]

Many teachers were unprepared for the new approach. They were not conversant with the doctrines and practices of progressive education, nor were they confident that the traditional mode of instruction was ineffective and needing modification. Newland and his associates recognized that while change was necessary, it had to come gradually. As a result, when the enterprise was introduced in 1936, it was not mandatory. Teachers were encouraged to experiment with it, but not until 1940 were they required to employ it.

When the changes were announced, in spite of the option clause there was considerable consternation among teachers. Newland, his co-workers on the Committee, and many on the faculties of the normal schools were immediately called upon to explain and to popularize the new approach. Judging from the output of materials and the number of instances where the changes were discussed the magnitude of the task was sizeable. Summer schools, columns in *The A.T.A. Magazine*, conventions, and reading lists were all utilized in an attempt to help teachers become adept in the use of the enterprise. Each year Newland reported to the Minister of Education on the use of the enterprise in the schools. His reports which were undoubtedly biased by his own preference suggest, contrary to the flurry of popularizing activity, that the majority of Alberta teachers understood and utilized the new approach.

The sources of help given to teachers during this phase of popularization varied, but the nature of the help was essentially the same. Emphasis was upon classroom problems. Teachers were given specific suggestions as to how the method was to be employed. They did not seek, nor did they generally receive, instruction dealing with the underlying philosophy of progressive education. This was in part due to the nature of the teaching force in Alberta. The large majority of teachers had been and were being prepared in the provincial normal schools. The period of instruction was brief, less than a year. The limited time available resulted in the philosophical and theoretical elements of teacher preparation being sacrificed in favour of the more immediate concerns of classroom effectiveness. Unfortunately, many teachers never progressed beyond this level of preparation and competence. They continued to concern themselves with questions about the "how" of teaching rather than the "why".

Newland was one of the few proponents of the new education who offered teachers a complete understanding of the reform. Newland commented frequently, both as an author and as a speaker, in a careful, articulate manner and offered Canadians much the same fare that Dewey, Counts and Kilpatrick were offering to their larger audiences. Those who heard or read Newland were not deprived if they had not studied the works of the better known American leaders of progressive education. Newland was selected along with Joseph McCulley of Ontario, M.E. LaZerte of Alberta and H.B. King of British Columbia to serve as a committee member of the essentially American organization, the Progressive Education Association. He was known as one of the more able Canadian spokesmen for the new education.

He defended the new program on two major bases: first, on the psychological principles of learning; and second, on what he believed to be the proper relationship between a democratic society and its schools. In describing Alberta's new curriculum before the Manitoba Education Association in 1940, he enunciated three basic principles of learning which he believed must be taken into account in providing adequately for child growth:

(1) Growth is dependent, not upon what is done for the child, but upon what the child does for himself. "The teacher cannot do the child's growing."[20] Similarly,

> Learning is not something that a child gets, but something that he does. The child grows into knowledge, skill, appreciation and culture; he does not take these things from the hands of the teacher.[21]

The child, then, must be active, not passive. The school must provide opportunities for him to learn by doing.

(2) Developmental growth is not segmental but total.

> A child does not shoot out an arm and then a leg. He grows all over all the time. Likewise, he does not grow intellectually one week and emotionally the next and physically the next; he grows totally all the time, physique, intellect, emotionality, character, personality and sociality.[22]

Thus the schools needed to allow ample opportunity for all these varied aspects of growth. As a corollary to this principle of total growth, Newland favored integration of subject matter. Learning, he argued, could not be fitted into water-tight compartments. The new program with its start at integration was an affirmation of his faith in this principle.

(3) Mental development takes place when efforts to reach a goal are evaluated. The school should therefore offer goals that are meaningful and

worthwhile to the child, that are within his reach, and that are sufficiently concrete or objective to allow the child to evaluate his efforts. In essence, learning was a process of problem-solving. The problem-solving approach was the most effective means of developing the capacity for critical thinking. According to Newland the new Alberta program honored all of these psychological principles.

The other major justification for the enterprise which Newland offered was related to his belief in total democracy. Nineteenth century democratic thought was outmoded according to Newland. In fact he believed that its continued existence jeopardized the future of any form of democratic government. The major fault with traditional democratic theory was its undue emphasis upon individual property rights. Adherence to this central tenet of the democratic faith had resulted over the years in the creation of a privileged economic class. This privileged class effectively controlled society of its own advantage and refused to share educational opportunities, essential social services and assurances of security. Newland feared that if this gap between the advantaged and disadvantaged continued to grow, the future of democracy would be at stake. Fascism, which was already attracting large numbers in Germany and Italy, appeared to many to be an attractive alternative. Newland regarded it as a despicable form of government. It was a philosophy of defeatism. It denied the free play of intelligence and faith in each individual which were so important in Newland's value system.

The threat of Fascism could be quelled, according to Newland, if people were willing to accept and work for total democracy. This meant that all people in society were to be a part of the essential decision making process. Total democracy then embodied a basic faith in the intelligence and goodwill of the masses of the common people. It meant that each individual in society, regardless of race, social position or economic circumstance, was to have equal access to the opportunities and advantages of society. This in turn suggested a much more conspicuous role for government in planning and regulating the resources of society.

The attainment of total democracy was impossible without the provision of total education. All people, children and adults, had to have equal access to educational opportunities or the system would falter. In explaining the connection between education and democracy Newland noted that "our theory of education must be our theory of democracy, for in a democracy education is government".[23] In another of the many elaborations of this theme which he presented Newland noted:

> We value our society as democratic, we accept the fact of social change, and we commit ourselves to the method of science, to the free play of intelligence and to the use of free-minded discussion. Since we rely on the intelligence and goodwill of all the people, our theory of education is democracy itself; and our task for education is to direct intelligence towards social welfare, and arouse the sense of social responsibility.[24]

Newland knew that there were numerous social changes which had to occur in the move toward total democracy. The educational system was to be an essential instrument in producing these changes. Divisive forces such as class prejudice and racial discrimination were to be consciously undermined. The retreat from reason was to stop, as was the continued dependence upon absolutes. The techniques of scientific enquiry and investigation were to be taught and were to be universally applied to all problems, even social ones. He also proposed that students be trained in the art of critical and independent thinking in order to be able to combat propaganda and tradition.

Newland believed that people in a democratic society were in a position to shape and to determine their future. Education had to provide the necessary skills and attitudes for the effective shaping of the future. Social progress was possible, but was dependent upon the growth of knowledge and on the reshaping of habits, attitudes and institutions by intelligence. The application of scientific knowledge and the scientific method was, in Newland's mind, the embodiment of intelligent action.

As he provided Canadians with his vision of total democracy and total education, Newland also identified for them the major problem standing in the way of the attainment of these two goals. He said:

> We Canadians have the resources, the physique, the intelligence and the goodwill to build a system of real education. Have we the courage?[25]

Teachers, Newland believed, were in the best position to show forth their courage and their willingness to assist in the realization of total democracy and total education. Traditionally, they had adopted a position of alleged neutrality. In effect they had been assisting the privileged few who manage democracy for selfish ends rather than for the welfare of the common man. Newland encouraged teachers to cease their neutrality and to adopt a position supporting the establishment of total democracy. In an address which he entitled "The Line of Action" he recommended among other things that teachers become students of economics. Armed with this knowledge base they needed to expound both within and without the classroom the view that political and economic democracy were inseparable. They needed to argue that modern society was obligated to provide adequate food, clothing, shelter, education, health and other social services for one hundred percent of its population.[26] In every aspect of social life, teachers were to be leaders.

Newland was a man well in advance of his times. His view of democracy embraced such policies as medicare, social insurance and extensive welfare services. During the Depression and early war years, the idea of permanent government responsibility for the common economic welfare of society was still a questionable and suspicious proposal.

As an educational reformer, it is evident that Newland was far ahead of the majority of his professional colleagues. From his early years in the Alberta Teachers' Alliance until the time of his retirement Newland offered teachers an exciting and challenging view of their responsibilities. He firmly believed that they had a significant contribution to make. He ordered his life in such a way that he provided both example and leadership to teachers. He knew that society could be improved; education could make a difference, and teaching could be an adventure in the great social frontier[27] of fulfilling the promise of democratic life. He wanted teachers to share his excitement for that frontier.

Notes

*The author wishes to express appreciation to Mrs. Patricia Oviatt. Her scholarly thesis on H.C. Newland was invaluable in the preparation of this chapter.

[1]H.C. Newland, "The Canadian Teachers' Federation, An Appeal for Support", *A.T.A. Magazine*, Vol. IV, No. 11, April, 1924, p. 17.

[2]*Ibid.*

[3]H.C. Newland, "Annual Report of the A.T.A. to the A.E.A.", *A.T.A. Magazine*, Vol II, No. 2, July, 1921, p. 22.

[4]H.C. Newland, "The Aims and Objects of the Alberta Teachers' Alliance", *A.T.A. Magazine*, Vol. I, No. 11, May 1921, pp. 11-12.

[5]*Minutes of the Executive Meeting of the Alberta Teachers' Alliance*, December 28, 29, 1919.

[6]H.C. Newland, "Editorial", *A.T.A. Magazine*, Vol. I, No. 2, July, 1920, p. 1.

[7]H.C. Newland, "The Aims and Objects of the Alberta Teachers' Alliance", *op.cit.*, p. 13.

[8]*Ibid.*

[9]*Minutes of the Executive Meeting of the Alberta Teachers' Alliance*, December 28, 29, 1919.

[10]*Minutes of the Annual General Meeting of the A.T.A.*, April 7, 1920.

[11]H.C. Newland, "Annual Report of the A.T.A. to the A.E.A.", *A.T.A. Magazine*, Vol. II, No. 2, July, 1921, p. 21.

[12]"Report of Meeting of the Law Committee", *Minutes of Executive Meeting of A.T.A.*, November 11, 1922.

[13]*Minutes of the Annual General Meeting of the A.T.A.*, April 2, 1923.

[14]A.E. Rosborough, "A Brief History of the First Twenty-One Years of the Education Society of Edmonton", unpublished document, p. 1. Included in *Proceedings of the Education Society of Edmonton*, Vol I, February 1927 - April, 1931.

[15]*Proceedings of the Education Society of Edmonton*, October 12, 1935.

[16]*Ibid.*, December 12, 1935.

[17]Peter Sandiford, "Curriculum Revision in Canada", *The School*, February, 1938, pp. 472-77.

[18]Arrigo Christe, "The Development of the Elementary Social Studies Programme in Alberta", unpublished Master of Education thesis, (University of Alberta, 1963), p. 71.

[19]H.C. Newland, "The Enterprise Programme in Alberta Elementary Schools". An address delivered to the General Session, Elementary Division of the Manitoba Education Association Convention, April, 1940, p. 21.

[20]*Ibid.,* p. 19.

[21]Province of Alberta, *Programme of Study for the Elementary School,* Grades I-VI, 1936, p. 3.

[22]H.C. Newland, "The Enterprise Programme in Alberta Elementary Schools", *op.cit.,* p. 19.

[23]H.C. Newland, "Education for Intelligent Living", *H.C. Newland — Collected Papers,* p. 8.

[24]H.C. Newland, "Education Grows Up", *H.C. Newland — Collected Papers,* p. 6.

[25]H.C. Newland, "Education for Future Needs", *H.C. Newland — Collected Papers,* p. 13.

[26]H.C. Newland, "The Line of Action", *H.C. Newland — Collected Papers,* p. 13.

[27]H.C. Newland, "A Sketch of Present-Day Education", *H.C. Newland — Collected Papers,* p. 13.

Progressive Education: Impetus to Educational Change in Alberta and Saskatchewan*

Robert S. Patterson

When Professor Hilda Neatby's book, *So Little for the Mind*, was published in 1953, denouncing progressive education for its harmful effects on Canadian education, it quickly became apparent that there were few stalwarts within the ranks of the educational establishment in Canada who possessed the conviction, the courage or the temerity to stand in defense of the ideas and practices which had been conspicuous in nearly all parts of the country during the previous twenty-five years. Clearly, Canadians had discovered what was well recognized elsewhere: it was no longer fashionable or prudent to be regarded as a supporter of progressive education.

Those who did choose to confront Neatby and her scathing attack on schooling in Canada tended to argue that the charges were ill-founded; they opined, in fact, that the influence of progressive education in Canada was not as extensive as claimed. One leading Canadian educational authority, H.L. Campbell, asserted that much of the criticism directed at the impact of progressive education actually arose in the United States and more appropriately applied to extreme examples of the reform movement in that country. In other words, just as some had claimed that the new ideas and practices were imported from the United States, Campbell was suggesting that criticism of the movement was introduced in a similar way and did not fit the Canadian circumstance. Essentially, it was his contention that

> Most American educators of the progressive school regard Canadian education as most benighted, traditional and conservative. Canada has never followed the progressive movement in education, though the strengths of progressivism have made their contribution. Dr. F. Henry Johnson says that "Progressive thought in Canada has been in line with the moderates. It has first passed through the screening process of our engrained essentialism".[1]

In the post-World War II period, as reaction to the earlier reforms became commonplace, critics were prone to attack progressive education both in the abstract and in the particular or applied form as it was seen to exist in Cana-

---

*From Howard Palmer and Donald Smith (eds.), *The New Provinces: Alberta and Saskatchewan, 1905-1980.* Vancouver: Tantalus Research, 1980. Reprinted with permission.

dian schools. Their contention was that Canadian education had been influenced markedly by this doctrine, and that the schools were doing a deplorable job. Therefore, progressive education was deemed unacceptable in both its theoretical and its practical manifestations. School authorities chose not to debate the relative merit of the phenomenon labelled progressive education nor did they challenge the claim that the progressive education movement had influenced Canadian education. Instead they focused on the extent to which these educational ideas and practices had permeated and altered the philosophy, the curriculum and the methodology of the schools. In this paper the educational reform of two neighbouring provinces Alberta and Saskatchewan, will be juxtaposed, examined and compared in an attempt to provide some insights into this issue pertaining to social and educational change in Canada. Coincidentally, by looking at the process, as well as the content of change, attention will be directed to the relative importance of the American progressive education movement and the indigenous Canadian social conditions as precipitators of and contributors to the reform of Canadian education.

Canadians, as one might expect, were relatively late in recognizing and expressing interest in the ideas and practices associated with progressive education. In 1938, twenty years after the founding of the Progressive Education Association and just at a time when criticism of the movement in the United States was on the increase, a leading Canadian educational authority noted that Canada was in the midst of a nation-wide curriculum reform based upon the "progressive element in American education".[2] He indicated that these revisions challenged the traditional belief that education was synonymous with the acquisition of useful knowledge and, alternatively, stressed the development of character, including qualities of citizenship. Among the other changes he identified as associated with this reform were the introduction of junior high or intermediate schools, greater recognition of and provision for individual differences in learners and increased emphasis on the whole child through elevating the status of such revised subjects as art, physical education, health and mental hygiene, household science and manual training. Lavell, commenting a year later on the same trend, observed that "in the precedence given to personality development over the mere acquisition of knowledge or skills, greater emphasis has been placed on such things as music, art, literature and drama".[3] Also central to these reforms was the introduction of and emphasis on activity programs which resembled in some instances the commonly known project method, but which generally bore the name of enterprise, derived from more acceptable British sources.

Many different practices and ideas surfaced under the rubric of progressive education. Spanning at least a half century in time, responding to widely ranging, rapidly changing socio-economic and educational conditions, and building upon new psychological and philosophical theories, progressive education, as Cremin observes, was of a pluralistic nature meaning "different things to different people".[4] There are clear distinctions to be made between pre- and post-World War I views of progressive education in the United States. Prior to the war, educational progressivism was closely allied with and was essentially an extension of the social and political progressivism of that era. Post-war progressive education, dominated by professional educators, came to have a variety of meanings and emphases. Graham describes the post-war era as follows:

> With the disuse of progressivism as a popular social and political sentiment after the war, the label "progressive" continued to be applied to schools, but these schools were of quite different kinds. In 1920 a "progressive" school was an experimental one, a school that attempted to include in its program some of the findings of the new psychology and to conform to the spirit of the emerging social sciences. These methods were tightly correlated with a sharp focussing of attention upon the individual child in the schoolroom. By the 1930's, when a quite different social reformist sentiment had boiled up as a result of the Depression, a "progressive" school could be either one bearing down hard on individual development and creativity or one that emphasized the school's responsibility in society. In the late 1940's, the term "progressivism" would take on still another shade of meaning, returning very briefly to an identification with the social views of an existing political party.[5]

It is the post-World War I era that tended to have the greatest impact on the Canadian educational reforms of the 1930's.

In keeping with these different emphases and to some extent reflecting the thinking and writing of John Dewey, the prophet and elder statesman of the movement, a number of soon to be overworked expressions emerged as common parlance. Learning by doing, activity-centered learning, educating the whole child, creating democratic citizens, focussing on the interests of the learner and utilizing a child-centered curriculum, were some of the frequently employed clichés which became synonymous with progressivism in education. For many educators these clichés also were indicative of the depth of understanding and the extent of the justification associated with innovative practices.

It is not difficult to find similar diversity and superficiality to that of the United States in the Canadian experience with progressive education. Yet, while it is possible to find instances where all themes and innovations were transplanted, it is evident that Canadians tended to be selective and, because they were, some aspects of the movement received greater attention than did others. Sutherland notes a similar tendency on the part of Canadians interested and participating in the child welfare movement of the early twentieth century.

> Clearly, whether lay or professional Canadian reformers borrowed, modified, or invented an approach or procedure in child welfare or education, they did so in accordance with their assessment of Canadian conditions.

> . . . In short, those who tried to improve the lot of Canadian youngsters looked upon the rest of the world selectively; with their characteristic self-assurance they took one idea from here, another from there, and added their own modifications and inventions. They were sure that they knew how each element fitted into the over-all and, in their opinion, superior systems they were creating.[6]

In Sandiford's 1938 article on "Curriculum Revision in Canada", an attempt is made to identify in order the provinces which had to that point undertaken and completed revisions in the spirit of progressivism in education. After observing how criticisms of American commentators on Canadian education and the findings of the English Hadow Reports had stimulated change, he indicated that Saskatchewan, in 1929, was the first province to embark on a course leading to the introduction of a new curriculum.[7]

Agitation for change in Saskatchewan's educational system had been mounting since the early years of World War I. In June 1915, the Honorable Walter Scott, Premier and Minister of Education, indicated that "the time was rapidly approaching, if it were not already here, when the system itself should be radically changed, with the purpose of procuring for the children of Saskatchewan a better education and an education of greater service and utility to meet the conditions of the chief industry in the Province which is agriculture".[8] School improvement became a topic of widespread interest as a variety of organizations responded to the encouragement of the government and the press to become involved. The Saskatchewan Public Education League was formed and became a forum for the expression of public opinion. One outgrowth of the deliberations of the League was a recommendation to the new Premier and Minister of Education, the Honorable W.M. Martin, "that a small and disinterested commission should be appointed to conduct a systematical and efficient research and survey of school education".[9] Stirred by this resolution and similar promptings from the School Trustees Convention and the school inspectors, the idea of the school survey was made reality in June 1917 when H.W. Foght, a specialist in rural school practice in the U.S. Bureau of Education, was appointed to undertake a survey of educational conditions in Saskatchewan with special reference to rural schools. The action taken by the Martin Government is a part of a trend that became increasingly apparent in both Alberta and Saskatchewan in the ensuing years in educational matters. First, there was the matter of seeking expertise and reform ideas in the United States. Second, was the belief that solutions developed in a foreign context could be applied, generally with modest modifications to a Canadian situation that appeared to bear considerable resemblance to the American problems that stimulated the development of the new ideas.

The interest shown in and concern for the rural school was not unique to Saskatchewan nor to the second decade of the century. In fact in the cases of Alberta and Saskatchewan, the issue of adequate rural school provisions remained in focus at least until the outbreak of World War II, with Saskatchewan of the two provinces being the more reticent to introduce basic reform measures. The Report of the Foght Survey was published in 1918, containing nearly sixty recommendations pertaining to such topics as school organization and administration, school inspection and supervision, attendance, consolidation, rural high schools, normal schools, teachers, vocational education, schools in non-English communities, examinations, school hygiene and health inspection and financial support. Despite the initial interest in the Report and the acknowledged need to improve the rural school situation, only limited gains were made. During the decade of the 1920's the issues associated with better educational opportunities, especially for rural students, continued to be prominent. Faced with a school population that had increased sevenfold in the period between 1905 and 1920, as well as with increased pressure for high school provisions, Saskatchewan, like Alberta, sought administrative, organizational, curriculum and methodological reforms that would provide solutions to the problems. The presence of numerous immigrant communities where English was not readily understood or spoken served to intensify and complicate the problems.

While many reformers, Foght being no exception, looked primarily to administrative and organizational changes to provide relief, a small number, not limited to professional educators, began to voice suggestions that reflected a changing perspective about the nature of childhood and the purposes of schooling. While Foght hints at this trend in his criticisms of extreme formalism in classroom management and mechanism in method,[10] it is during the latter part of the 1920's in Saskatchewan that such ideas gained prominence. The women of the farm movement in Saskatchewan were an important part of this development. They showed considerable interest in the problems of the rural school and sought to understand and to encourage the new ideas gaining acceptance among professional educators.[11] An examination of the records of the Department of Education, including the normal schools, and of the teachers' organization indicates that there was a growing sentiment in support of a more comprehensive view of the child, extending beyond the intellectual dimension to include mental and physical health and character or personality development. As early as 1922 teachers-to-be were receiving instruction on the project method made famous by H.W. Kilpatrick, a leading American authority on progressive education and a faculty member of Teachers College, Columbia University.[12] Normal school examinations of the latter part of the 1920's indicate that students were expected to be familiar with the theorists of the child-centered movement.[13]

The comments of J.S. McKechnie, Chief Superintendent of Schools for Saskatchewan, made in 1926 reflect this changing perspective and, as well, anticipate one of the ways that the Department would choose to examine the ideas and practices of progressive education. Under the heading "Some Recent Movements" he notes that

> The realization that children are not as alike as two peas is slowly making itself felt, and considerable thought is being given throughout the educated world to the question of individualizing instruction. In the past, efforts have been too much centred perhaps on mass production. . . . The problem now before school men is how to individualize instruction so that each pupil may advance according to his ability and effort, and at the same time do those things which are beneficial to and which fit him for society as a whole. . . . The plans which are receiving perhaps the widest interest are the so-called Dalton and Winnetka.[14]

Both of these individualized instruction approaches, named for the cities in which they originated, attempted to organize the learning of the child so that students could proceed at their own rate and according to their interests. This required the development of diagnostic tests, learning units and evaluation instruments.

Mckechnie's interest in providing for the individual differences of students was sufficiently strong to cause him to correspond in 1928 with Carleton Washburne, Superintendent of Schools in Winnetka, Illinois, in order to learn more of the Winnetka Plan. In seeking Washburne's help, the Chief Inspector revealed his concern for the quality of education in the "four thousand one-roomed rural schools" of Saskatchewan and his hope that the Winnetka Plan had been adapted successfully to such an institution.[15] The motivation behind the request for Washburne to visit Regina and meet with the school inspectors was not that Saskatchewan officials were considering adopting the approach. It was McKechnie's wish to keep the inspectors abreast of developments of the times. It was also felt that "the inspectors, having become familiar with the philosophy and methods, would be in a position to stimulate thought and discussion among their teachers as part of the general plan of training the teachers while in service".[16] Following Washburne's visit in January 1929, during which he spoke about progressive education and the Winnetka Plan, several teachers conducted experiments with the method. It was in the urban centres where the ideas received their most extensive application. With the encouragement of Superintendent C.A. Oulton, two teachers from Saskatoon attended summer session at Winnetka in 1929 in order to familiarize themselves with methods of individualizing instruction. Upon their return experimental classrooms were established and the Winnetka materials, without modification, were used.[17] Other teachers and inspectors attended Winnetka summer schools and made use of the ideas and materials in their schools.[18]

The Winnetka experience in Saskatchewan featured a number of developments that typified the reform movement of the period in that province. First, there was an acknowledged concern over the quality of schooling provided in the numerous rural one-room schools in the province. Second, it expressed an interest in the philosophy and practices of progressive education. Third, it relied on American expertise. People were imported from the U.S. to expound on the new approach, while teachers from Saskatchewan went to the U.S. to attend graduate schools and learn of current developments.

The revision of the Saskatchewan curriculum, announced in 1929 and undertaken over the next two years, culminating in 1931, coincided with the period of mounting acceptance of these new ideas and the recognition of the inadequate level of education in the province. Dr. John Huff, appointed Superintendent of Education in 1929, was in charge of the revision. His viewpoint clearly corresponded to that of the progressives in education. His own studies took him into matters related to the increasingly popular field of mental health and hygiene. His remarks to Saskatchewan teachers indicate that he saw the rural school as the chief concern of the period and that education should reflect a progressive perspective. In Deweyan fashion he contended that "education is a process of growth and development. It has no final stage; its ultimate aim can never be achieved".[19]

The new curriculum presented in 1931 reflected in a limited or modest way the new ideas fermenting in the province. Coming when it did, early in the Canadian exploration of these ideas, the revision was only a partial, tentative introduction of change. Although the revision did not incorporate changes which attempted to completely transform the schools, there is no doubt that the new curriculum definitely reflected the new ideas of the progressives which were in vogue in the United States and which had been introduced into Saskatchewan in the previous five years by officials of the Department and by teachers who had visited American summer schools. The most basic or fundamental shift associated with the revision was the introduction of a different purpose for schooling. Whereas, prior to this time, the emphasis was clearly on subject matter mastery, accumulation of information and skill development, these were now regarded as means to an end. Health, social and spare-time activities became the focus of attention. Due to the fact, as noted by the authors of the revision, that "there is a widespread tendency to overlook happiness and mental well-being as a basic objective of school education",[20] special consideration was given in the curriculum guide to the subject of mental hygiene.

The decade of the 1920's in Canada had witnessed a considerable growth of interest in mental hygiene. As early as 1920, W.A. White had indicated that education had too narrow a perspective and needed to become more concerned with "guiding the development of personality".[21] Eight years later, C.M. Campbell stressed that:

> If the school is an apparatus through which the community hopes to train the child for future citizenship it will be interested not only in pedagogic problems, but in the formation of character; it will pay attention to the emotional as well as to the intellectual life; it will be interested in the social adaptation of the child as well as in his scholastic progress.[22]

Whereas some viewed mental hygiene as a concern related primarily to the mentally deficient and to delinquent children, more were acknowledging it as a matter of prime importance relative to "normal" individuals. The elementary level of education became an important focal point for mental hygiene efforts because, as one authority noted, "mental health principles if applied in the elementary school will necessarily be carried over into secondary and university education".[23] The emphasis on mental hygiene which was conspicuous across Canada was also an important concern in the Winnetka technique. Saskatchewan, therefore, was subject to the influence of the movement in both respects, that is directly from the United States and from other parts of Canada. In fact, while schools in Saskatoon were experimenting in 1929 with the individualized learning plan from Winnetka, Dr. S.R. Laycock, Professor of Educational Psychology at the University of Saskatchewan, an authority on mental hygiene, undertook a special study of the personality and behavior characteristics of the children in one experimental school. His research was made possible through a grant from the Laura Speelman Rockefeller Foundation to the Canadian National Committee for Mental Hygiene.[24]

The interest shown in the Winnetka Technique in Saskatchewan surfaced in the revision in other ways. Just as Washburne and his associates distinguished between individualized and socialized activities, the new program made a similar distinction. Teachers were told, in the new curriculum guide that "certain activities are of a purely individual nature and instruction in these should be individualized in order that pupils may advance according to native ability. But all creative activities should be socialized".[25]

Another theme apparent in the revision, important to the time and clearly a vital aspect of the progressive education movement, was that related to self-activity of the child as a basis of learning. In language reminiscent of W.H. Kilpatrick, the authors of the new program agreed that "the spontaneous, vigorous, wholesome, purposeful self-activity of a child in his present stage of development will contribute more to the enrichment of his future life than any immediate consideration of future needs".[26] The language, however, is not the only link with Kilpatrick. In the new course, Citizenship and Character Education, the use of Kilpatrick's project method was outlined and encouraged as the way to ensure that students would participate in purposeful activity which was both spontaneous and socially desirable.

While there was much in the revision to indicate that progressive education had made its way into the school curriculum of Saskatchewan, much remained in the program that was associated with the traditional, subject centered, academic emphasis of the past. The eclecticism which fostered the retention of much of what was old and incongruent with the new doctrine being promulgated undoubtedly gave license to many teachers to lean toward the experience of the past. Inspectors acknowledged that teachers had not caught the spirit of the revision and continued to encourage students to pursue information accumulation and storage.[27]

The Saskatchewan curriculum revision of 1931 marks the first formal acceptance by a Canadian provincial educational authority of the ideas and practices associated with the progressive education movement. Characterized by an attempt to harmonize the old and the new, it stimulated further investigation and reform that extended the impact of progressive education in Saskatchewan and Alberta. Educators from Saskatchewan visited Alberta following the 1931 Revision to expound on their new ideas and practices just as Alberta educational leaders subsequently exported their new developments to Saskatchewan following their 1936 Revision.

The Alberta experience leading up to a major revision of curriculum in 1936 was not appreciably dissimilar to that of its neighbouring province. Throughout the decade of the 1920's and early 1930's dissatisfaction with the quality of schooling, especially in rural districts, increased considerably, precipitated by essentially the same conditions as those prevailing in Saskatchewan. Coincident with this wave of criticism was an apparent growth of interest in, and in some quarters, support for practices and ideas associated with progressive education.

The election of William Aberhart's Social Credit party in Alberta in 1935 attracted considerable attention. A number of interested observers wondered how Albertans could have been duped into believing Aberhart's preposterous theories about dividends being given to the public in order to stimulate the economy. Some were interested in examining the educational system that had contributed to the acceptance of such a claim. One such observer, Dean William Russell of Teachers' College, Columbia University, provided the following assessment as a result of his investigation:

> If there is any place on the American continent where the old conservative educational ideals hold sway, it is the Province of Alberta. They are guiltless of progressive education. They center their attention upon reading, writing and arithmetic. They keep the one-teacher country school. Their instructors have been drilled in the subjects they teach. No trick methods. No standard tests. . . . There is no over-elaborate curriculum. They read, they write, they spell, they cipher. Nevertheless, the citizens of Alberta voted to pay themselves $25.00 a month.[28]

H.E. Smith, a member of the School of Education at the University of Alberta, commenting on Alberta education four years later, was able to report, seemingly with some measure of pride, that in the intervening years Alberta, under that very Social Credit government, had introduced "an educational programme second to very few in America in so-called progressiveness".[29] Alberta, according to Smith, was in the midst of a province-wide educational experiment to test a theory. At the heart of this experiment are the theories caught up in the phrase "progressive education".[30]

What Dean Russell missed in his appraisal of Alberta education in 1936 was that many Albertans, especially a group of educators in the Department of Education and normal schools, shared his assessment of the educational system and were actively engaged in the process of encouraging and introducing sweeping reforms in that very year. In fact the major revision of the Alberta curriculum announced in April 1936 was simply the climax of rather lengthy discussions which had extended over most of the previous fifteen year period. At the heart of the debate was the plight of the rural school.

The existence of a farmer government, the United Farmers of Alberta, in office since 1921, helped to make people more aware of the disadvantages and seeming inequities faced by the rural populace. For some the solution was seen to reside in different economic policies. For others, particularly, for the members of the United Farm Women Association, the problems of rural living were acute in the context of the home and community and hence the solutions they sought were at this more basic level of existence. Nowhere was the inequity in the quality of life between rural and urban settings more obvious than in the provisions made for schooling. Rural schools, typically multi-grade, one-room, one-teacher institutions in isolated locations, frequently in non-English speaking communities, were the focal point of controversy and dissatisfaction throughout the period between the two World Wars. The same problems apparent in Saskatchewan prevailed in Alberta. As late as 1935 over sixty-five per cent of the province's classrooms were located in one-room schools.[31] The growing demand for secondary school instruction, the lower attendance in rural areas, the demands placed by multi-grade instruction on inexperienced, immature, poorly prepared practitioners and the unique needs of non-English-speaking students in some communities combined to add credence to the claim that the most serious educational problem of the period was the rural school.[32]

Perren Baker, the Minister of Education in the UFA government throughout its fourteen years in office, attempted during the last half of his administration to spearhead the adoption of the Baker Bill which attempted to deal with the rural school problem through the creation of large administrative units. In 1928, when the Minister presented his proposal to the annual meeting of school trustees, the response was overwhelmingly negative. Despite the obvious opposition to the Bill, it went before the Legislature in 1929 for approval. The valiant efforts of Mr. Baker notwithstanding, the Opposition and many of Mr. Baker's own party were not persuaded by his arguments, causing him to withdraw the Bill before third reading. In the 1930 session it was reintroduced with minor modifications, and again it was withdrawn because the Premier and Cabinet were not willing to force its passage. In retrospect Mr. Baker noted that with an election pending the government was concerned about staying in office. As he explained it:

The depression deepened and with the growing distress the popularity of the government throughout the province weakened. Its thought and its energies were fully engaged with marches of the unemployed to the legislation [sic] building, legislation for the protection of debt-ridden farmers threatened with fore closure, make-work schemes, and the distribution of "relief" all over the province. It is small wonder if the problem of survival, both of the Government and of the hard pressed families everywhere, seemed more urgent than the passing of a rather unpopular educational reform.[33]

While in this instance the UFA Government felt it was acting in accordance with the wishes of the farm population, no longer was it acting on the expressed will of the Annual UFA Convention. In fact the desire to stay in office resulted in a conservatism entering into the party which alienated a number of the more dogmatic and zealous agrarians. In at least two conventions, encouragement had been given the Minister to introduce anticapitalistic textbooks. His refusal to do so is yet another indication of the changed relationship between the members of the movement and the highly pragmatic and moderate government.[34]

Under Baker's leadership the Legislative Assembly in 1934 created a committee to investigate rural education. Many of the same issues as those giving rise to the proposed Baker Bill were identified to focus the deliberations of the Committee. In this setting it was learned that the Department had proceeded to advance the idea of the large unit through the creation of two experimental large districts in the Berry Creek and Turner Valley areas and that a three-member committee had been struck by the Minister of Education to prepare a revised elementary school program which was intended "in all material respects to satisfy the aims of an activity programme".[35] Mr. G. Haverstock, Principal of the Camrose Normal School, in speaking before the Legislative Committee provided the following quote from Dr. Dunn of Columbia University as a rationale for the new approach:

> The great handicap of the traditional type of one-teacher school is the large number of "recitations" required for many subjects in many grades. The progressive conception of education, however, replaces verbal recitation with socialized activity. Integration of subject-matter is effected through large units of work developed around genuine life interests and experiences. Children are not classified in closely homogeneous groups on a basis of achievements in skills or factual knowledge, but work together, as people do in life outside the school, on enterprises of common interest in which each participates according to his ability. Some are clever with figures, others show peculiar ability in finding and bringing in interesting objects for group use, others contribute clippings or pictures, others search whatever library facilities are available, and report what they have read. . . . The groups cut across one another, and the child who is the admired and respected leader in literary activities may become the humble follower of an erstwhile school

dullard when there is a sand table to be constructed, or a scenery to be painted for a school play.[36]

The ideas and practices associated with the anticipated revision were not new to the province. School officials in the latter part of the decade of the 1920's expressed growing interest in the need to break away from "the old formal reproduction and memorization types of method" and adopt instead "socialized study and problem methods, which encourage free and independent thinking".[37] Like people from Saskatchewan, some Albertans encouraged experimentation with individualized learning plans such as Winnetka and Dalton. As an Alberta normal school instructor of the period, G.K. Sheane, observed, "the decade 1920 to 1930 was characterized by a 'challenge to the recitation'. Patented techniques of various kinds were either developed or tested".[38] In 1924, the Dalton Plan, an administrative arrangement for individualizing high school instruction, was given a five-year trial in the Garneau School in Edmonton and the Winnetka Technique was investigated by the Department of Education, but was rejected because it was too costly to operate.[39]

Like their counterparts in Saskatchewan the women of the UFA organization provided support for the examination of and move toward these educational ideas and practices associated with progressivism. A number of them travelled to other countries investigating ways in which schools were dealing with what were perceived to be common problems. Mrs. Irene Parlby, a member of the UFA Cabinet, presented the Dalton Plan to the 1925 UFWA Convention by noting that the Plan "permits children to learn by the scientific method and to investigate for themselves. . . . The end of this education is the character development of the child. He becomes a wholesome, charitable and intelligent person".[40]

Mrs. Susan Gunn, during her presidency of the Educational Committee of the UFWA, reinforced the sentiments being expressed by a growing number of educational leaders in the Province. It was her claim that the UFWA felt that the "schools were too rigid, with too much routine".[41] They contended that schools should emphasize "training not for examinations, but training for life".[42]

In both provinces the farmer movement encouraged a shift from the competitiveness of the capitalist system to co-operation as the basis of the new order they were trying to establish. The terminology found its way into a statement of purpose in the 1931 Saskatchewan revision and into the rhetoric of many Alberta educators speaking of their new program. However, there is considerable cause to doubt that most teachers really understood or accepted such a fundamental value shift. For the better part teachers continued to focus on the practical methodological and curriculum concerns of the classroom.

A three-member curriculum committee was appointed in 1934 by H.C. Newland, Supervisor of Schools, to undertake a revision of the curriculum.

Within a year they had a proposal ready for trial in the schools. Seventy-five teachers, allegedly among the more effective teachers in their respective inspectorial districts, were chosen to pilot this program. Given the careful selection of the experimenting team, their overwhelming positive response to the proposed revision is not surprising. Thus in the spring of 1936 Newland announced that in the fall of that year a new program would be in effect.

The key figure in the implementation and popularization of these ideas and practices in Alberta schools was H.C. Newland, Supervisor of Schools in the Department of Education. Newland, a former high school Latin teacher in Edmonton and a key figure in the growth of the Alberta Teachers' Alliance, became interested in the ideas of progressive education during the latter part of the 1920's and became an active proponent of them in Alberta following his doctoral studies at the University of Chicago in 1932. While his commitment to the new doctrine was not unique in either province, his understanding of and promotion of the social reconstructionist role for the school was distinctive. Unlike the majority of his fellow teachers, Newland was interested in the philosophical ideas associated with progressive education. In speaking of creating a new social order through different purposes, curricula and methodology in the schools, Newland was identifying with the modern liberal views espoused by the prominent American progressive education theorists. They spoke of negative effects of extreme individualism in the capitalist system and in the school system. In its place they emphasized equality of educational opportunity and total democracy to combat the threat of Fascism. Very few Albertans endorsed the social reconstructionist ideas promulgated by Newland. Many, like William Aberhart, were speaking of creating a new social order, but for each user there was clearly a different meaning to the idea and a different method of realizing it. The common terminology gave the appearance of a compatibility between the proposed social and educational reforms that did not in fact exist. Much of the philosophical basis for progressive education was incompatible with Aberhart's basic beliefs, which suggests he did not study carefully the curriculum revision endorsed by his government in 1936 or, like most teachers, ignored its philosophical implications.

The year 1936 saw the introduction of a number of highly significant educational changes in education including the establishment of the large unit of administration, the creation of junior high schools, the requirement that all teachers affiliate with the Alberta Teachers' Association and the introduction of the Enterprise, a curriculum and methodology based on the principles of progressive education. The former UFA Government was aware of needed change and even had encouraged such through its interest in and experimentation with the large unit of administration and through the creation of a curriculum revision committee. Yet, hamstrung by a conservatism associated with its desire for re-election, the UFA administration failed to act. The election of Aberhart and his Social Credit colleagues introduced a new government with a fresh mandate based on the expectation of change. Nearly one-fourth of the elected Social Credit representatives formerly had been teachers. They knew firsthand the problems in Alberta's schools. Aberhart's acceptance of the Education portfolio along with that of Premier and Attorney General meant that G.E. McNally as Deputy Minister and H.C. Newland as Supervisor of Schools provided much of the leadership in this field, unencumbered by close ministerial supervision. Such latitude was suited particularly to the interests and liking of Newland, who used this as an opportunity to introduce the curriculum and methodological reform he and others had been preparing.

As the Calgary *Herald* announced the new developments to the public, it indicated that something new in the way of schooling was under way for Alberta schools. Whereas in the present system knowledge acquisition was the basic consideration, under the new scheme appreciation and interest were to rank first with knowledge following naturally and more quickly.[43] According to officials in the Department of Education the new elementary school curriculum was to be "in substance an 'activity programme'" based partly on the principle that "learning is not something a child gets, but something that he does".[44] The activities engaged in by the children needed to be worthwhile and important to the children. They would afford opportunities for the students to socialize as they worked together on problem solving tasks. A new method and curriculum designation called the enterprise, a name derived from British rather than American sources, was introduced as a way of providing for student activity, integration of subject matter and group planning and decision making. The new approach was explained in the curriculum guide:

> The name "enterprise" has been chosen to designate the "doing or activity", rather than the familiar "project" because it has a somewhat stricter meaning. An enterprise is a definite undertaking; teachers and pupils agree upon it and tacitly promise to carry it through as agreed. An enterprise is an undertaking chosen, after careful consideration, for its interest and value; carefully planned in advance, carried out according to plan, and brought to a definite conclusion, after which some reckoning of gains is made. An enterprise is not only a carefully organized undertaking in itself, but it is also part of a whole, a definite step in a course designed to cover three years of work. Each enterprise involves planning, the organization of ideas and of materials, and co-operation. Enterprises include both mental and manual work, the collection of information and the practice of skills.[45]

The Alberta reform was the most enthusiastic and extensive adoption of progressive educational practices of any in the country. Yet, even though Alberta generally was recognized as the Canadian leader in the movement, there was in the 1936 reform an evident reluctance to provide for an unconditional or unqualified adoption of the reform ideas. To ease the introduction of the reform teachers were not required, but instead were encouraged, to use the enterprise method and curriculum. In reference to the importance placed by many on knowledge acquisitions, some subjects were retained and taught as distinct courses outside of the integration in the enterprises. The basic skill subjects of reading, spelling, arithmetic and writing were among this protected group.

It was in the elementary school, as in Saskatchewan, where the new activity program was centered. While the enterprise technique was not legislated beyond the elementary school, teachers in the new intermediate school grades were encouraged to study it and to operate by a similar philosophy. They were informed that their program, like the one in the lower grades, was "also a great protest against formal methods of instruction and rigidly prescribed lesson material".[46] They were to understand that

> the basic principle of procedure in this course is that learning is an active process. The outline abounds in activities that call for pupil experimentation, individual research, and creative self expression. The social studies classroom instead of being a place where children "learn" history, geography and civics, is to be a real laboratory, where co-operation, initiative, originality and responsibility are developed.[47]

The announcement of the new program in the spring of 1936 caused a considerable stir within the ranks of the teaching profession. Teachers flocked to the summer school, resulting in a tenfold increase in attendance over previous years. The Department was inundated with requests for help in understanding and implementing the changes. Newland, his associates on the Revision Committee and members of the staff at the various normal schools became actively engaged in proselyting and winning converts to the progressive approach in education. Evident in this propaganda campaign, even in the original planning and development phase, was a heavy reliance on expertise and examples from the United States. There was an obvious attempt by these Albertans to rely on British sources,[48] where feasible, but clearly their greater dependence was on American expertise. Headline personnel for the summer schools were drawn from American universities and well-known American progressive schools, and they were given the responsibility of explaining the new phenomenon to Alberta teachers. At the same time that educators were being imported to introduce the reforms there was an exodus of Alberta teachers and members of the Department of Education's normal schools and inspectorial staff to the United States where they participated in graduate programs which had a similar purpose. This exchange of personnel was common across the country and was not limited to formal course work. Featured speakers for teachers' conventions were also American educators prominent in the progressive education movement. Beginning with Boyd Bode in 1938 a succession of such speakers came to Alberta to disseminate the doctrine of progressive education. A number of these went on to Saskatchewan and other Canadian locations to perform a similar function there. The visit of nine members of the executive of the Progressive Education Association in 1939 to the Alberta Teachers' Convention was evidence that the province had arrived as a convert to progressive education, all in the short space of three years since Dean Russell had acclaimed Alberta's education system as "old-fashioned, reactionary and effete".⁴⁹

The write-up of the convention provides insight into the way in which the profession viewed the proceedings:

> The 1939 Easter Convention is over, and if there is one regret that lingers, it is that all the teachers in Alberta could not have been there. . . . The central feature of the convention, of course, was the invading host of American educators (nine of them) to put before us the aims, doctrines, practices and hopes of the Progressive Education Association of the United States, that is to say, to point out to us what they regard as the Better Way in Education. This they did, and they did it in a way to win in conspicuous degree the respect and confidence of everyone.⁵⁰

The involvement of the PEA in this and subsequent Alberta conventions is a reflection not only of Alberta's interest in drawing upon this organization's expertise and reputation, but it is also an indication of both an endorsement by the PEA of the Alberta reform and a growing interest in Canada on the part of the American-based organization. In the absence of a Canadian organization to promulgate the doctrines of progressive education, educators in almost every province had sought affiliations that would place them in the mainstream of the movement. For the better part the choice was made in Canada to establish branches of the New Education Fellowship, a European centered counterpart to the PEA. During the decade of the 1930's branches of the NEF were established in Toronto, Halifax, Winnipeg, Calgary, Vancouver and Victoria.⁵¹ While the joining of the NEF indicates a formal link with Europe in the movement, there was a conscious effort on the part of Canadians to relate to and benefit from the American PEA. Toronto, the most active section, encouraged association and jointly-sponsored conventions with the PEA. When Joseph McCulley on behalf of the NEF in Canada expressed appreciation to the PEA for the opportunity of being able to participate in and benefit from the 1935 PEA convention in Buffalo, the Association went on record as "favoring cooperation with the NEF in Canada and being willing to cooperate with the NEF in Canada in any program or in any way the NEF desires".⁵² Two years later, Harold Rugg, Chairman of the PEA's Committee on International Cooperation, had encouraged greater involvement of Canada in PEA matters. In the involvement of the PEA in Canada we see not only the Canadian desire to draw upon American expertise, but also a conscious effort on the part of the American organization to extend its influence into Canada. Partly this was motivated by a response to Canadian overtures, but undoubtedly it was also related to the concern of many in the organization to find new membership strength for the PEA. As many as 104 Canadians became members of the PEA and at least five gained membership on Executive and Conference Committees of the Association.[53] It is significant to observe that two of the five, H.C. Newland and M.E. Lazerte, were Albertans.

Following four years of experimentation with the enterprise system, in 1940 Alberta produced another curriculum revision which marked the high-water point in the acceptance of progressive education in Alberta and for that matter in all of Canada. This revision made mandatory by all teachers the use of the enterprise method. The principles of student activity and subject matter integration were reaffirmed. The number of subjects to be included in the interdisciplinary, integrated part of the curriculum was increased. The content of the enterprises was not taught as discrete subjects but instead was centered on topics of interest to children and derived from several subject areas. Six fundamental ideas were acknowledged as basic to the revision:

1. The child and not the subject takes first place.
2. The child should enjoy a substantial degree of freedom.
3. The school should operate as a social organization.
4. The child as well as the teacher should have goals.
5. The work of the school should be organized, in large measure,
6. It is of the essence of such a programme that there be encouragement of initiative both for the pupil and for the teacher.[54]

It is interesting to observe that included in the new curriculum guide was the following statement about the origin and nature of the revision:

> Although the programme of studies here presented may be called an activity programme, nevertheless it is in no sense one which is borrowed from another system or applied without regard to the nature of the environment in which it must operate. Rather it is a home-grown product carefully developed in the light of the needs, opportunities, and limiting conditions as they are to be found in and about Alberta children in Alberta schools.[55]

From the outset Albertans were anxious to point out that while these new ideas were in the mainstream of education advancement, they had operated selectively to ensure that such obvious pitfalls as undue permissiveness and neglect of basic studies witnessed elsewhere were avoided in Alberta. It was their belief that they had achieved "a very happy balance between the extreme subject-matterists and the extreme activityists".[56] W.E. Hay, school inspector and member of the 1936 revision committee, provided a comment that many people endorsed.

> The new education procedures incorporated in our Revised Course of Study for Elementary Schools were not derived from forms of the Activity Program; they took form in accordance with progress toward a satisfactory selection of problems involved in the desirable improvement of our scheme of education for the schools of Alberta; particularly the rural schools. I

think that Dr. Dickie and Miss Fisher will agree with the contention that I am making for Enterprise Education and the corresponding procedures incorporated in our new course that they are "home-grown products". . . . Enterprise Education is the Alberta variety of a product more or less inevitable under the conditions of our times.[57]

There is no doubt that the new ideas were clearly an attempt to deal with the problems associated with rural schooling in Alberta. Just as Saskatchewan had sought help from Washburne for that reason, so Alberta looked to the U.S. for assistance in that same regard. Once introduced, the activity program was recognized by the Department of Education and by others as being available primarily to help rural schools. In an exchange of correspondence between F.G. Buchanan, Superintendent of Calgary Public Schools, and H.C. Newland in 1936 it is made plain that the new course of studies was intended principally for rural schools but was to be the basis of instruction for all schools, both city and rural.[58]

As in the case of Alberta, Saskatchewan, following its initial attempt to introduce progressive educational practices into its schools, eventually extended that revision, thus becoming, on paper at least, more committed to the new doctrine. Educators from Saskatchewan shared their 1931 revision in Alberta during the early part of the 1930's as Department officials such as Dr. Huff and Mr. Seeley visited teachers' conventions in the neighbouring provinces.[59] In turn, throughout the decade Saskatchewan had several occasions to benefit from Alberta's leadership. Dr. Newland was invited to present the key features of the 1936 revision to a convention in 1939. He used the opportunity to point out that in spite of the middle course followed by the Alberta revision, there was still much controversy over it.[60]

Even the imported messages introduced into Alberta, largely from the United States, made their way to Saskatchewan. When the major infusion of PEA personnel and ideas came to Alberta for the 1939 convention, Saskatchewan officials were present.[61] At least one of the cadre of visitors subsequently spoke in Saskatchewan as did other PEA officials in the following two years. Numerous teachers from the province attended summer and graduate schools in the United States to obtain further education.[62] The fact that a large number of these chose to attend Teachers' College at Columbia University, the acknowledged mecca of progressive education, is some indication that they were seeking an understanding of the new doctrine.

Impetus for further change beyond the 1931 Revision in Saskatchewan came from a variety of sources. Some was stimulated by the continuing concern over the poor quality of rural education in the province, some came from the expanding interests of teachers within the province and still others came from the examples of other Canadian provinces. Following Saskatchewan's ground-breaking move into the realm of progressive education, Nova Scotia in 1933, Alberta and British Columbia in 1936, Ontario in 1937 and Manitoba, New Brunswick and Protestant Quebec in the next three years, all introduced revisions that reflected the new philosophy. The earlier Saskatchewan revision, revolutionary in its day, subsequently proved to be a modest beginning when compared to the revisions of other Canadian provinces. Interest in another revision grew within the Province particularly after the 1936 changes in Alberta. In 1937, Miss S.S. Milner published an article for Saskatchewan teachers on the "revolutionary educational program" on which Alberta had embarked, outlining the underlining theory and basic practices associated with the new education.[63] In that same year the Regina Normal school, spurred by the studies of Mrs. Hay at Columbia University, and in co-operation with school inspector Muller, undertook an experiment using an integrated school program.[64] Also in 1937 the Director of Curriculum, A.B. Ross, indicated that

> committees consisting of inspectors of schools, normal school instructors, teachers, and others interested in education are being set up with a view to making such changes as will improve the course and emphasize more particularly its activity features.[65]

In the following year he forecasted more specifically the direction the revision would take. It was to "give a still greater emphasis to the social education of children".[66]

The exact nature of the revision was unveiled in 1940 by the Director of Curriculum, prior to its formal adoption in 1941. Much of the language used to describe and to justify the new program could easily be mistaken for similar material in the Alberta revisions of 1936 and 1940. The Director noted:

> The curriculum is definitely an activity programme i.e. the pupils participate more than ever before in all school activities because through these they develop and expand.
> . . . The new activity or enterprise programme implies a new concept of teaching, in which book learning and preparation for examinations give place to socialized classroom activities and learning procedures.[67]

The teachers in Saskatchewan like those in Alberta faced some problems in adopting and utilizing the new methods. Many chose to adhere to the old traditional methods of teaching. Many, according to the inspectors, were confused over the enterprise method of teaching.[68] While the Department on the one hand was trying to convey the message that the revision was being implemented successfully throughout the Province and that teachers were behind the new program, it was, on the other hand, engaged in a series of activities designed to counteract the struggles teachers were facing in relating to the changes. A series of annual conferences were sponsored by the Department to provide practical help to teachers. In both 1942 and 1943, the focus was on the use of the enterprise in the rural school.

Even though there was much similarity between Alberta and Saskatchewan in the process and the content of reform, it is apparent that Alberta revision was a more enthusiastic and complete conversion to progressive education than was that of Saskatchewan. One place, among numerous others, where this was evident was in the view held with respect to the enterprise. Saskatchewan officials accepted it as one of several useful classroom procedures rather than as "the basic procedure for the whole school programme".[69] Alberta, at least by 1940, had clearly opted for the more encompassing use of the enterprise.

The uniqueness of Alberta, as the leader and most enthusiastic Canadian convert to the new doctrine, is attributable essentially to the existence of a forceful, extremely talented leader, H.C. Newland, who was imbued with a philosophy of education that give pre-eminent place to the potential power of the school and the teacher as agents of social change and to the activity, problem-centered curriculum as the best way to stimulate change. When opposition to the new ideas arose, as it did in the 1939 Calgary civic elections, Newland was able to successfully counteract the opposition. Of course, Newland was not alone in his crusade for sweeping educational and social reform, although few there were who actually identified with his social reconstructionist role for the school. As influential as Newland was in this transformation process, he could not have succeeded on his own. G.F. McNally, the affable, well-liked deputy minister, played a key role, as did Donalda Dickie, Olive Fisher, W.E. Hay, W.D. McDougall and others who formed a cadre of hardworking, practical-minded support personnel, working out the details of the revisions. The fortuitous timing of a momentous political change in Alberta which brought to power a former teacher espousing ideas for a new social order, yet too busy with establishing a government to attend closely to departmental business in education, left the forceful Newland in an ideal position to introduce the new doctrine.

On the surface it would appear that both Alberta and Saskatchewan during the 1930's and 1940's were converted to progressive educational theory and practice. The curriculum revisions of the period clearly pointed in that direction. Leading educational spokesmen confirmed that emphasis. Yet, in the stress upon selective adoption, on home-grown products and on trying to adopt a middle way between the so-called "progressives"and "traditionalists",[70] it would seem that even among the leadership of the movement in these two provinces that was hesitancy about complete conversion and a desire, as Sandiford observed, to "provide a brake for the too enthusiastic 'Progressive'".[71]

At the level of classroom implementation there is considerable reason to question the extent to which progressive education permeated the system. The outcry of teachers in both provinces for help in utilizing the new ideas and practices indicates that teachers were poorly prepared for the innovations. Further, if we accept Cremin's claim that the prescriptions of the progressives in education made "inordinate demands on the teacher's time and ability"[72] and in turn related that observation to the fact that most teachers in Alberta and Saskatchewan in the interwar years received little more than a brief eight month training after completing Grade XI in high school, it should come as no surprise to discover that many teachers experienced difficulty with the enterprise and reverted to traditional methods and content. This fact, coupled with the fact that the school facilities and resources were extremely limited in this period, provided ample reason to doubt that the new ideas and practices were properly represented in the schools. Saskatchewan officials noted one additional concern which only added to the problem in both provinces:

> Various factors have interfered with the development of the enterprise method of teaching in the rural schools since the introduction of the 1941 curriculum for elementary schools. The chief factor has been the serious egress of teachers to the armed forces and to occupations more directly concerned with the war, and the consequent influx of correspondingly large numbers of young, inexperienced teachers, some with academic qualifications below the normal standard.[73]

In conclusion, then, it would seem reasonable to claim that in both provinces an interest in progressive education, precipitated by an acknowledged need to improve rural education and stirred by new ideas about children and their learning, gained from other Canadian sources, but especially from the American progressive education movement, expanded to the point that both Alberta and Saskatchewan modified their curricula along these lines. However, while the language and ideas of the progressives were incorporated into these curricula, in both instances there was an obvious attempt to persuade observers that the borrowing from the progressive education movement was limited and had been selectively undertaken. While there is reason to question the degree of selectivity in the process, there is no reason to doubt the fact that these reformers clearly wanted to limit the impact of the new ideas and avoid the shortcomings being criticized elsewhere. Thus we see, just at the level of policy, there was hesitancy or only a partial commitment to the doctrine. When the examination of the reforms is taken to the level of the classroom to determine the extent to which policy was implemented, there is additional reason to question the actual impact of the reform. Conditions within the profession and the numerous rural classrooms made it difficult to successfully utilize the proposed ideas and practices. That teachers experienced such difficulty and reacted to it was apparent from the efforts made to respond to their pleas for help. The revisions were the work of a select few in each province located mainly in the Departments of Education, the normal schools and the urban school systems. Their thinking was clearly influenced both by reformers in the progressive education movement and by the more conservative element in their own systems. Given the moderate courses followed at the level of formal adoption and the apparent problems with implementation in the classroom, there is cause to doubt that there was a system-wide commitment to the doctrines of progressive education. The rhetoric employed in the curriculum guides and official pronouncements of the period belies the extent of the impact of the reform movement on Alberta and Saskatchewan education in the pre-1945 era. The outcomes of the educational changes of the period suggest that the proposed alterations of the curriculum were not widely supported by the public or profession and that the educational bureaucracies of the two provinces were able to attempt reforms not fully understood and endorsed by the political leaders of Alberta and Saskatchewan.

Notes

[1]H.L. Campbell, *Curriculum Trends in Canadian Education* (Toronto: W.I. Gage & Co. Ltd., 1952), pp. 48-49.

[2]Peter Sandiford, "Curriculum Revision in Canada", *The School* (February 1938): 475.

[3]W. Stewart Lavell, "The Theories at Work in Canadian Schools", *Queen's Quarterly* (Autumn 1939): 319.

[4]Lawrence A. Cremin, *The Transformation of the School* (New York: Alfred A. Knopf, 1961), p. x.

[5]Patricia Albjerg Graham, *Progressive Education: From Arcady to Academe* (New York: Teachers College Press, 1967), pp. 12-13.

[6]Neil Sutherland, *Children in English-Canadian Society: Framing the Twentieth-Century Consensus* (Toronto: University of Toronto Press, 1976), p. 235.

[7]Sandiford, "Curriculum Revision in Canada", p. 474.

[8]Harold W. Foght, *A Survey of Education in the Province of Saskatchewan* (Regina: King's Printer, 1918), p. 5.

[9]*Ibid.*, p. 6.

[10]*Ibid.*, p. 83.

[11]Le Roy John Wilson, "The Education of the Farmer: The Educational Objectives and Activities of the United Farmers of Alberta and the Saskatchewan Grain Growers' Association" (Ph.D. dissertation, University of Alberta, 1975), p. 198.

[12]Lecture notes for January 4, 1922, *F.M. Quance Papers*, University of Saskatchewan Archives.

[13]Department of Education Professional Examination 1927, 1928 in History of Education, Provincial Normal School Records, PAS.

[14]Province of Saskatchewan, *Annual Report of the Department of Education*, by J.H. McKechnie, 1926, p. 101.

[15]Letter to Carleton Washburne from J.H. McKechnie, October 22, 1928, Winnetka Plan File, PAS.

[16]"Saskatchewan", *The School* (March 1931): 698.

[17]Province of Saskatchewan, *Annual Report of the Department of Education*, by C.A. Oulton, 1929, p. 114.

[18]Letter to Brother Chrysostom from the Deputy Minister, June 17, 1935, Winnetka Plan File, PAS.

[19]Dr. John Huff, "The Commissioner's Message", *The Saskatchewan Teacher* (January 1930): 3.

[20]Province of Saskatchewan, *Public School Curriculum and Teachers' Guide, Grades I - VIII* (Regina: King's Printer, 1931), p.8.

[21]W.A. White, "Childhood: The Golden Period for Mental Hygiene", *Canadian Journal of Mental Hygiene*, 11, 2 (1920): 148.

[22]C.M. Campbell, "The Prevention of Mental and Nervous Disorders", *Mental Hygiene of Children*, 1928, p.4.

[23]W.T.B. Mitchell, "Mental Hygiene in the School System", *Social Welfare*, X (April 1928): 149.

[24]Province of Saskatchewan, *Annual Report of the Department of Education*, by C.A. Oulton, 1929, p. 115.

[25]Province of Saskatchewan, *Public School Curriculum and Teacher's Guide, Grades I - VIII* (Regina: King's Printer, 1931), p. 10.

[26]*Ibid.*, pp. 7-8.

[27]Province of Saskatchewan, *Annual Report of the Department of Education*, 1932, p. 44.

[28]William F. Russell, "Straws from Alberta", *Teachers College Record*, 37 (January 1936): 272.

[29]H.E. Smith, "The New Education in Alberta", *The School* (November 1940): 187.

[30]*Ibid.*

[31]Province of Alberta, *Report of the Legislative Committee on Rural Education*(Edmonton: King's Printer, 1935), p. 7.

[32]W.E. Macpherson, "Canada", *Educational Yearbook of the International Institute of Teachers College, 1924* (New York: The Macmillan Company, 1925), p. 82.

[33]Quoted in Le Roy John Wilson, "Perren Baker and the United Farmers of Alberta: Educational Principles and Policies of an Agrarian Government" (M.Ed. thesis, University of Alberta, 1970), p. 46.

[34]*Ibid.*, p. 47.

[35]Province of Alberta, *Report of the Legislative Committee on Rural Education* (Edmonton: King's Printer, 1935), p. 20.

[36]*Ibid.*, p. 19.

[37]Province of Alberta, *Annual Report of the Department of Education*, by John Scoffield, 1929, p. 43.

[38]G.K. Sheane, "The History of and Development of the Elementary School in Alberta" (Doctor of Pedagogy dissertation, University of Toronto, 1948), p. 86.

[39]*Ibid.*, p. 87.

[40]Honorable Irene Parlby, "Creative Education", *Minister of the U.F.W.A. Convention*, Glenbow Foundation, Calgary.

[41]S. Margaret Gunn, "President's Address", *U.F.W.A. Convention Reports*, January 1926, p. 5. Glenbow Foundation, Calgary.

[42]*Ibid.*

[43]Calgary *Herald*, May 9, 1936, p. 4.

[44]Province of Alberta, *Programme of Studies for the Elementary School: Grades I - VI* (Edmonton: King's Printer, 1936), p. 3.

[45]*Ibid.*, p. 288.

[46]Province of Alberta, *Annual Report of the Department of Education,* 1937, p. 18.

[47]Province of Alberta, *Programme of Studies for the Intermediate School: Grades VII, VIII and IX, 1935* (Edmonton: King's Printer, 1935), p. 36.

[48]The British Hadow Report, studies on child development and education, and a variety of British experimental schools were commonly cited as authority for changes in Alberta. As well a range of British educational leaders such as Sir John Adams were invited to Alberta to present their ideas on the new education.

[49]Russell, "Straws from Alberta", p. 272.

[50]*A.T.A. Magazine,* Vol. XIX, No. 9, May 1939, p. 2.

[51]*The School* (February 1931): 513.

[52]*Minutes of the Executive Committee of the Progressive Education Association,* May 11, 1935.

[53]*Ibid.,* December 16, 1939.

[54]Province of Alberta, *Programme of Studies for the Elementary School, Grades I to VI* (Edmonton: King's Printer, 1940), pp. 23-25.

[55]*Ibid.,* p. 22.

[56]*A.T.A. Magazine,* Vol. XVII, No. 4, p. 32.

[57]Letter from W.E. Hay to H.C. Newland, June 19, 1936, *Newland Papers,* Department of Education Archives.

[58]Letter from H.C. Newland to F.G. Buchanan, August 26, 1936, Department of Education Archives.

[59]*The School* (April 1931): 800.

[60]"Report of Convention", *Dr. Thompson Papers,* University of Saskatchewan Archives.

[61]Province of Alberta, *Annual Report of the Department of Education,* 1939, p. 39.

[62]*The School* (October 1933): 133.

[63]S.S. Milner, "Enterprise Education in Alberta", *Saskatchewan Teachers' Federation Bulletin,* IV, 12:11.

[64]Letter from J.H. McKechnie to the Minister of Education, March 20, 1937, PAS.

[65]A.B. Ross, "Report of School Curricula", *Annual Report of the Department of Education,* 1937, p. 26.

[66]*Ibid.,* 1938, p. 28.

[67]*Ibid.,* 1940, p. 31.

[68]*Ibid.,* 1942-43, p. 31.

[69]"Enterprise Procedure", *Annual Report of the Department of Education,* 1943-44, p. 40.

[70]*Annual Report of the Department of Education,* 1946-47, p. 18.

[71]Sandiford, "Curriculum Revision in Canada", p. 476.

[72]Cremin, *The Transformation of the School,* p. 348.

[73]*Annual Report of the Department of Education,* 1942-43, p. 37

VI

Education in Contemporary Society: The Search for Canadian Identity

The history of Canada and the history of Canadian education are essentially histories of regions, each of which has responded in a unique way to outside influences and local conditions, each of which has sought to create and maintain a unique identity. This Canadian tendency, already well-established by the middle of the nineteenth century, was confirmed and strengthened by the British North America Act, which placed the responsibility for educational policy and practice at the provincial level. Thus, as has been demonstrated in the earlier chapters of this book, the societies of Quebec, Ontario and the Prairie Provinces, including their educational traditions, differ significantly, not only in their development but in their contemporary character. And what is evident in these central regions is even more noticeable in the peripheral provinces of Newfoundland, the Maritimes and British Columbia. All have had unique and widely differing metropole relationships and all have succeeded in creating widely differing educational traditions and practices.

So idiosyncratic has been the development of each region and its education that observers, both Canadian and foreign, have pointed not only to the lack of any coherent national educational policy but the absence of a distinctive Canadian identity. And in a sense, it is true that Canada in the 80's continues to be a country seeking to establish an identity and defend its autonomy in the face of the all pervasive influence of a metropolis. In this respect, Canada's situation replicates that of its various regions, as well as its diverse social, linguistic and ethnic groups, all of whom exist in some form of metropolis-hinterland relationship. Economically, politically and culturally, Canada stands in a dependency relationship with the United States. The resulting "hinterland psychology", which is attracted to and at the same time resentful of the culture of the metropolis, is a major determinant of Canadian educational practices and policies. Thus the impact of metropolis ideas presented in the media and through school textbooks is profound, universally recognized, universally condemned and universally tolerated. Indeed, it is the dominant values of the metropolis which provide the rationale and legitimization of the public school system in Canada.

This is not to say, however, that the influence of metropolitan ideas and values has resulted in a lack of awareness of or concern for uniquely Canadian problems. Indeed, as in Canada's past, the metropolitan perception of problems coupled with an awareness of the extent of metropolitan influence has stimulated the hinterland to become somewhat more introspective and thus somewhat more sensitive to the value of its cultural heritage, somewhat more serious in planning its future. Such issues of bilingualism, multiculturalism, native rights, regional disparity, all have taken on a distinctively national character. In the determination to provide distinctively Canadian solutions to distinctively Canadian problems, formal education is invariably called upon to play an important role.

In this final chapter we will consider a number of contemporary educational issues which have a national, social and educational significance. In his article "From the Swinging Sixties to the Sobering Seventies" J. Donald Wilson tackles two of the most serious problems facing educators today, the disillusionment and loss of confidence in public education, and the lack of any national consciousness of or consensus about the essential purposes of education. He relates how the optimism of social reformers about the ability of education to build a better society was unbounded in the 1960's and early 1970's. This resulted in great increases in educational expenditure and enrolments, accompanied by demands for a more relevant curriculum, free schools and various radical alternatives. But the climate of economic uncertainty of the late 1970's produced reaction against such experimentation. In many ways the optimism of the 60's and the disillusionment of the 70's reflected similar tendencies in the U.S. — suggesting that the direction of Canadian education is still very much determined by metropolitan influences. Education, then, has not proven to be a panacea for the nation's ills. Nor has it seemingly forged a clear vision of the future of society.

The concern with the influence of the American metropole on Canadian society is so widespread in Canada that it constitutes a part of the national character and one of the few reliable national rallying cries. This concern is given a particular focus in Manoly R. Lupul's article "Multiculturalism and Canadian Identity: The Alberta Experience", which provides a personal interpretation of the official policy of multiculturalism within a bilingual framework. He argues that a distinctive Canadian identity can be found in the heritage of the country's diverse ethnic groups. The importance of language is stressed, above all, as the key to this heritage. Arising from this position is a uniquely Canadian education experiment in which minority languages and cultures are given official recognition in the schools.

Finally, in his article "Education and Inequality in Canada", John Young considers what for many people is the most crucial issue in contemporary education, the social function of schooling in promoting equality or inequality. Although this is an issue which has aroused greatest interest in the United States, Young's article treats the problem primarily in a Canadian context.

He argues that large scale investment in education has not produced an egalitarian society. Canada is still very much a hierarchically stratified society featuring substantial inequalities in the distribution of wealth, power and prestige. The equality of opportunity supposedly provided by universal education has proven to be an illusion. Those children born into the elite group invariably end up with the most prestigious and lucrative positions in society themselves. Conversely, the children of the poor rarely manage to rise above the deprived conditions of their birth. In fact, educational credentials serve to justify the existing inequalities by making it appear that all had equal chances in the social steeplechase. The reality, then, is that schools are not agencies of social change, but agencies of social control — a fact that was explicitly admitted by the founders of school systems in Canada.

What then can schools accomplish? Can they foster a distinctive Canadian identity, and if so what will characterize this identity? Can they serve as mechanisms for greater social justice? Or must they merely legitimize existing inequalities and buttress a status quo? These are complex questions, to which there are no simple answers. They are complex questions primarily because, although a society may ignore its past, it cannot escape it. Contemporary educational problems, indeed the very questions we ask about them, are rooted in the responses which past societies made to the conditions which beset them. Our ability to get a grip on these problems and to come to workable solutions depends largely on the depth of our understanding of the rich diversity and, above all, the significance of these reponses, to recognize, in fact, the essential and inescapable relationship we have with our own history.

From the Swinging Sixties
to the Sobering Seventies*

J. Donald Wilson

Towards the end of 1976 an article on education in British Columbia appearing in the *Vancouver Sun* suggested: "The political kudos all lie in a return to the Three R's. Parents, frightened by continual publicity about the illiteracy of their children, not only would welcome it, but are demanding it. Professional educators are increasingly of the view that innovation has outdistanced value".[1] What ever happened to the popular demands for educational change and reform of the late sixties, the sort of reform advocated by Ontario's Hall-Dennis Report in 1968 and British Columbia's *Involvement: The Key to Better Schools* which appeared in the same year? In all, there were fifteen major provincial commissions of enquiry into education between 1960 and 1973, with the bulk of them in the last ten years. Not one provincial educational system was unaffected, since every one launched at least one inquiry, and four provinces — Alberta, New Brunswick, Ontario, and Prince Edward Island — each had two major royal commissions on education in that period.

The recommendations of these commissions often called for sweeping and costly changes. This was particularly true in the case of Quebec, Ontario, Newfoundland, and Alberta. Nationwide expenditures on public education, sky-rocketed. In the period between 1960 and 1975 expenditures on all levels of public education including universities increased sevenfold from $1,706,000,000 to $12,228,000,000.[2] By 1969 Canada led the major industrial countries in the share of its Gross National Product devoted to public expenditures on education. Its figure of 7.6 per cent compared favourably with the USSR at 7.3 per cent, exceeded the United States at 6.3 per cent, and almost doubled the percentage figure for France, Japan, and West Germany respectively.[3]

At the time all this expenditure of public money seemed worthwhile. Faith in education as a panacea for society's ills persisted, despite the hard historical evidence of a century of free, universal and compulsory schooling that education could not reasonably be expected to solve social problems which in fact presupposed more fundamental reform. Moreover, distinguished economists ranging to the lofty heights of the Economic Council of Canada promised that

---

*From Hugh A. Stevenson and J. Donald Wilson (eds.), *Precepts, Policy and Process: Perspectives on Contemporary Canadian Education.* London, Ontario: Alexander, Blake Associates, 1977. Reproduced with permission.

increased "investment in human resources", as they phrased it, would insure an increased Gross National Product for the nation and an increased standard of living for individual Canadians. High pressure advertising campaigns in the sixties blatantly urged students "to learn more to earn more". Such campaigns paid off with increased retention rates in Canadian high schools and much higher enrolment rates for the normal post-secondary age cohort. The estimated retention rates for grades 9 to 11 increased dramatically between 1956-8 and 1969-71, reflecting the success of provincial government efforts to retain adolescents in school for longer periods of time for their own and the state's benefit. (See Table I)

The significant transformation of the high school from a screening institution to a holding basin is clearly apparent from the above table. No longer would the high school by its curriculum and rigorous discipline remain essentially a training ground for the university, an obstacle course to sort out the sheep from the goats. In future the sorting-out of late adolescents would in large measure be transferred to post-secondary institutions. Thus universities and high schools came to play the same roles. While this made universities "important", as evidenced by the vast sums of public money lavished on them in the sixties, it also made professors annoyed and bitter at the alleged functional illiteracy of their students. These same professors conveniently forgot that of the thirty students they now faced in a university classroom, twenty

Table I

Estimated Retention Rates, Grades 9 to 11, by Province (percent)

Province	1956-8	1969-71
Newfoundland	54	81
Prince Edward Island	51	71
Nova Scotia	62	79
New Brunswick	61	80
Quebec	48	92
Ontario	53	84
Manitoba	63	86
Saskatchewan	65	83
Alberta	75	92
British Columbia	76	91

Source: David Munroe, *The Organization and Administration of Education in Canada* (Ottawa: Information Canada, 1974), 215.

would not have made it there fifteen or so years before.[4] The personal rewards of a mass system were most welcome but not the concomitant responsibilities.

Between 1960 and 1969 enrolment ratios doubled in Canada for the twenty to twenty-four age group. By the latter date one of every four in that age cohort was enrolled in some sort of post-secondary institution. This figure was roughly comparable to the USSR but trailed the United States where close to 50 per cent of that age cohort was similarly engaged.[5] By the late seventies many university professors refused to accept that the university had become in effect part of a tertiary level of public education. They valiantly set up a rearguard action designed to perpetuate the myth of the university as a place for seekers of knowledge for its own sake. In the meantime politicians aware of their electorate, university administrators conscious of formula financing, and the clients themselves desperately aware that the "BA isn't worth much anymore" and lacking strong scholarly inclinations, all demanded a "relevant" education geared as much as possible to practical pursuits. Desmond Morton sums up the situation beautifully in his essay: "As both educator and analyst of its society, the university community can look forward to being more needed and less wanted than at almost any earlier period in its history".

The full-time enrolment figures for all levels of schooling are even more startling. In 1970 one out of every three Canadians was attending an educational institution of some sort, a figure which corresponded precisely to that for the United States. In the United Kingdom, by contrast, only 20 per cent of the entire population was enrolled in "school". Once again Canada and the US topped the list of industrialized countries.[6] These figures serve to underline the central position of schooling in Canadian life, especially in the life of young Canadians.

In the late sixties and early seventies there was a lot of talk in Canada about educational radicalism and innovation. For many the 1968 Hall-Dennis Report, entitled *Living and Learning*, on the aims and objectives of education in Ontario was the harbinger of a new progressivism of the John Dewey variety. The needs and interests of school children were taken into account. Students, teachers, and parents demanded a larger role in formulating educational policy and making educational decisions. From various quarters demands were made for a more "relevant" curriculum, for more student choice in courses of study, and for student representation at all levels of university policy-making from individual departments to university senates and boards of governors. There was even some evidence in larger cities of high school student activism. Canadian high school students began forming "inter-high" unions, mostly at the local as opposed to the provincial level.

By the early seventies, however, the student power movement had dissipated almost as quickly as it had appeared. As the job market tightened and as the hopes of a new democratized university dimmed in student leaders' minds, there was a return to a conservatism among students which resembled the early sixties. Graduating from university — and with some distinction —

became a goal again for many students amid the intense competition for suitable jobs and places in the professional schools, especially law and medicine. 'Confrontation politics', once a student watchword, became a historical term. The practice of 'stopping out' — the process of interrupting their education with the intention to study at some future time — became as infrequent as it had formerly been in the fifties.[7]

In the sixties, amid the expansion of public education, the need for more teachers forced the public to accord relatively higher status to and to place a higher monetary value on teaching as a profession. Regular and often substantial salary increases resulted. Highly structured systems of classifying competence for purposes of payment were introduced. The widespread success teachers experienced in regard to status and salary encouraged them to become more vocal in subsequent demands around the negotiating table. In the face of galloping inflation teachers became more and more militant. Strikes ensued, often bitterly fought following the familiar pattern of trade union-management confrontations. Many parents and taxpayers were appalled at the so-called "unprofessional" tactics of striking teachers. Newspaper editorials generally made forthright condemnations of teachers' strikes, especially in Ontario and Quebec. Parents were angry at the prospect of lost schooldays and their children roaming city streets and suburban plazas unsupervised. Senior students worried about the possible deleterious effects on their projected university careers. Confronted by such opposition, teachers were confused, convinced as they were of their value to the community in return for which they argued at length that they were as concerned about improved educational settings for their students as they were about salaries and working conditions.

The late sixties also saw the advent of a new form of parent power. Of course, the PTA or the Home and School dated form the interwar period in Canada, but less than a decade ago parent pressure for involvement in educational decision-making became intense. A great deal of attention was given to the concept of community schools, public schools which would function at the behest of a community-based council rather than follow the dictates of a downtown school board office. Critics began to advocate the abolition of school boundaries so as to enable parents to send their children to public schools of their own choice rather than be stuck with the educational philosophy or practice of their neighbourhood school.[8] Why shouldn't parents, one advocate queried, "be allowed the same privilege that most school systems give their teachers — the chance to request a transfer to the school of their choice?"[9] That same observer was to write in 1975 an entire book on the subject of parent power in Canada.[10] By that time, however, many "parent power" advocates had lost their enthusiasm for community-controlled schools. The *Zeitgeist* of late sixties reform had clearly passed away, media support had abated, and in any case their children were now out of elementary school. But all had not been lost. Many school districts now allowed for cross-boundary enrolment and parental advisory councils, thus taking the steam out of the movement.

Such innovations were not likely to be reversed despite the clamoring of "back to the basics" people demanding a return to rigid discipline and the three R's. Ironically, the cross-Canada support for the "back to the basics" movement emphasized the continuing desire of parents to share in educational decision-making.

Other proposals for change in the sixties included Frank MacKinnon's suggestion in *The Politics of Education* (1960) that the immense bureaucracy of public education be replaced by a system of individual schools organized as public trusts on the model of crown corporations. Financing would continue to originate from public funds but purely 'educational' decisions, such as curriculum planning , would be left to each school's teaching staff (with no suggestion of student involvement). Nothing came of MacKinnon's proposal and teachers no less than parents seemed unaware of the potential for positive change that resided therein.

In the late sixties the widely publicized "voucher system" attracted a great deal of attention in the United States but went largely unnoticed in Canada. Disillusioned with many aspects of the public system, both civil rights advocates and militant Black Power groups called upon US federal and state authorities to put public moneys into the hands of the consumer of education instead of into the institutions which dispensed the education. This "client-oriented" suggestion saw many variations but all of them came under the general rubric of the "voucher system".[11] In Canada such an assault on the traditional common school could have been (and could still be) a godsend to native peoples who want their children to have native teachers and curricula and linguistic identity, and to religious minority groups, such as Roman Catholics (in those provinces without separate school systems), Jews, and Christian Reformed, as well as atheists and agnostics opposed to the Christian ambiance of the public schools. Of course, as critics pointed out, a system of weighting vouchers in favour of the poor would be necessary to offset the imbalance that would result otherwise. In any case the public system as constituted over the past century held its ground in both Canada and the United States.

Another alternative given a great deal of play in the late sixties was the "free school" movement. Inspired by the model of A.A. Neill's Summerhill and drawing spiritual inspiration from Rousseau and Tolstoy, the "free school" made a distinct impact upon education in Ontario and British Columbia with lesser spillover effects in other provinces. The Everdale Place, northwest of Toronto, even managed to gain North American attention through publication every two months of Canada's most lively education journal, *This Magazine is About Schools* (now *This Magazine*). But like the student activist movement, free schools began to close down or be absorbed in part into the public system. Tom Durrie, teacher-founder of Saturna Island Free School in British Columbia, spoke in late 1971 of the deleterious effect of the "political and internal hassles" encountered in running a free school. Survival itself eventually became the sole goal.[12] Likewise, Bob Davis, one of the founders of

Everdale Place, conceded by the early seventies that the aim to make Everdale a model for others to imitate had been futile. There was, he concluded, "no alternative to the public schools and . . . all our energies must go into changing that system".[13] In Vancouver Knowplace and the Drop-Out School of the sixties were replaced by the likes of Ideal School and City School operated by the Vancouver School Board. Now they are not called free schools but "alternatives". "Some of them", one observer noted, "are as free as a public school system could be expected to tolerate, others structured in an enlightened way". The same writer continued: "What is left of the free schools, what we have to thank [A.S.] Neill for, has been reduced to a very simple idea. Choice. We no longer need to accept the inflexible institutions of the fifties . . .; nor need we tolerate the ecstatic experiments of the sixties that produced so many unhappy illiterates. We have moved into the supermarket era: we can shop around for the right school for our children, and although the choice is limited, the concept is at least accepted".[14] Other school boards also attempted to establish "free schools" within the public system. Certainly, by mid-decade several aspects of "free school" practice were apparent in many "freer" Canadian elementary and secondary schools. Some of these very practices, ironically, were responsible for calling into being the back-to-the-basics movement with its contention that schools were no longer hard or rigid enough.

The most radical alternative of all was that proposed by the Jesuit thinker and educator, Ivan Illich — namely, to abolish schools altogether.[15] Illich, head of the Centre for International Documentation [CIDOC] at Cuernavaca, Mexico, flashed onto the Canadian scene in 1970 speaking to packed audiences right across the nation and reaching the attention of many Canadians through the pages of *Saturday Review, The New York Review of Books*, and *Weekend Magazine*. For him the greatest myth we operate under today is that schooling means education. This is not so, he asserted. Schools are harmful because they are compulsory, graded, competitive, and contribute to "job discrimination in favour of persons who have acquired their learning at a higher cost". Further, like all bureaucratic institutions created in the nineteenth century, schools suffered from basic paternalism. Illich saw schooling as a rite that functioned from the masses in much the same way as the church used to ("Alma mater has replaced Mother Church"). He identified the school as we know it, with its universality for children between five and sixteen, as an historical phenomenon dating from the last century. It may have been needed then, but since we have entered a new historical age, he argued, we have now outgrown the need for such an institution. Soon the school would be considered an "historical relic".

For two or three years the notion of "de-schooling society" captured the imagination of North American leftists, left liberals, and counter-cultural people. Then Illich too faded from the scene like a shooting star.[16] The whole idea of breaking up the public school system was much too radical a step to contemplate. In fact, the concept was downright revolutionary since it struck at the very heart of North American society. After all, the educational establishment in the United States was as big as the defense industry, and in Canada even bigger than the defense industry.

In the face of all these alternatives and the overall enthusiasm of their proponents and supporters, why did so little come of the reform ferment? For one thing the failure of the economy to fulfill its promises undercut the premises of an ever-expanding education system. Thus the affluence that allowed for "play" in the schools could not be sustained. Moreover, severe problems were posed by the very large pool of young people and older women entering the job market already shrunken by recession. Secondly, it could be seen in the late seventies that many reforms were merely superficial manipulations in any case — what Michael Katz has referred to as moving objects around in a box but not altering the box itself.[17] Thirdly, in some quarters there was failure to understand the nature of bureaucratic power. The bureaucracy was loath to share real decision-making power and therefore, although a great fuss was made about decentralization, important decisions still tended to be taken "downtown" and in the provincial capital. As one student of school bureaucracy has pointed out, "From the most cynical point of view, it is an old and usually brilliant trick of school people, like any bureaucrats, to dilute the strength of an attack by appearing to adopt the language of the enemy".[18] Fourthly, the very success of many reformist activities resulted in the co-opting of many activists. Finally, the media in both Canada and the United States had the effect of blowing out of proportion the limited number of people actually desiring educational change.

In Ontario one Cassandra, James Daly, a historian at McMaster University, in a book critical of the Hall-Dennis Report, predicted a day of reckoning, however, estimating, quite correctly as it turned out, that the recommendations of the Hall-Dennis Report would be terribly expensive to implement. He summed up the situation as follows: "There is always a discrepancy between what people expect and what they are willing to pay. Everyone wants more and more from government; fewer and fewer are willing to pay for it. To bathe in illusions of far greater expenditure, and to encourage the public to expect results, beyond the dreams of avarice, is to play with the future of the whole system. If people come to expect miracles, and see no sign of them, the result could be a subtle but massive growth of resentment which would deeply shake public confidence in the whole process of education".[19] In actual fact, we are very close today to such a lack of public confidence in the public schools.

To attempt to restore the schools' credibility, both British Columbia and Ontario announced new core curricula late in 1976.[20] Both were clearly political moves, both in the crass sense of currying favour with the public and in the sense of responding to public demands that something be done about the seeming chaos in public education. The BC booklet, complete with public "reaction sheet", expounded thirteen goals of the core curriculum. The first four set the tone for what followed: "to develop the skills of reading, writing, listening, and speaking." Primary students, for example, "should learn to print and write neatly and legibly" and "should learn to read and understand material written for children". How ironic after the excitement of the sixties that the teaching of basic human skills should become an innovation. Although studiously avoiding mention of reform and preferring instead adjectives such as "refined", "modified", and "improved" to describe his new curriculum, Ontario Education Minister Thomas Wells did, however, concede that: "We are now convinced that, in our enthusiasm for curriculum flexibility, we may have gone too far in decentralizing the responsibility for the preparation of the courses of study at the elementary and secondary levels. In championing the concept of local autonomy in curriculum development, I believe that we have relinquished to too great a degree the element of central direction and central expectations and standard of student achievement".[21] This was exactly what many parents wanted to hear: "back to the basics". Every student was to have a "well-rounded program, with the required subjects forming the foundation upon which optional subjects can be carefully chosen in the student's best interests".[22] Even the formerly militant provincial teachers' organizations fell into line without a whimper of protest. The Ontario Secondary School Teachers' Federation was quick to accord approval to the new departmental guidelines which presuppose less local autonomy and a much greater degree of centralized control over curriculum.[23]

One of the most startling revelations of the recent OECD Report on Education in Canada (1976) was the statement that "Canadian education policy may be one of the least 'politicized' in the world". "Indeed", the report continued, "it is as if the attempt has been made in this field since the beginning to avoid party-political controversy at any cost".[24] One need only peruse the various provincial Hansards to note how little political controversy is ever aroused in the area of educational policy. Exceptions are rare, as, for example, the occasional debates on whether public financing should be extended to separate and private schools. Political parties rarely make statements on specific educational matters, preferring instead to concentrate on questions of the most general nature and to convert education platform planks into motherhood statements. Demands for "quality education" and "back to the basics" tend never to be defined in specific terms. One slate of candidates for the Vancouver School Board in 1976 calling itself the Genuine Education Movement promised to "halt the alarming decline of literacy, the high instances of vandalism and the growing drug problem"[25] — all this without reference to a framework of general social policies presumably essential before schools could effectively offset such widespread social ills.

In the last two decades only Quebec's *revolution tranquille* was a case where intense politicization of most aspects of that province's social life was subsequently reflected in fundamental educational changes. These reforms came in the train of the Parent Commission Report (1961-5), which deliberately sought to link education with the deep economic, political, and cultural changes going on in Quebec life. Elsewhere in Canada, as the OECD Report concludes, "reforms in education are almost totally pragmatic, or so generally conceived and relying so heavily on United States, British, and French models, more or less adapted to Canadian conditions, that the opportunity for party political conflict is, for all practical purposes, excluded".[26] The absence of open political controversy, of course, lends support to the perpetuation of the *status quo*, of what Hugh Stevenson calls the "business as usual" syndrome.[27] A sharpening of political party debate about public education would, on the other hand, improve the level of public discussion and force governing parties to take a closer and harder look at the bases for educational policy decisions. If politicians and educational policy-makers and bureaucrats are unwilling to engage in debate over fundamental policy issues in education, then planning for alternative futures is unlikely to take place. In the absence of a future orientation to educational policy-making, the future of education is likely to be pretty much like the present, or in other words to see a continuation of "business as usual".

Concluding that Canada has experienced a predominantly unplanned development within and beyond education, the OECD examiners caution that the past fortuitous outcomes of this lack of planning may not persist down the road. The fact that most things have gone along well to date has lulled Canadians into a certain smugness about the likelihood of continued future happiness. For the examiners, however, the absence of an "explicitly-stated, overall conception of the country's interests" seems "intolerable".[28] Of course, they seem to have overlooked or underplayed the simple historical fact that education is a provincial matter by the BNA Act and almost certain for various reasons to remain subject to provincial jurisdiction. It is hard to imagine the federal government playing an any more obvious role in public education than it now does. Various provinces, and not just Quebec, are jealous of their control over education and unlikely to concede a stronger hand to Ottawa. This is especially true when increased decentralization seems a probable solution to the threat of Quebec separation and to general Western Canadian alienation. The likelihood of effecting a "fit" between ten different education systems and the federal government's version of the country's national interests seems very remote indeed. Nonetheless, the political leadership which the report urges could conceivably be found at the provincial level. After all, what is at issue in this regard is not so much the political and economic future of the nation but hard-nosed measures designed to offset the severe public backlash against future educational development in Canada.

The reformers of the sixties who seemed to have caught wind of that period's exhilarating mood of change were to find by the turn of the decade that the formerly prevailing wind was coming from a decidedly less favourable direction. Retrenchment became the order of the day. From a point where there seemed to be money for buildings, teachers' salaries, educational research and development, and such like, all of a sudden the well seemed to have run dry. The excitement of the late sixties was replaced by an atmosphere of disillusionment.[29] The change was partly a result of concern over rising costs but much more so a growing sense that education had failed to live up to the extravagant promises made for it in the previous decade. Crime and vandalism were on the increase especially in metropolitan areas. The "drug problem", if anything, had expanded, seeping down into elementary schools and becoming acceptable at fashionable middle-class parties. Venereal disease was said to be near epidemic proportions. Divorce rates were doubling and common-law marriages were becoming more and more common. Where would it all end? The wisecrack, "Is nothing sacred?" was no longer funny; it had become a serious question. The feeling of despair must have matched that of educational reformers at the turn of the century when even after a full generation of free, universal, and compulsory schooling, it was patently clear to every thinking Canadian that the nation was coming apart at the seams.

Clearly schools have not delivered on the promises of the sixties. Despite this fact, youngsters continue to stay in school well beyond school leaving age and faith in education persists among parents convinced that, as usual, only curriculum changes are necessary to restore merit and value to education. "Back to the basics" has become genuine *cri de coeur* for many parents. They tend to associate a formal, ordered structured mode of teaching with the "basics" and recoil at the supposed permissiveness of the public schools. They believe that once attained, this policy will effect miraculous change for the better. Such advocates remain, consciously or not, completely oblivious to a permanent scarcity of work in the "post-industrial" age. As Lazerson and Dunn make abundantly clear, unemployment and underemployment cannot be solved by resort to more or different schooling. "The essential problem", they stress, "is not the supply of workers, but the demand for them". Yet there is little sign that any province or the federal government are attempting to make some sort of innovative adjustment to this situation which now seems permanent.

Perhaps the main educational question facing Canadians today can be reduced to this: Is education to be seen primarily in terms of its cultural or its economic benefits? A decade ago I wrote an article critical of the vocational orientation of Ontario's educational system. I objected to this trend because I felt it prevented schools from "educating" in the traditional sense of the term, from emphasizing individual social and cultural objectives for a society where leisure activities were bound to be more important than in the past.[30] I considered then and still believe the "investment in human capital" dogma to be misplaced. But is there currently a recognizable philosophy of education in any provincial ministry of education? The core curricula of both British Columbia and Ontario, while speaking interminably about goals, have nothing to say about the philosophy underlying those goals.[31]

Notes

The preparation of this article was greatly assisted by the comments of my colleagues William Bruneau and Marvin Lazerson at the University of British Columbia.

[1]*Vancouver Sun*, 4 Nov. 1976.

[2]"Expenditures on Education, Selected Years", in Organization for Economic Co-operation and Development, *Reviews of National Policies for Education: Canada* (Paris 1976), 28 [hereafter OECD Report, *Canada*].

[3]*Ibid.*, 29.

[4]Alexander Lockhart, "Educational Policy Development in Canada: A Critique of the Past and a Case for the Future", in Richard Carlton, Louise Colley, and Neil MacKinnon, eds., *Education, Change and Society* (Toronto 1977), 80.

[5]David Munroe, *The Organization and Administration of Education in Canada* (Ottawa 1974), 212.

[6]OECD Report, *Canada*, 23.

[7]*Globe and Mail* (Toronto), 11 Nov. 1971. Reprinted in H.A. Stevenson, R.M. Stamp, and J.D. Wilson, eds., *The Best of Times, The Worst of Times: Contemporary Issues in Canadian Education* (Toronto 1972), 309-11.

[8]See, for example, Robert M. Stamp, "Let's Abolish School Boundaries", *Alberta Teachers' Association Magazine*, LI, 1, Sept.-Oct. 1970, 38-9. Reprinted in *Best of Times*, 436-8.

[9]Stevenson, Stamp, and Wilson, eds., *Best of Times,* 438.

[10]R.M. Stamp, *About Schools: What Every Canadian Parent Should Know* (Don Mills 1975).

[11]See, for example, Theodore R. Sizer, "The Case for a Free Market", *Saturday Review,* 11 Jan. 1969. Reprinted in *Best of Times*, 480-6.

[12]Tom Durrie, Introduction to "Free Schools: Threat to the System or Harmless Lunatic Fringe?" (fall 1971) in *Best of Times*, 474.

[13]"Where Have all the Free Schools Gone?" in Douglas Myers, ed., *The Failure of Educational Reform* (Toronto 1973), 90.

[14]Audrey Grescoe, "Working Classrooms: Alternative Education in Vancouver", *Vancouver*, IX, 1, Jan. 1976, 24-5.

[15]Ivan Illich, *Deschooling Society* (New York 1971).

[16]It is noteworthy that by mid-decade Illich was back in the limelight thanks to the controversy sparked by a book which opened with the statement, 'The medical establishment has become a major threat to health'. *Medical Nemesis: The Expropriation of Health* (Toronto 1975).

[17]Michael B. Katz, "Class, Bureaucracy and Schools", in Myers, ed., *Failure of Educational Reform*, 20.

[18]Katz, "Review of *Radical School Reform*", in *Best of Times*, 455. See also Clarence J. Karier, "Elite Views on American Education", in Walter Laqueur and George Mosse, eds., *Education and Social Structure in the Twentieth Century* (New York 1967), 150-1.

[19]James Daly, *Education or Molasses? A Critical Look at the Hall-Dennis Report* (Ancaster 1969), 73.

[20]B.C. Ministry of Education, *What Should Our Children Be Learning?* (Victoria 1976); Ontario Ministry of Education, *The New Core Curriculum in Secondary Schools* (Toronto 1976).

[21]Thomas L. Wells, "Major Change in Curriculum Development". Address to Ontario Association for Curriculum Development, 12 Nov. 1976.

[22]Ontario, *The New Core Curriculum* (pamphlet).

[23]*Globe and Mail*, 15 November 1976.

[24]OECD Report, *Canada*, 19.

[25]Election brochure for the NPA, Vancouver, Nov. 1976.

[26]OECD Report, *Canada*, 19.

[27]Hugh A. Stevenson, "Public Education: A Choice for the Future". Address to Ontario Association of Education Administrative Officials, 28 Oct. 1976, 5.

[28]OECD Report, *Canada*, 21.

[29]Hugh A. Stevenson, "Public and Professional Disenchantment: The Spectre of a New Crisis in Canadian Education", *Lakehead University Review*, IV, 2, 1971, 83-99.

[30]J. Donald Wilson, "Vocationalism in Education: Some Comments from Ontario", *Journal of Educational Thought,* II, 2, Aug. 1968, 91-6. Reprinted in *Best of Times*, 274-9.

[31]The consistent "ad hockery" of Ontario's educational system — "the lack of planning associated with specific goals" — is clearly set forth by Walter Pitman in "The Big Blue Schoolhouse: The Davis Era in Ontario Education", in Myers, ed., *Failure of Educational Reform*, 147-8, 155.

Multiculturalism and Canadian National Identity:
The Alberta Experience*

Manoly R. Lupul

Notwithstanding the fact that the government of Manitoba was the first to subsidize a province-wide multicultural conference,[1] today the province of Alberta probably leads in implementing the many facets of a comprehensive multicultural policy. The introduction of "A New Cultural Policy For the Province of Alberta" by the former premier, Harry E. Strom, at the Alberta Multicultural Conference on July 16, 1971,[2] was undoubtedly an important first step, but the Lougheed administration's own high regard for multiculturalism as state policy has been demonstrated in several significant ways.

The appointment of Mr. Horst A. Schmidt, a first-generation Canadian of German (Bavarian) background, as Minister of Culture, Youth and Recreation was most fortunate, for his dedication to multiculturalism has been as unequivocal as his infectious humor and penchant for hard work. By June 17, 1972, the new minister had organized "The Alberta Cultural Heritage Conference," a kind of parliament of ethno-cultural groups approximately three times the size of the earlier conference. In keeping with the Conference's recommendations, *Heritage*, a folksy bi-monthly publication strong on historical vignettes, appeared (January-February 1973); an Alberta Cultural Heritage Council consisting of approximately sixty-five members designated by the ethno-cultural groups and fifteen appointed by the minister was organized (October 1973); a director of the Cultural Heritage Branch (Mr. Orest Kruhlak) was appointed (September 1974); and a monthly "Bulletin" to facilitate communication for the above-named Council was issued (March 1975).

The usual grants have been made available for a great variety of cultural projects, including a study of how Edmonton's multicultural heritage might best be represented in Fort Edmonton Park, the city's future historical showcase. But probably the most significant, and certainly the most unique, grant was the $150,000 given by the Department of Education (with the Department of Culture fully informed) for a three-year Ukrainian-English bilingual program which began in September 1974 in Edmonton's public and separate school systems with approximately 115 pupils,[3] and more than twice that number a year later. Although supported for the time being as a pilot project, the response of the parents has been so favorable and the fluency in Ukrainian

---

*From Alf Chaiton and Neil McDonald (eds.), *Canadian Schools and Canadian Identity* (Toronto: Gage, 1977), pp. 105-175. Reproduced with permission.

209

acquired by the pupils so gratifying that there is no doubt that enrolments will continue to rise and that the program will be extended beyond Grade three. In June 1975 the federal Government, through its multicultural program, made $56,605 available to the Department of Education through the Ukrainian Canadian Professional and Business Federation for the publication of the five-booklet language development series which the Department has prepared for use in Ukrainian bilingual classes in Grade two. The Federation, it should be clear, obtained more than money. It led the way in bringing about the much-needed dialogue between federal and provincial officials in the vital field of education as it affects multiculturalism. The major breakthrough has made similar funds available to other ethno-cultural groups prepared to embark upon a serious program of bilingual education with fluency as the ultimate goal — and such initiatives as will it is hoped, emerge, for other bilingual combinations will have profound implications for Canada's identity as a multicultural and bilingual nation.

It is not possible to say what definition of either term the government of Alberta espouses. To the writer, who has been deeply involved in the Ukrainian bilingual movement, the two terms carry meanings which define Canada's national identity without excluding any of its many peoples. Thus, outside the province of Quebec, bilingualism refers to all languages other than English. In Alberta French is a second language, but so is Polish, German, Ukrainian, or Cree. To many, this is a controversial definition because bilingualism is automatically associated with French. In the writer's view, this is an overly simplistic approach to the subject. A bilingual Canada is a desirable goal, but neither bilingualism nor multiculturalism will amount to much until they are seen as umbrellas embracing the whole country with the application of each varying specifically from region to region according to how the people themselves perceive their needs. To think otherwise is to render meaningless such oft-repeated statements as 'No one in Canada will be forced to learn French' or, for that matter, 'No one in Canada will be forced to learn English.'

The world knows that Canada is a land of immigrants and their descendants. It should also come to understand that because of this a Canadian today is someone who (unlike the essentially unilingual American) is likely to be able to speak more than one language: English-French, but not necessarily English-French. Nothing would do more to give Canada that most illusive and much-sought goal - a distinctive national identity. Most Canadians also realize that Canada is a land of minorities, but what very few seem to appreciate is that all minorities stand or fall together. Nor does the important Official Languages Act change the situation, for the Act does not make the French minority an official minority; nor does it make French an official language of communication without restriction:

> The English and French languages are the official languages of Canada for
> all purposes of the Parliament and Government of Canada, and possess and

enjoy equality of status and equal rights and privileges as to their use in all the institutions of the Parliament and Government of Canada.[4]

Thus, the Official Languages Act recognizes French as a language of communication within the federal Government and the agencies of the federal administration. The Act gives French Canadians the opportunity to communicate with the federal Government in French from coast to coast. Of necessity, outside Quebec all other communication will have to be in English most of the time. This is not a reason for rejoicing, but facts cannot be ignored. If the French had settled the Prairies and British Columbia in greater numbers in the nineteenth century, the situation today would be very different, and there would be no room to speak of English-Polish, English-German, English-Ukrainian, or English-Cree bilingualism. But whose fault is it that French-Canadians preferred New England to western Canada? Demographic realities simply cannot be ignored or dismissed. We have done that for far too long in the province of Quebec by making English the main language of work, and we all know the bitterness in Canada. Yet that is just what we will get if we grant that individuals can be bilingual in different ways but at the same time insist that French-speaking Canadians who speak English and English-speaking Canadians who speak French are 'official' bilingual persons.

The second term, multiculturalism, is far less controversial because to date very few have tried to define it. Yet once the attempt is made not only is the task difficult, but controversy too readily emerges. Most Canadians probably realize that multiculturalism is today's equivalent for two older terms, 'mosaic.' which had wide currency between the two world wars, and 'cultural pluralism,' a term very popular since the second world war. Multiculturalism, then, is associated with pluralism, diversity, and variety, which, it is confidently maintained, are the essence of Canada's national identity. Besides mosaic, various other symbols have been advanced to express this plurality: flower garden, rainbow, cathedral, tapestry, the sun streaming through stained-glass windows, and the much more pedestrian vegetable soup and fruit salad. The symbols need not detain us; what is significant is the relationship between the variety of cultures and Canada's identity as a nation.

Canada, we have recently been told by Prime Minister Trudeau, has no official culture[5]; its culture, then, is in the process of evolution, definition, or formation. Clearly creativity is involved - and what becomes important is the source or basis of that creativity. The writer's approach, recently reflected in the first annual report of the Canadian Consultative Council on Multiculturalism,[6] may appear deceptively simple and it may even be wrong, but it can be stated in one word: ethnicity. In ethnicity or in our ancestral roots as exemplified in Canada's successive immigrations lies the well-spring of a distinctive Canadian identity, if multiculturalism is to be the essence of that identity. But — and this is the crucial point — the emphasis must be on ethnicity as a well-spring, as a point of departure for creativity. To cultivate ethnicity for its own sake, as ethno-cultural groups have been doing in an atmosphere largely hostile to ethnicity, is to freeze ancestral ways into forms which can never thrive on Canadian soil because they have been transplanted from their original, relatively isolated milieu (frequently peasant or peasant-based) into one of large homesteads, rapid transportation, quick communication, growing urbanization, and the pressure of competing values. But properly understood and encouraged, Ukrainian culture, for example, can release the creativity of discriminating, bi-cultural individuals who will then blend selective aspects of Anglo-American society with the feelings, attitudes, and impulses rooted in ethnicity into cultural forms which will be distinctively Canadian: Multiculturalism, then, is the development of a consciousness of one's ancestral roots or ethnicity for creative purposes to the end that a distinctive Canadian identity will emerge which is neither wholly European nor wholly North American but which incorporates elements of both. It seems obvious that the better one understands the ancestral language, the deeper will be the understanding of one's ancestral culture, and the stronger will be the creative base for the talent that exists.

The emphasis on creativity as the core of multiculturalism is an emphasis on cultural development as distinct from cultural preservation. In the past, ethno-cultural groups have been encouraged (even forced) to stress mainly preservation and the result has been much alienation of the young, who cannot readily identify with norms, institutions, and customs imported from other parts of the world. As a result, today the survival in Canada of groups as strong as the Ukrainians or the Indians, or even the French is seriously in doubt. The key to continuity is immersion in, for example, Ukrainian culture, including the language, not for the sake of Ukrainian culture but for the creative springboard Ukrainian culture can provide for the development of a distinctive Canadian identity. And language is important if the classridden nuances or the juxtaposition of humor and pathos in such operettas as "Natalka Poltavka" or "Zaporozh za Dunayem," or the inspiring sentiments of Shevchenko's "Zapovit" are not to be missed. Literal translations like Ilia Kiriak's *Sons of the Soil* are poor substitutes, though they are infinitely better than the strained versions of the 1930's provided by such well-intentioned persons as John Murray Gibbon."

The definition of multiculturalism presented above is undoubtedly a difficult one. It is one in which very few Canadians can really share except vicariously through financial contributions because it entails the cultivation of artistic talent, which is in the main hereditary. Yet, until we come to a full realizaiton of what is required to make multiculturalism a truly viable alternative for Canada — instead of just a cliché or slogan — we are doomed to equate the stimulus for the creation of a distinctive Canadian identity for the identity itself. This may give dances like the Ukrainian "hopak" a temporary reprieve but the "hopak" can never be part of Canada's identity any more than can the highland fling, which belongs to Scotland. The Canadian equivalent of the highland fling is the reel — a square dance — and the goal of learning the "hopak" is to incorporate its tempo and spirit into some such art form as the ballet, with or without the Ukrainian dress (depending on the theme). Here "Fiddler on the Roof" is a case in point. Its Jewish character is as unmistakable as the appeal of its tuneful American music. Another example are the paintings of Alberta's William Kurelek, which so poignantly express the joys, the sorrows, and the struggles of the Ukrainian spirit in the Canadian environment. No one unfamiliar with Ukrainian culture and the Ukrainian psyche — which presupposes a knowledge of the language — can do the Ukrainian-Canadian experience justice. And without the experience of Ukrainians and others like them — without taking into account the experience of all the peoples who have developed Canada — what can the Canadian experience (and by implication Canada's identity) be?

Languages like Ukrainian thus emerge as the entrance points to the development of a distinctive Canadian identity which we may term multiculturalism. But this multiculturalism must be meaningful — neither an exotic and curious nor sentimental preoccupation with static or frozen relics of the past but a living, creative source of Canadian art forms and Canadian values. Hence the importance of a broad or liberal understanding of bilingualism in Canada and the significance of Edmonton's Ukrainian bilingual elementary school program referred to earlier.

What are some of the more specific implications of this approach to multiculturalism for Canadians in general? Among the most significant, several affect the school. Students, for example, need to explore concepts like mosaic or tapestry for their meaning in concrete or specific terms. At present they merely mouth slogans like "Canada is a mosaic and not a melting pot like the United States." That is not good enough. The meaning of such terms and the reality behind them needs to be examined. What is a melting pot, and who says Canada is not one? Is the United States with its large pockets of Germans in Milwaukee, Poles in Chicago, Jews and Italians in New York, Irish in Boston, and Chinese in San Francisco really a melting pot? In what sense?

Another cliché which students need to examine is cultural pluralism. Paens have been and are still sung to it by scholars, intellectuals, and politicians, but the reference points are primarily religious and political. That is, we are all free to worship and to vote as we please, but the pluralism rooted in ethnicity and thus the pluralism of language is ignored in the hope that it will somehow go away. And thus a self-fulfilling prophecy is set in motion, for what the opinion-makers ignore the young tend to discard. Little wonder that ethnicity as a source of cultural creativity has had so little currency in our society.

The sources of creativity are of course many, but why should ethnicity be ignored? Is it because reference to ancestral customs or practices associated with the rites and high-feast days of life, which invariably require at least a passing acquaintance with the language and history of a group, may prove embarrassing to our largest minorities by revealing the overt and subtle ravages of Anglo-conformity — the cultural remnants with their badly battered linguistic bases, the poorly understood folkways, scraps in the personal or private lives of 'nationalistic,' 'old-fashioned,' or just plain unwanted human beings? In short, will exploration reveal what can be termed truncated multiculturalism — a multiculturalism defined in the 1920's and 1930's and confined to folk dancing, native costumes, special foods, handicrafts, decorative arts such as Easter egg painting, instrumental music or even folk songs (including Christmas carols) with atrocious English translations or adaptations.

All students (not just those who study second languages) need also to learn a good deal more about the peoples who have come to Canada, including the dreadful manner in which some immigrants were and are still received and most were and are still being exploited. We admire the pioneer, but the bigotry and racial pecking order inspired by the theory of Anglo-conformity is never mentioned.[9] Yet, like the melting pot which continues to simmer, the effects of Anglo-conformity are still very much with us. Thus the Anglo-Celtic is still at the top[10] and others who have come to Canada and are still ranked roughly according to their distance from London, England, the centre of 'civilization.' Accordingly, the French from Normandy and Brittany, the Protestant Belgians, the Scandinavians along with the Protestant Germans and Swiss are the best immigrants of all, infinitely superior to all peoples from southern, central or eastern Europe. Among the latter, Czechs are better than Slovaks, and Czechoslovaks are better than Poles, Romanians, Bulgarians, or Hungarians. The last four in turn are better than Ukrainians, but being white the Ukrainians are much more desirable than the Hindus, who have generally been at the bottom, and the African Blacks, who have not counted at all. The Native peoples, over whose entry only God presumably presided, have been somewhere near the bottom, together with the lighter-skinned colored people like the Japanese, Chinese and Gypsies.

In bringing the facts of John Porter's *Vertical Mosaic* into the classroom, we must get rid of what may be termed 'the contributions approach,' so popular with the Canadian Citizenship Branch and the United Nations clubs. This approach is full of name-dropping and statistics, with the emphasis on politicians, scholars, and oat kings. The best adult example, on which much school material is modelled, is *The Canadian Family Tree*, which came out in 1967 and is now being up-dated for a second printing. The weakness of the 'contributions approach' is that it ignores such basic questions as the following:

> How did the various peoples and their children fare in Canada? What were their main occupations, and how much has that changed? What specific problems did they pose for Canada? What problems, in turn, did Canada pose for them? What problems do each still pose for one another? What were their cultural and linguistic aspirations and how well have they been realized? In what ways have they helped to develop a distinctive Canadian identity? Were their efforts encouraged by the Anglo-Celtics and French?

How? Could each generation have done more if their languages had been given the same encouragement as their handicrafts, folk dances, and cooking? Why is no attention paid to the cultures (including the languages) of Canada's 'other' peoples when the crisis of Canadian culture and identity is discussed? Will the glib assumption that progress is being made and time will take care of the rest suffice? "Since large-scale immigration ceased in 1930," according to Lower and Chafe,[11] " the various peoples of our country have been settling down together and the process by which the newcomer becomes a citizen and a Canadian has been speeded up." Speeded up in what direction? In short, what is the content of the Canadianism being 'absorbed'? . . . Some of Canada's 'other' peoples have always been more visible than others; who have they been and why have they stood out?[12]

Another specific implication of multiculturalism for Canada's national identity is the study of Canada's immigration policies not only for their racism, but also for the peculiar predicaments which certain groups already in Canada face. For example, the Latvians, Lithuanians, Estonians, Ukrainians, the Native peoples and the French in Canada share a predicament peculiar to themselves. Other peoples in Canada — whether Norwegians, Germans, or Bulgarians — do not much care about the fortunes of their language past the second generation. Most, in fact, are quite prepared to disappear in Canada because abroad their ancestral cultures and languages are secure. The Native peoples, the Ukrainians, the Baltic peoples, and the French Canadians are not so fortunate: the Native peoples because they are the indigenous peoples and have no ancestral culture overseas; the Ukrainians and Baltic peoples because their culture and language overseas is behind the high walls of the Soviet border where both are subjected to direct and indirect processes of unrelenting Russification; and the French Canadians because their culture and language in Quebec are being subjected to similar processes of Anglo-Americanization.

Canadians must come to understand the above situation for several reasons. The first, and most important, is psychological. Presently, besides the Anglo-Celtics, most offspring of German or Scandinavian background (two of the largest groups in Canada) also have little sympathy for peers descended from nationalities who live with the constant threat of potential extinction. Among Anglo-Celtic, German, and Scandinavian offspring is to be found the most pronounced impatience with all who emerge as hyphenated Canadians. Our schools must teach that at least *some* people in Canada have no choice but to remain hyphenated Canadians. Our schools must teach why certain groups continue to cultivate organizations and activities which differ from the norm — why they attempt to exert political pressure through briefs or even bloc voting and why they continue to follow European developments closely or are even reluctant to participate in activities in Canada (such as multicultural centres) which are likely to accelerate the galloping forces of assimilation. Schools which encourage such understanding among the young will have a powerful effect on children who come from homes which have to live with predicaments they cannot easily escape. The main effect on 'the peculiar' young will be to feel less peculiar and become more comfortable about the activities which are important to their parents and thus more willing to assume the concerns of their parents. The maintenance of a second language, it must be strongly underlined, usually takes first place among these concerns, and the efforts in this respect among some families are truly prodigious. Needless to say, these efforts would be greatly strengthened if the young of what may be termed the non-beleaguered groups in Canada understood not only how the learning of second languages contributes to the development of a distinctive Canadian identity, but also how language enjoys practically a holy status in the eyes of some distraught groups who, unlike the majority of Canada's peoples, simply cannot afford to become , in the glib phrase of the uninformed, 'Canadians pure and simple.' They must remain hyphenated Canadians or through linguicide risk genocide.

This leads directly to still another implication. Two main groups have been singled out. The majority who like to see themselves as 'pure' Canadians and either ignore multiculturalism and comparable terms or through lip-service bring them down to the level of slogans and clichés; and the minority who believe in multiculturalism and the importance of ancestral backgrounds and ethnic roots. Neither group, however, will amount to much without attention to the economic soil in which each is supposed to grow. A curriculum which does not give the young the opportunity to examine the content of 'pure' Canadianism and multiculturalism is bad enough; but a curriculum which does so in the same economic vacuum in which most governments have been promoting the policy of multiculturalism is largely a waste of time. It has already been stated that Quebec feels beleaguered by Anglo-Americanization. If the French Canadians with their strong demographic base in Quebec and decades of cultural evolution find it difficult to withstand the pressures of Anglo-American culture, what chance have other ethnic groups with non-existent or much weaker linguistic bases? Yet the American empire grows and grows in Canada, and American values and ways of doing things capture the young so effectively as to practically mock all talk about developing a distinctive identity for Canada through multiculturalism. The Americanization of Canada was bad enough before the era of massive American investment; since the latter, one wonders whether there is any hope at all for the emergence of a distinctive Canadian identity. Certainly judging by the attitude one frequently encounters in places like Calgary towards multiculturalism and bilingualism, there is little room for optimism.

The next implication is irresistible, for it follows naturally from much that has been said above. The schools must give far more attention to the fine arts and other humanities, especially at the junior and senior high school levels, where they are now largely options. This may well be our greatest challenge in developing a distinctive national identity, for North America with its numerous opportunities for growing rich has encouraged education for marketable skills, and that always with an emphasis on mass production. As a result, we have not placed a high value on developing creative artists. Singers, composers, poets, writers, etc. have had to fend for themselves with predictable results. Artistic talents have been subordinated to numerous dull and prosaic careers as librarians, university professors and school teachers, factory and office workers, and department store clerks. Youngsters have generally been encouraged to pursue the equally dull but well-paying professions. Only a few — a very odd few — have pursued the fine arts, literature, philosophy, and the social sciences where the techniques (and perhaps even the products) of creativity are best exemplified. This is particularly true among children of ethnic groups where the sheer struggle for existence still commands first place - as it must always among those low in the socio-economic scale. This puts more of a burden than ever on those concerned about the bases of creativity, for the poor can feel ethnicity as easily as the rich, and the poor can be as talented as the rich. Expose the ethnically-conscious, talented poor to humanistic studies and these studies become the pathway to riches, for the poor can comment with rare depth about life and in this very commentary reveal important aspects of the emerging Canadian identity, as in Mordecai Richler's *The Apprenticeship of Duddy Kravitz*

It should be obvious that the implications of multiculturalism outlined above, if taken seriously, should greatly ease the burden of second language learning — and, although the situation in Alberta is yet far from perfect, the fact that Ukrainian as a language of instruction in the elementary grades is used as much as possible in a cultural context, with specific reference to customs, the arts, history, and literature, is most encouraging. Since 1971, Grade Ten social studies has given the better teachers ample opportunity to treat sympathetically the tragedy of cultural disintegration and the intriguing process of adaptation and modification which is always a part of the Canadianization process.[13] Important for the future would be to saturate the curriculum at the elementary school level with facts about Canada's peoples from many lands in English or (in Quebec) in French and English in order to arouse the curiosity of the young about the nature of the languages spoken today. In short, the multicultural horse must be placed before the language cart to encourage second-language learning. There has been far too much talk about language and language learning in Canada and far too little talk about the people who speak or spoke the languages and the significance for culture and national identity of spoken languages.

But whether it be the aspects of a people's culture or their language, the study of both should begin early — at the pre-school level in play schools and kindergartens wherever possible. This is what the French, the Cree Indians, and the Ukrainians in Edmonton are attempting to introduce at the present time. Progress in the kindergartens and in the elementary classes has exceeded all expectations. The play school dimension has still to be developed and, to some extent, the much needed improvement in the study of second languages at the junior and senior high school levels has taken second place to developments in the lower grades. However, bilingualism to the point of fluency can only be built on solid foundations and, once accomplished, the skill and understanding acquired will revitalize the work in senior classes. In the meantime, it is well to remember that the key to bilingualism is multiculturalism and both together, liberally understood and applied, are the keys to the development of a distinctive identity for Canada. But the task is momentous and time is fleeting.

Notes

[1] *Report of Manitoba Congress, October 13-17, 1970, Manitoba* (Winnipeg: University of Manitoba, Extension Division, 1970).

[2] *A New Cultural Policy For the Province of Alberta* (Edmonton: Queen's Printer, 1971).

[3] For details see M. Lupul and P. Savaryn, "The Politics of English- Ukrainian Bilingualism in Alberta," *Ukrainian Canadian Review 1974* (Edmonton Ukrainian Canadian Professional and Business Federation, 1975), pp. 18-22.

[4] *Statutes of Canada*, 17-18 Eliz. II, s. 2 (1968-69, second session).

[5] *House of Commons Debates*, 1971, col. 8545.

[6] *First Annual Report of the Canadian Consultative Council on Multiculturalism* (Ottawa: Queen's Printer, 1975), pp. 4-12.

[7] Ilia Kiriak, *Sons of the Soil* (Toronto: Ryerson, 1959).

[8] J.M. Gibbon, *Canadian Mosaic: The Making of a Northern Nation* (Toronto: McClelland & Stewart, 1938).

[9] For an historically confined but thorough study of the subject, see H. Plamer, "Responses to Foreign Immigration: Nativism and Ethnic Tolerance in Alberta, 1880-1920" (unpublished Master's thesis, University of Alberta, 1971).

[10] See, for example, M.C. Cohen, "McTavish: An Underside Perspective of Canada's Smug Majority," *Star* (Toronto), May 1, 1971.

[11] A.R.M. Lower and J.W. Chafe, *Canada — A Nation: And How It Came to Be* (2nd rev. ed., Toronto, New York, London: Longmans, Green, 1958), p. 433.

[12] M.R. Lupul, "The Portrayal of Canada's 'Other' Peoples in Senior High School History and Social Studies Textbooks in Alberta, 1905 to the Present," *The Alberta Journal of Educational Research* Vol. xxii (1), (March, 1976), 1-33.

[13] *Senior High School Curriculum Guide for Social Studies* (Province of Alberta: Department of Education, 1971), pp. 28-30.

Education and Equality in Canada

John Rowland Young

One of the most striking features of Canadian society is the great disparity which exists in its reward structure and the consequent vast inequalities in the distribution of 'tangible goods' among its members. These 'tangible goods' include such realities as health, disposable income, education, social privileges and, most importantly, the power to influence others. Also striking is the fact that these goods are not allocated independently of each other. That is, those who possess most of one usually possess most of the others. This differential allocating of rewards leads to what is known as a stratification system in which Canadians are grouped according to the share of the rewards they have at their disposal as the outcome of their participation.

Not everyone feels that these inequalities are necessarily bad for the country. Indeed some feel that inequalities are inevitable and even necessary to maintain a high level of motivation. On the other hand, there are those who oppose inequalities because they are seen as an affront to the basic principles of justice and humanity, or because pronounced inequalities lead to crime, apathy and other social disorders which threaten the *status quo*. Consequently, various theories of stratification have been developed to explain and justify this inequality. The theory chosen to explain inequalities is to a degree determined by one's assumptions about human nature, the most desirable goals to which society should aspire, and what are reasonable financial or social costs to bring about desirable change. However, if one assumes that Canada as a whole will benefit from the most effective utilization of talent of the largest number of people, regardless of where this talent is found in the stratification system or occupational structure, then it is clear that talent wastage is negatively affecting all of its citizens, either directly or indirectly.

In Canada, the determining factors which are associated with the stratification system are class, region, race and ethnicity, religion, and sex. John Porter's[1] classic study of Canadian society showed that the elite (i.e. those who have most access to the greatest rewards of society and are thus at the top of the stratification system) is composed of individuals with relatively similar backgrounds. Furthermore, Clement's[2] more recent study indicates that in the twenty years following Porter's initial work there has been little change in the composition of the higher strata of Canadian society. Mobility, either upward or downward, is more the exception than the rule.

If we look at a particular social phenomenon at the lower end of the stratification system, such as poverty, we find that again the aforementioned factors. It is important to remember that when we are talking about poverty we must see it as a relative condition and not as an absolute condition. Poverty in Canada would be quite different in an absolute sense than poverty in India. Using relatively conservative estimates, the Economic Council of Canada and the Senate Report on Poverty claim that more than one in five Canadians live in poverty. However, the chance of being in this category of poverty is not randomly distributed. Those Canadians most prone to poverty are those who are female, less educated, resident in the Maritime provinces, rural, over the age of 65, single parents, and/or Native Canadians. Contrary to popular belief the majority of the poor are not on some form of social assistance, but rather work at jobs which keep them below the poverty line or are on some form of pension, which we tend to think of as a just reward for years of service. For example, according to the National Council of Welfare,[3] 66% of the total poor in the province of Alberta are working poor.

As we are focussing on the relationship between the educational system and inequality, it is perhaps most pertinent to look at children in poverty. Most Canadians would like to believe that all children are born with equal opportunities to achieve as much as their abilities allow them. However, the realities are not so kind. Poverty has a devastating effect on children. Specifically:

> To be born poor is to face a greater likelihood of ill health — in infancy, in childhood and throughout your adult life. To be born poor is to face a lesser likelihood that you will finish high school; lesser still that you will attend university. To be born poor is to face a greater likelihood that you will be judged a delinquent in adolescence and, if so, a greater likelihood that you will be sent to a "correctional institution". To be born poor is to have the deck stacked against you at birth, to find life an uphill struggle ever after.[4]

What role does education play in either creating these structural inequalities or bringing about their demise? If one looks at the educational objectives as stated by departments of education of the various provinces in Canada, one is made constantly aware of a recurrent theme — namely that of equality of educational opportunity. Although it is stated in many different ways it boils down to the assumption that in Canada children, regardless of their class origin, sex, religion, ethnicity or physical location are to be given an equal opportunity to make the greatest possible use of their talents in school at all levels. It is further assumed, if not overtly stated, that it is the educational institution over all others that has the greatest possibility to alleviate social inequalities. This has almost reached the level of an article of faith among many Canadians. As Manzer states, the basic assumption guiding those in power is that

> opportunity to secure educational advantages based on a person's ability to profit from them must be regarded as one of the most important parts of the opportunity structure of an advanced industrialized society.[5]

However, if there is general agreement as to the desirability of fostering equality in society, there is less agreement as to whether this should take the form of equality of condition or equality of opportunity. Porter differentiates between the two possibilities in the following manner:

> Equality of condition . . . implies that whatever 'is valued' as good in the society — material resources, health, personal development, leisure — should be distributed among all the members of society in relatively the same amounts regardless of the social position which one occupies. Equality of opportunity on the other hand, implies a society in which resources are distributed unequally — as indeed has been the historical experience — but in which access to the structured inequality should be open to all without regard to the individual's social class origins, their parental resources, their religious affiliations and, in more contemporary discussions, their membership in minority groups or their sex.[6]

In Canada, the principle of equality of condition has not been embraced to any degree, other than in such alternate social groups as the Hutterites. The principle of equality of opportunity, on the other hand, has been an important part of the general liberal ideology which has influenced the development of public education in the past one hundred years. The guiding principle has been the assumption that education would provide equal opportunities for all individuals to achieve whatever position in society they desire through the use of their abilities and motivation. In other words, every child should have the opportunity to make fullest use of his or her potential and the means by which this would happen would be the educational system. Although education would not eliminate inequality completely, the argument goes, talent found among children in the lower structures of society would be fostered and unfair advantages open to children in higher positions would be reduced. In other words, education would be a means of assuring that children would end up in a position in society commensurate with their abilities and motivation and not merely their place of birth.

However, when one looks at the realities of the educational system in Canada, one finds a very close and persistent relationship between the hierarchical occupational structure that exists at a particular time and levels and type of education gained by the children of adults holding them. This is often quite independent of the child's ability and motivation. In other words, those adults who have been allocated to higher positions in the occupational hierarchy have their experiences and characteristics recognized and rewarded by the educational system; in turn these can be passed on to their children assuring that they will be allocated to like positions through the educational qualifications they gain. Consequently, inequalities which exist are by and large reproduced in the next generation by the educational system. The best predictor of determining who is most likely to make the greatest use of education and consequently be allocated to the highest positions in society is not the ability or motivation of the individual but rather the position that his or her parents occupy. It is important to remember at this juncture that many of the factors which influence the unequal distribution of rewards are structures into which a child enters at birth such as sex, class, region, ethnicity and religion.

If we focus for a moment on this allocative function of education we find ample evidence that *inequality* of educational opportunity has been and is today more the rule than the exception in Canada. Pike[7] provides evidence that students from higher class backgrounds tend to have higher aspirations and are more likely to attend universities or institutions of higher learning. Breton[8] provides evidence that this is true even among those students of equal intelligence. Other studies show that males are more likely than females to be allocated to higher class positions by the educational system. The link between educational achievement and occupational achievement seems very strong. However, one must be somewhat cautious about assuming a direct relationship between these two realities. Jencks[9] has shown that in the United States 'chance' factors such as luck may have an influence on educational outcomes.

One way to determine how effective an educational system is in promoting equality of educational opportunity is to look at the degree of social mobility that exists in a society. If inequalities exist in one generation then the educational system will, according to the original argument, allow or encourage children to move up or down the hierarchically ranked occupation structure according to their ability. Himelfarb and Richardson review the studies of social mobility in Canada and reach the conclusion,

> First, most mobility is short distance mobility. It appears that the changes in occupational status which people experience are usually quite modest; few rise from the very bottom to the top of the social hierarchy, even fewer make long falls downwards. Second, there is less social mobility than there would be if there was complete equality of opportunity. To put that another way, parents' status still influences what happens to sons and daughters.[10]

Also social mobility has not increased appreciably over the last century in Canada, despite the massive increases in expenditures in education. This does not mean that opportunities for various groups have not changed in Canada over time. But the relative change of positions has not occurred because as opportunities in the educational system changed, all students were exposed to them and those coming from more advantaged positions were also able to make greater use of them than students from less advantaged positions. Consequently, relative positions remain unchanged.

For some individuals who realize the limitations of the educational system as it presently exists in solving problems of inequalities, the solution is seen in increased expenditure on education and educational growth. However, recent studies of the relationship between the educational system and the economy conducted by Bowles and Gintis,[11] Carnoy,[12] Feinberg,[13] and Martell[14] provide a cautionary note. In the words of Feinberg:

> The higher the educational growth, the higher the disparity. Countries with high educational growth show high educational disparity, and countries with low educational growth show low educational disparity . . . In other words: *educational growth as it is known in the world today does not lead to educational equality.*[15]

What we may be doing is simply spending an increasingly larger portion of the Gross National Product to increase the disparity between those who receive the greatest rewards, both financial and social, and those who receive the least. Participation in the educational system has expanded greatly in the past century to where presently nearly one-third of the total Canadian population is enrolled in educational institutions, and expenditures on education have increased accordingly. Presently, one-fifth of the total of all governmental expenditures is directly allocated to formal public education. All these resources have little effect on structural inequalities.

What has been shown so far is *not* that schools have no influence on society. On the contrary, we have seen that schools have successfully forged clear linkages between educational attainment and the occupational structure. But what is clear is that faith in the ideal that the educational system can be the means to bring about equality in society is misplaced. Schools have not been successful as vehicles of mobility for children of lower class positions or as agents of social change. What is evident is that schools reproduce the inequalities that already exist in society and that the credentials awarded by schools are used to justify an individual's allocation. Schools, indirectly if not directly, legitimize inequalities. Contrary to the professed goal of those who control schools of using education as a means of restructuring society by allocating individuals according to talent and motivation rather than according to characteristics ascribed at birth, schools are themselves directly shaped by the realities of the broader society. Consequently, the goal of social change is in reality changed to one of social control.

In this respect, early social reformers were perhaps more honest or realistic in their goals for education. Schecter's study of early educational developments in Canada lead him to the conclusion:

> What is so striking about Canadian early school reform is the frankness with which the reformers acknowledged that its basic purpose was the social control of an emerging working class. In practice this meant the establishment of a state-controlled system based on the principles of centralization and uniformity — standardized textbooks, the development of a Normal School, the establishment of an effective inspectorate.[16]

Compulsory schooling was initially conceived to be an agency of social control. It was to be a means of turning out a loyal, obedient and unquestioning work force by teaching students the habits of honest hard work, punctuality and a respect for those in authority. This is not to deny that literacy was not also an assumed outcome. Educational reformers may have changed the language of educational goals, but they have done little to change the actual outcomes.

Bowles and Gintis, in their book entitled *Schooling in Capitalist America*, provide considerable empirical evidence to show that contemporary schools reproduce the personality characteristics and values desired by a subtly repressive industrial society. This is done through what is referred to as the hidden curriculum which is the unstated but still effective outcome of norms, values and dispositions learned within a total educational experience. Schools, they argue, are less concerned with the skills and knowledge to be transmitted to students and more concerned with assuring the outcome of compliancy, efficiency, obedience and apathy. In this regard they credit schools with considerable success. How schools accomplish this is described by Hurn in the following way:

> Therefore, schools whose graduates enter predominantly low status occupations stress rule following, provide minimal discretion in choice of tasks, and teach obedience to constituted authority. Schools and universities that prepare students for elite positions, by contrast, encourage students to develop some capacity of sustained independent work, to make intelligent choices among many alternatives, and to internalize norms rather than to follow external behavioral rules. If we compare junior colleges with elite universities, for example, or the college preparatory tracks of a suburban high school with the vocational curriculum, we will find not only differences in curriculum, but also differences in the social organization of instruction. In junior colleges and in the lower tracks of a high school students will be given more frequent assignments, have less choice in how to carry out those assignments, and will be subject to more detailed supervision by the teaching staff. By contrast, the college preparatory tracks of many suburban high schools and elite universities have an educational environment a great deal more open and flexible. Such differences mirror both different class values (the preference of working class parents for stricter educational methods and the preference of professional parents for schooling that encourages initiative and independence) and the different kinds of qualities of personality needed for good performance in high and low status occupations. The social organization of particular schools — the methods of instruction and evaluation, the amount of choice and discretion permitted the students — reflects the demands of the particular occupations that their graduates will eventually obtain.[17]

This leads us to the pessimistic conclusion that discussions about educational change in Canada may be considerably misguided if not incorrect.

Changes may be more in what educators say they are doing than in what is actually happening in schools.

It has been shown that it is not just the structural factors outside of schools which have a profound effect on what schools actually do. We have also seen that both the hidden curriculum and educators' assumptions about educability and future allocation exert a significant influence on the different values taught to students. A third factor is also important. Inequalities and their stratifying outcomes are built into the very structures of schools themselves. Streaming and tracking are two such structures that assure differential allocation of students. For example, Raymond Breton[18] showed that academic stratification (streaming) is considerably more important in influencing students' aspirations to utilize higher education than is measured ability or class background. Cicourel and Kitsuse[19] concluded that where a child is allocated by the educational system is more a function of decisions made for students by counsellors, teachers and principals, whom he calls the academic decision-makers, than are outside structural factors. Basil Bernstein's[20] studies of linguistic codes provide some evidence that the actual language used in educational discourse may be geared to assure the success of middle class students over students from working class backgrounds.

Females differ from males not only in their levels of educational attainment and in their rates of educational participation but also in the kinds of education they receive. In that subject knowledge is stratified into a hierarchical ranked structure and in that sex role socialization occurs in schools as well as other institutions such as the family, females may be exposed to different kinds of pressures and expectations which create different aspirations and lead to allocation to occupations which are differentially rewarded.

What has been argued here is that the educational system is not just an 'innocent bystander' when it comes to the creation of inequalities in society. We have shown that it has been not only relatively ineffective in alleviating inequalities which exist in the broader social structures, but, more importantly, that these inequalities are naturally generated by the educational system itself. Furthermore, the educational system legitimizes and justifies the inequalities that are perpetuated. Schools not only serve the purpose of economic reproduction of inequalities in Canada; they also engender cultural reproduction and further preserve and perpetuate inequalities.

This paper has attempted to look "through" what educationalists in Canada say they are doing and better see the reality of educational outcomes. This has led to a fairly pessimistic conclusion. But it does not mean that teachers are totally helpless. Changes in teacher training, curriculum, and pedagogic practices may be required and useful if for no other reason than providing a more humane and stimulating environment for students who spend the better part of each day for twelve years or more within these institutions. However, we must be realistic in our assessment as to what changes and reforms within one institution can do about factors which are fundamental structural problems in society. Alternative educational structures and institutions have also failed to bring about any fundamental changes. For the most part they were predicated on the assumption that one institution, the school, was socially and economically independent of the 'deep structures' of society. In Canada, as elsewhere, "most educational innovations have little or no impact on the society as a whole and may even strengthen the *status quo* by rechanneling and diffusing discontent".[21]

Given this fact, is there any hope for significant change in education and ultimately society? The author is convinced that such changes will occur only when the majority of Canadians share a goal based on a theory of social justice which is concerned not with equality of opportunity but rather equality of condition. This would be a commitment to make open and accessible the reward system to the least advantaged members of society. It would be along the line of thinking of Apple:

> For a society to be just it must, as a matter of both principle and action, contribute most to the advantage of the least advantaged. This is, its structural relations must be such as to equalize not merely access to but actual control of cultural, social and especially economic institutions. Now this would require more than mere tinkering with this social engine, for it implies a restructuring of institutions and a fundamental reshaping of the social contract that has supposedly bound us together. This theory of social justice which lies behind such a program needs to be generated out of more than personal ideology. It has its basis in a number of empirical claims as well. For example, the gap between rich and poor in advanced corporate nations is increasing. The distribution and control of health, nutritional, and educational goods and services is basically unequal in these same industrialized nations. Economic and cultural power is being increasingly centralized in massive corporate bodies that are less than responsible to social needs other than profit. After some initial gains, the relative progress of women and many minority groups is either stagnant or slowly atrophying.[22]

This goal is no less controversial than it would be difficult to obtain. However, if we accept that the inequalities that exist in Canada are costly in both an economic and social sense, inimical to our sense of social justice, and destructive of the realization of authentic democracy, then we may wish to do something about it. And here is where education can play its part. It seems reasonable to assume that, if schools have been so successful in teaching docility and compliance, they could also teach the norms of distributive justice and the principles of equality. Rather than teaching loyalty and commitment to the *status quo*, schools could teach sincere questioning and critical analysis. Rather than accepting the role of allocator of credentials which reduce students to products, schools could foster knowledge and skills which would lead to students seeing themselves as producers of reality. But ultimately this commitment to the values of social justice and equality must be directed toward society as a whole, and not simply to just one of its institutions. We have seen the failure of educational reform to solve social evils within Canada. Schools alone cannot alleviate racial, sexual, ethnic and religious discrimination, poverty, regional disparities or social disorganization, for they are all directly or indirectly the outcome of a distribution system which fosters and perpetuates inequalities. This situation will be challenged only when a sufficiently large number of people are aware of and committed to a theory of social justice which directly opposes this inequality. Perhaps schools can play this more modest role.

Notes

[1] J. Porter, *The Vertical Mosaic: An Analysis of Social Class and Power in Canada*, Toronto: University of Toronto Press, 1965.

[2] W. Clement, *The Canadian Corporate Elite: An Analysis of Economic Power*, Toronto: McClelland and Stewart, 1975.

[3] Ottawa: National Council of Welfare, *The Working Poor: People and Programs*, March 1981, p. 5.

[4] Ottawa: National Council of Welfare, *Poor Kids*, March 1975, p. 1.

[5] R. Manzer, *Canada: A Socio-Political Report*, Toronto: McGraw-Hill Ryerson, 1974, p. 188.

[6] J. Porter, *The Measure of Canadian Society: Education, Equality and Opportunity*, Toronto: Gage, 1979, p. 244.

[7] R. Pike, *Who Doesn't Get to University . . . And Why*, Ottawa: Runge Press, 1970.

[8] R. Breton, "Academic Stratification in Secondary Schools and the Educational Plans of Students", *Canadian Review of Sociology and Anthropology*, Vol. 7, No. 1, 1970.

[9] C. Jencks, *Inequality: A Reassessment of the Effect of Family and Schooling in America*, New York: Basic Books, 1972.

[10] A. Himelfarb and C. Richardson, *People, Power and Process: Sociology For Canadians*, Toronto: McGraw-Hill, 1979, p. 194.

[11] S. Bowles and H. Gintis, *Schooling in Capitalist America*, New York: Basic Books, 1976.

[12] M. Carnoy, *Education as Cultural Imperialism*, New York: David McKay, 1974.

[13] W. Feinberg, "Equality Under Two Conflicting Models of Educational Development", *Theory and Society*, Volume of 2, No. 2, 1975.

[14] G. Martell, ed., *The Politics of the Canadian Public School*, Toronto: James Lewis and Samuel, 1974.

[15] W. Feinberg, *op.cit.*, p. 185.

[16] S. Schecter, "Capitalism, Class and Educational Reform in Canada" in L. Ponitch, *The Canadian State: Political Economy and Political Power*, Toronto: University of Toronto Press, 1977, p. 378.

[17] C. Hurn, *The Limits and Possibilities of Schooling: An Introduction to the Sociology of Education*, Toronto: Allyn and Bacon, 1978, p. 50.

[18]R. Breton, *op.cit.*

[19]A. Cicourel and J. Kitsuse, *The Educational Decision-Makers*, New York: Bobbs-Merrill, 1963.

[20]B. Bernstein, *Class, Codes and Controls*, Vol. I, London: Routledge and Kegan-Paul, 1971.

[21]A. Himelfarb and C. Richardson, *op.cit.*, p. 218.

[22]M. Apple, *Ideology and Curriculum,* London: Routledge and Kegan-Paul, 1979, p. 12.